Stealing the Sky

First printing October 2023

Library of Congress Cataloging-in-Publication Data

Hughes, Daniel
stealing the sky lowercase / by daniel hughes

Paperback ISBN: 9798864211366
Hardcover ISBN: 9798864211571

Published by AR PRESS, an American Real Publishing Company
Roger L. Brooks, Publisher
roger@incubatemedia.us
americanrealpublishing.com

Edited by: Robin Konger
Interior design by Eva Myrick, MSCP

Printed in the U.S.A.

STEALING THE SKY

A Tale of the Espionage Behind America's Race to The Moon.
Based upon a true story.

DAN HUGHES

Table of Contents

Prologue

Americans in the late 1950s and early 1960s lived in fear. The Post War generation feared nuclear devastation unleashed by our enemy the Soviet Union designed to end our way of life. School age children were taught to "duck and cover" by a cartoon turtle wearing an army helmet and fallout shelters were constructed in most metropolitan areas. And we waited. Waited for mushroom clouds over the horizon. Waited for what we thought was to be the inevitable. Those who were our allies just a few years previously had now become a perceived threat overshadowing the fun-loving and carefree images Norman Rockwell painted so well for the cover of The Saturday Evening Post. We wanted his images of America to be real. We forced ourselves to believe they still were.

The more we enjoyed sock hops, shiny new cars with tail fins, and barbecue grills in the backyard, the more we feared it would all end in a fireball of science's creation. The Russians were defined as evil and we as Americans with our wholesome way of life therefore must be the good guys. What frightened us most was the thought the bad guys knew more than we did.

We had proven ourselves the greatest "superpower" in the

world: we had defeated the Axis powers in Europe and the Japanese in the West, and we had done it almost single-handedly. Or, at least to us Americans, it was the mindset. We were heroes, and we liked the feeling which came from thinking we had saved the world.

Twenty years earlier, our country was in the grips of a Great Depression with twenty-five percent of our workforce unemployed. Many remembered being hungry and no one wanted to go back to "the good ole days." This was supposed to be our time. We had earned it. We deserved to enjoy it.

We were smarter than the Russians, harder workers, better educated, and possessed a stronger moral fiber. We were winners. Good guys are supposed to win. Yet, the headlines on October 4, 1957, shocked all Americans: Russians launch the first satellite into Earth's orbit...Sputnik Circles the Globe.

The definition of the word stealing is for one to have taken another person's property without permission or legal right and without intending to return it. The word can be as innocuous a stolen base in baseball...but this was different.

America was the greatest country on Earth. With our long history of manifest destiny, had we not conquered lands once occupied by others of a lesser value for the betterment of what we represent? It made for simple common sense that we as the leaders of the free world should conquer the uncharted vastness of space simply because we thought of ourselves as worthy and others as less so. Space itself was to be an American domain.

The Russians launched three more satellites before we successfully launched Explorer 1 on January 31, 1958. Our own attempts failed several times, including one in front of our nation's television cameras in a debacle making all American's gasp as the rocket exploded a few hundred feet above the gantry. It all served to remind our nation the Russians were ahead of us, not only technologically but also in propaganda.

President Eisenhower was embarrassed. As the supreme commander of the Allied forces in World War II, he had brought victory home to America and earned a seat in the Oval Office because of it. Now the Russians were boasting of their world domination and there seemed to be little he could do about it. If the Russians could launch a satellite into orbit, then they could also gain the capabilities to launch nuclear payloads from space as well.

We had granted full immunity to Germany's smartest scientists, among them, Wernher von Braun, a ranking officer in the SS during the war and the primary force behind the development of the V-2 rockets which took the lives of countless British citizens. Braun's rocket factory in Germany, located on the Baltic Sea and called Peenemunde, was an underground facility built on the backs of 60,000 slave laborers. Most of which died either from starvation or sheer exhaustion. Those who survived were shipped to extermination camps in Germany and Poland so the secret location of the factory would remain just that...a secret. Sins forgotten for the sake of the better good, and beating the Russians was now the better good.

The Cold War and the Space Race was the end of innocence for The United States of America. Espionage and covert operations became the rule of the day and have continued into the present. The unspoken motto of our own government had become, "The end always justifies the means," and it all began with the noble goal of conquering the final frontier.

The story I am about to tell you is true. Recently declassified documents from the CIA and NASA will bear witness to the events I will tell you. Our government has not completely cleansed itself of its actions in those frightening days of the 1950s and early 1960s, but enough information has surfaced for one willing and diligent enough to dig for it. I have changed some names for the sake of privacy to those involved in the story. I fully admit to creating dialogue of conversations which will never appear on paper or in any documents. My publisher has labeled my writing "Historical Fiction," and to some degree I guess it has become my genre over the years, but I can assure you there is more fact here than fiction.

The Russians were out to steal our American way of life, and they would do so by beating us into space. Nuclear satellites aimed directly at our heartlands would be the deciding factor and we were not about to let it happen. It was time for America...to steal back the sky.

Chapter 1

Moscow: 13th of April, 1961

Nikita Khrushchev pounded his fist repeatedly on his desk in the Kremlin on that mild day in Moscow. A balmy day in Moscow in April might reach forty-five degrees. The sound of his large fleshy hands hitting the wooden desk once owned by the Czar Nicholas II resounded with an echo that those who stood outside the closed doors had heard many times before. Khrushchev had been an ironworker in his younger life and his hands were forged like the metal he used to work with. Those outside in the hallway turned their backs and looked down at their shoes. That sound usually meant someone would die soon.

The young Russian guards standing just outside winced but said nothing. It is what Russian soldiers do. He does not ask questions, lest you find yourself to be the next one with your head on the chopping block. The scholarly man they had escorted into the premier's office earlier was a man they did not know, but it did not matter they thought. 'Better him than me,' they reasoned.

The next sounds the young officers heard took them by surprise. Was that...laughter? Both guards looked at one another and relaxed with a sigh of relief. Today would be different.

The new dimples punctuated into Nikita Khrushchev's desk had not been caused in anger but in excitement. The man Nikita Khrushchev now pounded on the back and embraced was Sergei Korolev, the chief engineer on the Vostok 1 project. He had traveled from the Baikonur Cosmodrome in Kazakhstan last night by rail and had not slept in almost forty-eight hours. Still, it was important he personally tell the Russian Premier of his success before anyone else might think to take credit for what was his to boast about.

The Premier had been in constant phone contact with the Cosmodrome the day before, but Korolev thought it a good idea to piss on newfound ground to mark it as his own before anyone else could get the chance.

Yuri Gagarin, a twenty-seven-year-old Soviet Air Force pilot, had done what no other human being had ever done. The boundaries which separated the Earth from space had been broken. Gagarin was a national hero, but he had not done it alone, and Korolev wanted...no, he needed the Premier to know it was his thinking which had put the very first man into outer space.

The flight of Vostok 1 would become the shortest on record for a successful human space flight, lasting just 108 minutes. Gagarin orbited the globe just once—but once was all which was required to embarrass the Americans once again. Gagarin was to be the face people would remember, but the chief engineer wanted his due. Korolev had personally controlled the spacecraft, and designed the engines which would propel the young cosmonaut to an unprecedented speed of five miles per second, allowing him to be the first human being to break free of the bond's gravity held. They had done the impossible; but in Korolev's mind Gagarin was merely a passenger. Just like the three dogs he had launched into space a month earlier.

The old saying, "Whatever goes up must come down," does not always hold true in space. Gagarin's spacecraft was never designed to return to Earth. That technology had still eluded the best of Russia's scientists. Going up was the easy part—if you consider sitting on top of what was no less than a ballistic missile with no controls and hanging on as 'easy.' Returning a spacecraft from outer space and back into the atmosphere requires hitting a paper-thin window of trajectory, and if the engineers miscalculated the numbers, the spacecraft skips off the surface of our atmosphere and ricochets into space with little hope of ever returning. Mathematics was the greatest hurdle to overcome in space travel and the Russians had yet to figure out the numbers. The Americans had been working on solving the same equations for over five years without plausible success. Gagarin had ejected himself from the capsule while still almost five miles up and had parachuted back to Earth. Gagarin's free fall record of 26,000 feet was one of the few records which the Russians were not willing to brag. They were hoping to keep this one a secret.

Khrushchev waived the front page of that morning's Pravda paper while dancing a little jig. "We have beaten them again Korolev," the premier said in his deep tenor voice. "The Americans must be shitting themselves," he added enthusiastically.

Korolev wishing to please the man who stood before him. He said, "It is a great day for Mother Russia, brother General Secretary."

Korolev had used the official party title for the leader of the U.S.S.R. in hopes he would bring himself additional favor with the man few had ever seen this happy. The misuse of protocol in America will raise eyebrows, in Russia it can still get you shot.

Khrushchev was a master at political manipulation and wise enough to have grown through the ranks of Soviet politics during their most trying of times. He fully understood why Korolev was standing in front of him. He knew the game better than most. He had survived the same game in the early days of the Russian revolution and the execution of the Czar's entire family in a cellar of an obscure farmhouse on July 17, 1918. The brutal gunning down of Czar Nicholas II along with his wife and five children had ended 300 years of imperial rule and heralded in the rise of communism in Russia. Khrushchev had pulled himself out of the muck of his peasant parent's existence and risen to serve Vladimir Lenin in the aftermath which comes at the end of any dynasty.

After Lenin's death in 1924, he had ingratiated himself with a man who had no friends, a man whose paranoia was so great his own family lived in fear. Joseph Stalin had brought victory against Hitler and in doing so, twenty million of his own citizens had paid the ultimate price for the victory. Nikita Khrushchev had assisted Stalin in his purge of political dissidents before the war. Nikita Khrushchev was the man chosen by Stalin to manage the slave labor in the Ukraine during World War II, which supplied the armaments and labor that had defeated Nazi Germany. He was not a man opposed to breaking a few eggs in order to make an omelet. The newfound Space Race would be no different.

Korolev waited patiently until he felt the right opportunity to detail to the Premiere the victories of the previous day, victories he hoped would grant him favor or at the very least minimize some scrutiny. Before speaking he wiped his brow twice with the handkerchief he always kept in the breast pocket of his tweed jacket.

Khrushchev listened to what he was already aware of and

enjoyed watching his chief engineer squirm. Yet today was different. Today was a good day and Nikita Khrushchev had what he wanted, there was no need to change the mood of victory.

There had been victories. Khrushchev let his mind wander as Korolev continued to speak. The Russians had launched the first living animal into orbit in November of 1957. The flight was meant to test the safety of space travel for humans. For Laika the dog however, it was a suicide mission with no expectations of ever returning safely. Laika was a stray picked up off the streets of Moscow just over a week before the launch. Thirty days later, they had launched the first satellite into orbit with Sputnik and the Space Race began.

It had taken almost three additional years before Soviet technology allowed two dogs to be launched into outer space and returned to the earth safely and both Khrushchev and Korolev knew it had happened by pure luck alone. In all thirty-six dogs were sent into space before yesterday's launch of Yuri Gagarin, and all had died but two. Eight months before Gagarin's flight, two scrappy little female mutts named Belka and Strelka were found in an alley of Moscow and presented with the titles of Russian cosmonauts. Chosen for their small size and calm demeanor, they would be the next furry eggs in Khrushchev's omelet aboard Sputnik 5.

A thruster rocket malfunctioned while the satellite was in orbit, and it burned just long enough to project the spacecraft into the slim envelope of successful re-entry. The primitive computers on board and those on the ground were not able to record the data and duplicate the maneuver, but both dogs survived, and the Russians took the victory.

The world's press had applauded the technological advance of Russia's brilliance and both Belka and Strelka became international superstars. The Russians had successfully put something living into outer space and then successfully returned them back to Earth.

There was no mention whatsoever in today's Pravda newspaper that Yuri Gagarin had parachuted back to the ground...let the American's think and worry the Russians knew more than they did. Khrushchev knew this was politics. It is *not* what you know, it's what the other person *thinks* you know.

Nakita Khrushchev chuckled to himself as he remembered the masterstroke of his own propaganda which followed Belka's and Strelka's return to Earth. He had sent both dogs to the Moscow Zoo and demanded both be bred as soon as possible. Belka never conceived, but Strelka produced puppies roughly six months later. One of which, named Pushika, the Russian equivalent to "fluffy," was then presented to the newly elected American president's daughter Caroline. What father could reject such a kind offer? John F. Kennedy had been elected in November of 1960 and Khrushchev wanted a daily reminder of his superiority pooping on the White House lawn. There was no kindness in the offer...again, *this* was politics.

Khrushchev did not even hear the last of Sergei Korolev's ramblings on that day in the Kremlin. The Premier had what he wanted. They had put a man into space and the man was still alive to talk about it. Gagarin would never attempt space travel again; he had no choice in the matter. Khrushchev fully understood the dangers involved and he would not allow his biggest asset to be risked in what might just be another failure of shoestring technology. Gagarin was a national hero and Khrushchev was not willing to risk this egg if it meant tarnishing his own image.

Sergei Korolev left the Kremlin feeling very good about his successes. He was sure he had accomplished what he had set out to do on a warmer than usual day in April 1961. The sky was blue, and it felt good to be alive. He was sure even with his failing health his future was secure. His life had certainly changed.

Just twenty-three years ago, he was a prisoner in a labor camp in Eastern Siberia, sent there by lies told from the mouth of a younger man he had trained himself. His protégé had wished to climb the political ladder faster than his skills allowed and well-timed rumors in the ear of a paranoid dictator were enough to see him convicted without trial. Joseph Stalin sentenced him to a ten-year term he would not have survived. Twelve-hour days working in a gold mine and continuous beatings which broke his jaw and cost him most of his teeth had taken their toll on him. It was only Stalin's death and Nikita Khrushchev's rise to power which allowed for his early release and his return to his passion for rocketry and space exploration.

Khrushchev had no love of space or for exploration; his concerns were about military might and embarrassing America, plain and simple. Rockets were his answer to both. The meager budget Korolev worked within had produced tremendous results and the Premier seemed happier than Korolev had ever seen him. Yes, today was a good day indeed. They were beating the Americans and the world knew it. Korolev had put a man beyond the top of the world, and it felt good.

What Sergei Korolev did not know, however, was in less than four years he would find himself being replaced once again by the very same man who had once spread those lies. In another year after, he would die of mysterious causes. In Russia it is the price you pay, for making one mistake to many.

Chapter 2

Washington D.C. – 5th of May, 1961, The Oval Office

The young newly elected president to the United States was still on the phone when Allen Dulles, the Director of the CIA, walked into his office. John Fitzgerald Kennedy pointed to a chair and Dulles sat down. The thick carpeting and lush upholstery of the Oval Office did little to muffle Kennedy's thick Boston accent as he spoke to the person on the other end of the line. Dulles, in an attempt at being polite, pointed at himself and then at the door. He gestured towards his watch saying silently he could come back at a better time.

JFK just patted the air with his hand as if to say, "No sit down, I will only be a minute."

Allen Dulles did not bother to try to listen to the conversation because he already knew who was on the other end of the line. Alan Shepard had just piloted America's first rocket to reach sub-orbital heights and safely return; they had brought an American astronaut home. The Russians had beaten them to the punch by almost a month, but it meant they were in the game. Shepard's Freedom 7 capsule, which sat atop the Red Stone 3 rocket, had not achieved orbit. But that was not the mission at hand. Before you can beat your opponent on any playing field, you first have to find your way onto the field at hand.

"Thank you, Mr. President," Alan Shepard said on the ship to shore telephone aboard the aircraft carrier USS Lake Champlain. "I am happy to have just done my part."

"You've done more than just that, Commander," the president said, "you're a hero to all Americans. Plus," the President added, "you've given those damn Russians something to think about."

"Thank you again, Mr. President."

Before Alan Shepard had spoken the last syllable, the President of the United States had already hung up the phone.

The president turned his attention to Allen Dulles. "Well at least we didn't screw that one up. Allen, what do you have for me?"

"If you're looking for concrete answers Mr. President, I don't have them," Dulles reported. "I wish I did," he added, "I'm working on it."

The president paused and rubbed both his eyes. He had not gotten much sleep the night before, and even less in the last few weeks. "Allen, please knock off the Mr. President crap, you and I have known each other since 1955. Just tell me what you know."

"Damn it, Jack. You're right, we *have* known each other a long time. But after what happened last month, I am afraid to tell you much of anything until I have all my ducks in a row. You hung my ass out to dry like Sunday's laundry buddy," Dulles said, not afraid to mince his words.

Allen Dulles was referring to the unmitigated disaster the press had dubbed "The Bay of Pigs invasion of Cuba." Eighteen days before, American backed Cuban rebels had attempted a coup d'état against the government of Fidel Castro. Fourteen hundred Cuban exiles had stormed the beaches at the Bay of Pigs on the Southern coast of Cuba, moments after eight B-26's sent by the CIA from an airstrip in Cabeza Nicaragua bombed three Cuban airfields. The Cuban exiles, trained and armed by the CIA, were told additional air power would reinforce their efforts. The air support never arrived.

President Kennedy, in a twelfth hour decision, over-rode the CIA directors' initiative and the additional bombers were called back to America.

Kennedy had only become President a few months earlier, and the Cuban attack had been an Eisenhower administration initiative. Kennedy and his advisors agreed to the covert operation, but only with the assurances it would look purely as if had been an anti-Castro operation without any assistance from the United States. Cuba resided just ninety miles from the nearest U.S. coast and with the concerns about the Cold War, Kennedy feared political blow back from the Russians if American support leaked out...

Allen Dulles had been in his position much longer than the newly elected president had been in his. When administrations change hands, there are always power struggles within and the C.I.A director was not immune to this. Allen Dulles had been the director of the CIA since 1952, and in that time, he had made one enemy in particular, both professionally and personally.

J. Edgar Hoover had directed the Federal Bureau of Investigation (FBI) since the days of President Calvin Coolidge. His household name was built on the successes of capturing (or killing) the likes of Bonnie and Clyde, John Dillinger and "Baby Face" Nelson. J. Edgar Hoover was an investigator; Allen Dulles was a spy, and there is a big difference between the two. Few people outside of Washington even knew Allen Dulles's name, while Hoover made sure every American knew his own.

Hoover investigated everyone. He kept personal files on many with a position of authority. Hoover's professional mandate was that of holding up the Constitution of the United States, but his mind set was controlling the power of others. The law meant nothing to the Director of the FBI—if he could get his hands on something which gave him the upper hand, then so be it.

Allen Dulles had grown up in the shadows of a father who was a Presbyterian minister. His older brother was Dwight D. Eisenhower's Secretary of State. His sister Eleanor was a diplomat. His maternal grandfather was John W. Foster, who was Secretary of State under Benjamin Harrison, while his uncle by marriage, Robert Lansing, served as Secretary of State under Woodrow Wilson.

Allen Dulles considered himself a patriot. Those around him and those who knew him well most often thought the same. It just so happened one of those individuals was the young newly elected president of the United States.

Allen Dulles sighed deeply. The Bay of Pigs had embarrassed his president, and his good friend. He was hoping to prevent more of the same. There *had* been a leak on the invasion. Dulles knew he had put confidence in what had turned out to be unreliable sources. Both men in the Oval Office that morning had solid suspicions as to where the leak had come from; both also had a more than reasonable judgment on who would benefit from the sabotage. Hoover wanted Allen Dulles to lose face.

If a few hundred Cuban exiles got their asses shot up, well, Hoover was the type who would think it was worth the cost.

The morning of the invasion, The New York Times ran an article for all to see of almost the entire operation. The CIA had overpromised on how Cuban citizens could rise up and defend the rebels. They completely underestimated Fidel Castro's forces and their ability to repel such an attack. The airstrikes on Fidel Castro's bases were ineffective and Castro was sitting with his forces in mass waiting at the beach. Had Kennedy sent in the additional bombers it would have most likely started World War III.

Jack Kennedy had fallen on his sword and taken blame for the debacle, but both Allen Dulles and the president knew it would eventually cost the CIA director his job. Not yet though. The president still needed his friend's covert skills in securing information others did not want known.

Allen Dulles paused, mostly out of frustration and out of a true affection for the man who sat on the corner of his desk looking at him. "Jack, you're premature on all of this space stuff. You want to go before Congress in less than three weeks and commit yourself to a plan of action where you have *no* plan. You have no infrastructure to support a plan, no budget to pay for it, and need I remind you; we don't even have the technology to support any of it yet."

The president sat patiently, allowing the CIA director to vent. It was as if Jack Kennedy, who was twenty-four years younger than Dulles, had assumed the role of a loving father listening to a rebel son. Kennedy was a master politician; he knew exactly how to use his public persona to his best advantage with television cameras and smiles, whereas Dulles did all his work as far from public scrutiny as possible.

"Jack, in light of last month I can only recommend you re-think this before you make another big mistake in the first five months of your presidency which could cost you your re-election," Dulles told him.

Kennedy paused long enough to make sure the man sitting in the chair in front of him was fully paying attention. "You about done Allen?" The president paused once again, only this time to allow his rising anger to settle. "Cuba was a mistake Allen, and I signed off on it because of what you personally told me. I have spent the last eighteen days bailing your ass out of the fire. You had bad intel and even worse expectations. Jesus, Allen, did you think Fidel Castro was just going to throw up the white flag because America came knocking on his back door?"

Allen Dules wanted to respond, but Kennedy kept hammering in on him.

"Damn it, you promised me a covert operation with no visible American support, and you screwed the pooch, and damn it, I am supposed to be the big dog around here. You might as well have had your Cuban refugees hum the star-spangled banner as they walked up the beach. You and I will spend the next six months just doing damage control on this one," the president said. "We need heroes right about now, Allen. The damn Russians have been kicking our ass in just about everything lately and I am tired of us looking like monkeys screwing a football! Every evening newspaper in America will have Alan Shepard's picture on the front page and Cuba will be pushed to page six. Allen, I need your support on this one."

Dulles slumped back in his chair and rubbed his forehead. "OK Jack, you're the big picture guy...what do you need?"

Kennedy leaned down from the corner of his desk, his favorite place to perch when he was dressing you down or trying to inspire you. Dulles wasn't sure which one this was—maybe both.

"I need a miracle Allen, the type of miracle people dream of, but no one in human history has ever accomplished. Americans have short memories. Right now, they have too many reminders of just how imperfect this country is. The economy is good, and the median income is the highest it has ever been. Most people are working a five-day workweek instead of the seven most people in our father's generation had to work."

Allen Dulles scooted to the end of his chair, wondering where the President was leading to.

"Allen, you and I both come from privilege; most people do not. You give an average man freer time to think, and they start looking for answers. Damn it, I have white people killing Negroes in the streets of Alabama right now. This whole civil rights movement is not going to go away, and it shouldn't. Women want equal pay for equal work and more and more women are registering to vote. Any time in world history which created change has the old guard worried they will have less in the outcome. This country is divided, Allen."

Kennedy was a politician who chose his words carefully. Allen Dulles was listening. The CIA director was not hearing the words of yet another Washington bureaucrat, he was listening to his old friend.

"If I am going to make a difference...a *real* difference in this country's future...then I need something which brings every American together, regardless of race, creed, religion, income, or any other God damn thing that draws lines in the sand. We need to think of ourselves as Americans without any prefixes."

Kennedy let his last words linger in the air.

"OK Jack" Dulles responded, "What exactly is it you're looking for, and what is it you're asking of me?"

President Kennedy leaned in even farther and said, "...I want the moon Allen, and I want it before the Russians can get their hands on it."

"I think you're being premature—" Dulles started to say. Kennedy cut him off.

"Allen, we just put an American into space, and yes we're behind, but we're in it. We must strike while the iron is hot. Alan Shepard and his wife will be here at the White House in three days, and we will present him with America's highest civilian Medal of Honor." Kennedy smiled.

Dulles looked confused. "Jack, Alan Shepard is a naval military officer and test pilot, not a civilian."

President Kennedy raised an eyebrow and Allen Dulles caught on. He chuckled. The man who sat on the end of his desk was truly a master of public perception.

"It is an American achievement Allen, not a military achievement," Kennedy explained. "I am going before Congress in less than three weeks to ask for the funding which will allow *all* Americans to get to the moon. The Russians are way ahead of us...and your job is to tell me personally what it is they know that we have not figured out yet. If the Russians get there first, we lose everything, don't let that happen."

Allen Dulles hung his head before speaking, "And just how am I supposed to do that, Jack?"

John Fitzgerald Kennedy looked down on his dear friend and said, "You're the spy...figure it out!"

Twenty days later on May 25, 1960, President Kennedy addressed a joint session of Congress. In his thirty-two-minute address, he asked for and would later receive the largest appropriations of money a President had ever asked for outside of a time of war.

"First, I believe that this nation should commit itself to achieving the goal, before this decade is out, of landing a man on the moon and returning him safely to the Earth. No single space project in this period will be more impressive to mankind, or more important for the long-range exploration of space; and none will be so difficult or expensive to accomplish."

"Let it be clear—and this is a judgment which the Members of the Congress must finally make—let it be clear that I am asking the Congress and the country to accept a firm commitment to a new course of action, a course which will last for many years and carry very heavy costs: 531 million dollars in fiscal '62—an estimated seven to nine billion dollars additional over the next five years. If we are to go only halfway, or reduce our sights in the face of difficulty, in my judgment it would be better not to go at all."

The Presidents stirring words galvanized his audience and the country as well. He had thrown down a gauntlet for Congress and they responded with increased funding for the Apollo program. Apollo 11 would land on the moon with 164 days left in the decade, just as the President had asked. On July 20, 1969, Neil Armstrong would plant an American Flag at the Sea of Tranquility on the lunar surface. President Kennedy would not be alive to witness the historical event. His famous words spoken in front of Congress are written in textbooks for every future generation to read. The few words he spoke to Allen Dulles in his office twenty days before were never recorded.

As Allen Dulles stood up from his chair and headed to the door of the Oval Office, Jack Kennedy stood up and said, "Allen, you report only to me on this matter, do I make myself clear? I need to know everything the Russians know. Now go, do what you do best."

All Allen Dulles could do was respond by saying, "Yes, Mr. President."

"And Allen...this time, don't get caught."

Allen Dulles closed the door behind him without looking back.

Chapter 3

London, end of May 1961

The Soviet Union was on a roll; they had achieved great technological advancements and wanted to take full advantage of showing off the superiority of the Soviet way of life. So, Nikita Khrushchev had decided to take his show on the road.

Khrushchev had scheduled several exhibitions throughout Russian and the Ukraine, all to inspire national pride and a further sense of Soviet patriotism. Khrushchev had started the practice way back in 1958 in Moscow with a joint American-Soviet exhibition Vice President Richard Nixon had attended. It was the Soviet leader's podium to debate the merits of Communism over Democracy. The shows drew such massive crowds the exhibition schedule was extended to include major cities across the globe, highlighting supremacy in all aspects of Soviet living. His timing could not have been better...for the Americans.

The first international show was in late May in London of 1961. Everything from modern kitchen appliances to women's fashion would be on display in the "Hall of Modern Living." The "Industrial Exhibition" displayed scale panoramas of the world's first nuclear power plant to go online. The London audiences stood mesmerized by displays of the world's first lasers and rudimentary and somewhat blotchy holographic 3-D images in the "Hall of Achievements."

The Russians even blew the dust off of earlier innovations and were willing to take credit for such inventions as the television, videotape recording, solar cells, and even the first helicopter. The Russians failed to mention that although a Russian pioneered each invention, those men had emigrated from Russia years before having created them. Vladimir Zworykin *had* invented the cathode ray tube called the kinescope back in 1929, without which television would never have been possible. But Zworykin's research was done in Pittsburgh, not Russia. Igor Sikorsky's first practical helicopter was unveiled in 1939 at his factory...in Connecticut.

But the Russians were happy to have Londoner's muttering to one another, "I didn't know that those were Russian inventions."

The exhibit hall all wanted to see, and thousands lined up for was entitled, "The Mastering of Space."

Nikita Khrushchev had purposefully chosen not to display military hardware or any other militaristic presence...with one exception. A Russian soldier guarded every display in the Space Hall with a SKS held across his chest, not shouldered, but at the ready. The visual of stone-faced sentinels standing next to shiny metal spacecrafts reinforced the importance of each item on display.

A copy of Sputnik 1 was proudly displayed with its shiny orb there to represent the Russians first step into space. Laika, the first animal in space was there in effigy, stuffed and smiling—

though she had burned in re-entry. And yet, there she was, replaced by some other poor animal to be seen by the fascinated British public, peering back at the audience from the window of a full-size replica of Sputnik 2.

Russian pressurized space suits, false mockups of Rocket engines, and other gear were on display. People flocked to see and meet Yuri Gagarin and see a model of the Vostok 1 capsule he had "piloted" into space. No cameras were allowed in the "Mastering of Space" hall, disappointing young children and adults alike, who had hoped to get a photo with the first man in space.

Scale models of the solar system hung from the ceiling while every Russian space vehicle ever launched floated from invisible silk threads suspended from the rafters.

In a corner of the exhibition hall, in a separate area cordoned off by the Russian guards, was a display which currently created the most attention for those who were following the Space Race closely. For one woman, it was her reason for being there. To enter the display area, one first walked by television monitors blaring a British newsreel entitled, "Soviet's amazing triumph wins world's congratulations." The one minute eleven second film was shown in cinemas across Europe but was never shown in America. In the early 1960s, cartoons and newsreels preceded feature films in theaters and for many it was how they kept themselves informed and entertained. This news story highlighted the third flight of the Soviet Union's latest achievements: The Lunik program, or "The Luna Programme," as the Russians had originally called it.

Luna 1 was launched in January 1959 and was intended to impact the moon in hopes of discovering soil depth and crust density. The Russians missed. In what scientists now call the "sling shot effect," the satellite achieved near moon orbit, only to be slung far out into space never to return. But now, Russia could boast they had the first satellite to orbit the sun. They took full credit for the achievement.

Luna 2, launched in September 1959, successfully hit the moon, becoming the first man-made object to do so.

The newsreel which welcomed visitors into the display was that of Luna 3, and the Soviets had indeed done something no one had ever done before. Launched in October of 1959, Luna 3 orbited the moon and sent back to Earth photos of the never-before seen "back side of the moon." As the moon revolves around the Earth, it does so at the same rate in which it revolves around its own axis. Because of this, people here on Earth only ever see the near side in what physicists and astronomers refer to as tidal lock.

Huge blown-up pictures of the photos shot 300,000 miles away were breathtaking, and the Russians were once again able to claim another first. The Russians were jubilant; the Americans outdone once again!

A twelve-foot diameter moon hung from the ceiling with detailed topography never seen before. Luna 3 was touted as "Russia's next step towards the moon," and once again, Nikita Khrushchev wanted everyone to know the Soviet Union would be the ones to get there first with a manned flight.

In an interview with the Soviet leader just hours after Alan Shepard's flight on May 5, Khrushchev was asked if he was concerned the American's were catching up. Khrushchev commented, "We put a man into space first, our satellites have reached the surface of the moon first...we will beat the Americans in anything they attempt to do." His next sentence was the one which scared American scientists and our government the most, because most thought it might just be true." The moon is ours for the taking." Khrushchev said, "The Americans are not up to the task of taking it from us."

A woman wearing a yellow sundress with a flower brooch on her lapel stood in line patiently to see the display. She faced the video which greeted all who waited before her, but her eyes were taking in other things. She had seen it before. She spent no time looking up at the gigantic lunar orb which hung from the ceiling because she had already seen stolen photos of what Luna 3 had captured from the dark side of the moon. What she wanted was a closer look at the vehicle that had taken them.

The woman was petite at five foot four inches, stunning by nature but dowdy when her role required it. No one noticed her that day in London and it was by design. Her black hair was pulled up under a scarf and the sundress she wore was two sizes too big for her frame.

As she stepped closer to the mock-up of the Luna 3 capsule, the tiny camera imbedded in her flower brooch came to life with silent clicks no one heard. Four Russian guards stood nearby and the simple fact there were four instead of just one, like every other display, told her the Luna 3 module was of supreme importance. While standing behind the velvet ropes which kept her at bay, she accomplished what she had been sent there for.

As the silent camera snapped photos, she scanned everything she could see, remembering even the smallest of details. Her own photographic memory was one of the reasons her skills came at such a high price tag. She counted the number of armed guards, remembering the rank of each one she visually investigated. She noticed wedding rings and facial expressions, who looked bored and who did not. Nothing escaped her gaze. Each guard wore a plastic identification badge clipped to his uniform and she memorized as many names and faces as she could see. If a guard had a roving eye, he was check marked in her mind for later reference.

The photos would be analyzed later that evening in a hotel room in London paid for by Allen Dulles and the CIA. The pretty, dark-haired woman would then wait for future instructions, as she always did.

Chapter 4

London, Later that Evening

The Ritz is one of London's most famous hotels. The Ritz opened its doors in 1906 and had long been a favored resting spot for European kings and queens. But this was definitely not the Ritz. Less of a hotel and more of a "boarding house," The Shoreditch was carbon covered and dark. There was no room service and from the look of the building, no housekeeping or maintenance staff either. The Shoreditch resided in the heart of Whitechapel, a seedy area on the East End of London best known for the man who slashed and disemboweled prostitutes in 1880.

The two adjoining rooms were large enough for the three men to work without bumping into each other, but not much more. One of the bathrooms had been turned into a makeshift dark room. The photos taken by the raven-haired woman earlier today would be developed soon.

The woman lay on the bed with her bare feet hanging off one end. She had escaped the sundress she had worn earlier in favor of something more fitting her own sense of style. The cream-colored pantsuit was daring for a woman in 1961—her choice not to wear a blouse underneath the jacket even more so.

She thumbed her way through the latest issue of Vogue as two of the men peppered here with questions.

"How close were you able to get to the Luna 3?"

The woman did not look up as she said, "Roughly ten feet away, three meters."

"And describe its size for us please. We'll have the photos soon, but we need a frame of reference," one man said.

She flipped another page and said, "It was cylindrical in shape, with a wider flange at the top that must have held the camera equipment. I would say average diameter ninety-five centimeters or just over thirty-seven inches. The flange at the top was 120 centimeters across or just under four feet. There were four probes on the top and my guess was each was thirty-six inches give or take. No more though. Let's call it thirty-five and seven-eighths." She looked up at the man asking the questions and said with just a little tone of indignation, "Two of the photos have one of the Russian guards in it. He stood five feet, eight inches, I am sure of that. You can use his height in comparing measurements."

Gravda Nemiroff was twenty-nine years old. She was just eight years old when Hitler invaded Russia. Her Russian father had met and fallen in love with a German tourist while vacationing on the Baltic Sea ten years earlier. It was a love affair worthy of a Tolstoy novel. When Germany attacked Russia, Joseph Stalin rounded up as many German nationalist as he could find and sent them to labor camps in Siberia. Gravda's mother had been one of them. They never saw each other again.

Gravda's father was a low-level bureaucrat in Moscow. His

responsibility was making sure the street sweepers did their job. He was not a politician; he was just a hard worker who adored his wife and daughter. His public outcry for the way his wife had been treated would later attract the attention of the Russian dictator and in 1944, Stalin had him executed as an enemy of the state.

Gravda was thirteen years old on that day. Two Russian soldiers held her by both shoulders as they forced her to watch her father be shot by a firing squad.

The government sent Gravda to a "children's home" in Kiev for the remainder of the war. Like her mother, she had blossomed early in life and her "caretaker" took full advantage of her early development. She was raped repeatedly from the time she arrived in the sod-roofed house of the man who forced her to call him "papa."

On May 7, 1945, Germany surrendered and the war in Europe was over. On the same day, young Gravda stood behind the kitchen door with a butcher knife determined to stop her own misery. She was fourteen.

"The condition of the capsule?" one man asked.

"It looked brand new, no signs of wear and tear," she said. "Well, other than the usual streaks of obvious black paint to make it look like it had been in outer space. I don't think it was a mockup though. Stage props are usually thrown together, and this thing looked well engineered. My guess is that this was a working backup to the Luna 3 the Russians modified for display."

She would be right. She usually was.

"Could you see any equipment inside?" her interrogator asked.

"No, I couldn't get close enough," she said. "There was definitely some instrumentation but at that distance I couldn't make anything out."

"Total height?" the second man asked.

Gravda put down her magazine and sat on the edge of the bed. "Bigger than I would have thought," she said, "The capsule itself was maybe 130 centimeters or a little taller. Add to that the antenna on the top and the thrusters on the bottom—I would say just over six feet tall. It looked heavy," she added. "It was supported in a framework of steel tubing so it would stand upright for the display. I think we're talking three to four hundred pounds at least."

The third man exited the bathroom with a stack of photos in his hand. "Nice work Betty, these photos are excellent."

Gravda bent down and slipped on her pair of low-heeled cream-colored shoes she had sat at the foot of the bed. "You boys have fun with your research, I'll be back at 8:00 a.m."

"You don't want to stay here with us in such lavish surroundings?" one of the men joked.

Betty...Gravda...grabbed her lightweight London Fog raincoat off the back of a chair, slipped into it and was cinching the belt when she said, "No boys, the CIA is about to get an expensive bill for room service in a nicer part of town."

As Gravda closed the doorway and walked down the dimly hit hallway towards the rickety elevator, she noticed the aged wallpaper peeling from the walls.

One of the men in the room behind her said chuckling, "Damn she's hot."

Another one said, "No...she's cold."

All three chuckled louder.

Gravda heard their laughter but could not make out the words. It didn't matter, she knew they were talking about her, and she had heard it all before.

She tied a flowered scarf over her head and reached into the pocket of her raincoat feeling for the passport residing there. As she walked out the front door of the Shoreditch Hotel, she once again became Betty Miller, a fashion buyer for Macy's department store. She was in London to check out the upcoming fall designs.

The woman had seven different passports at her disposal, none of which offered her real name. There we only two men living who knew her as Gravda and they would not be talking. One was her boss, Allen Dulles, who respected her tremendously for her willingness to do whatever it took to get the job done. The second was the man who had recruited her, a man she had come closest to falling in love with three years earlier. That man knew most of her dirty little secrets, but she was confident he would never share them with anyone. He couldn't, he had his own secrets to hide, because that man was the sixty-fourth United States Attorney General and the younger brother of the President of the United States.

Gravda spoke six languages fluently. Her passports were changed frequently so none would show the extensive amount of travel she incurred. She had no permanent residence. There were safe houses in several cities with considerable wardrobes for her to select from when the job or even her mood changed. Her clothing allowance rivaled the First Lady's, but Allen Dulles was willing to pay her what most C.E.O.s did not make. She had earned every penny.

She had no family, few friends if any, and no home. What

she did have was a burning disdain for the Soviet Union and everything it stood for. Russians who thought of themselves as better than someone else had destroyed everything she had ever loved, but this was not about revenge. Revenge is a broad brush which paints the color red over too many people. This was all about fairness and restoring order in the world. Revenge clouds your judgment and to Betty Miller, Sharon Wilkerson, Bianca Verti, or any other name she might be going by, a clear mind was her biggest asset. If someone was out to take something from another human being and she could change that, then she was just tipping the scales in favor of humanity.

She felt she owed it to her parents. Gravda Nemiroff had long ago decided she was damaged goods, and nothing could save her. Maybe, just maybe, she could save someone else from the same fate.

As she walked out of the front door of the boarding house, she reached into her coat pocket and felt for the key that would unlock the roll up door in the garage she had rented a block away. The dark streets of Whitehall seemed incongruent to the fashionable woman who strolled casually towards the corner.

As she reached the other side of the street, she heard a muffled whimper coming from the alley. Without hesitation, she turned into the blackness and came upon a bloated man in a cheap suit with his hand around the throat of a woman who looked to be in her late thirties. Her plastic skirt was well above the knee and her white go-go boots were no longer white. Even heavy makeup could not conceal the puffiness of her left cheek the man had slapped before she had arrived.

"Thirty quid, bitch!" the man spat at the woman he held at bay. "Yah brings me thirty quid or yah pay the consequences. I ain't doing this for me health! We's been over this before, Rita. When is yah gonna learn?"

Rita's eyes grew wide as she saw Gravda walk up behind the man.

"Let her go," Gravda said.

The man spun quickly out of surprise, his chubby hand still around Rita's throat. The man regained his composure and chuckled. "This ain't 'ave nuffin to do wiff yah, lady."

"Yes, it does," Gravda said, and before he could react, she kicked him hard to the groin.

The man moaned and stumbled.

She had already deduced he would have held Rita with his dominant right hand, leaving his jugular vein exposed on his left side. Gravda took one step inward and delivered a crushing blow with the side of her hand to the man's neck. He crumpled to the ground, face first, into the cobblestone.

It took a second for the unconscious man to release his grip on the frightened Rita, dragging her to the ground with him.

Gravda helped her to her feet, noticing her fish net stockings were now torn and her left knee bloody.

"Oh me bloody God, you fuckin' killed 'im," Rita stammered out of panic.

"No, I didn't," Gravda said, "But when he wakes up, he is going to be pissed...and if he ever sees you again, he *will* kill you. Rita...it is time you made some new career choices."

Gravda reached into the right pocket of her pantsuit and pulled out all the money she had, one thousand British pounds. Gravda pushed it into Rita's palm and simply said, "Now go...and don't look back."

Rita limped to the corner and disappeared. Gravda walked

the rest of the way and unlocked the roll up door, slipped behind the wheel of a new Jaguar, flipped down the visor to find the ignition key, and drove off to the Ritz where a reservation was waiting in her name...one of her names.

Chapter 5

Goddard Space Center, Green Belt Maryland

James E. Webb had scarcely had enough time to set up his new office at Goddard Space Center. The cardboard box which lay on the floor still contained the framed photos of his wife Patsy and his two children. The newly appointed director for the National Aeronautics and Space Administration was used to eighty-hour workweeks, but this was different. He had been the undersecretary of State in the Truman administration, and a successful attorney before that. His greatest skills were in management, organization, and the successful delegation of responsibilities.

He was well-versed in aviation and was still on the board of directors for McDonnell Aircraft Corporation but was tapped as the new director of NASA solely for his skills in uniting a workforce. President Kennedy had needed a leader, and James Webb was the right man for the job.

Webb looked more like a union boss than a bureaucrat. His

stocky frame and slicked-back hair made few argue with his authority. His voice was loud, and he demanded the best out of his people. "Tough but fair," is how most who worked for him described his personality, the emphasis was on the word tough.

Five days before President Kennedy's address to Congress, Alan Shepard circled the globe in a sub-orbital trek across the sky. Within twenty minutes, Kennedy had phoned Webb telling him of his plans to address Congress.

Webb had done his best to talk the President out of it.

Webb's argument was rational and based in reality. The United States lacked the technology, the infrastructure, facilities, and the trained workforce to make it all a reasonable goal.

The President's comment was simply, "James, make it happen."

James Webb had hung up the phone, his first words after having said, "Yes sir, Mr. President," were, "Shit, that's just like a democrat. Literally promise people the moon then expecting someone else to figure out how to get it done!" Webb would have his hands full.

America's space program in May of 1961 was a disjointed array of several research centers across the country with very intelligent scientists, but little formal communication. If James Webb was to honor President Kennedy's wish of putting a man on the moon and safely return him to Earth within a single decade, then he had better get people united to the cause.

Goddard Space Center is located approximately six-and-a-half miles from Washington D.C. in the rolling green hills of Maryland. Goddard acted as mission control for all the Redstone rockets Wernher von Braun and his team of sixty-five ex-Nazi scientists had designed. The Redstone rockets were not much more than enhanced intercontinental ballistic missiles and the big brother to the V-2 Braun had developed to terrorize England during the war.

Braun and his team knew well enough to stay away from Webb and therefore spent most of their time at the Redstone Arsenal in Huntsville Alabama. If James Webb had things his way, Braun and his cronies would have been locked up and charged with crimes against humanity. The sad part though was Webb now needed them more than ever.

In 1960, NASA wrote checks to 10,000 employees and civilian contractors. In 1961, the number would grow to over 50,000. In 1962, the number would double.

President Kennedy had personally helped to broker a real estate deal between two major oil companies and the William March Rice University, (often just called Rice), in Houston Texas which would allow NASA to build a sprawling 100-building complex on 1620 acres of newly donated land. The new Manned Spacecraft Center would pull several research centers from across the country and put them under one roof. The center would act as mission control and astronaut-training center, as well as a hub with offices for such contractors as Grumman International and Lockheed aircraft.

When the President wanted a man on the moon within the decade, every hour counted. No longer would astronauts take their classroom training in Langley Virginia, their physical preparedness and interaction with space hardware in Huntsville, and their briefings at Goddard.

Webb was to orchestrate the construction and the move to Houston in less than fourteen months. The pace would be exhausting, and Webb wanted an edge. Twenty-five thousand American engineers and scientists were about to embark on mankind's greatest challenge. They were behind, and Webb knew he needed help. And he was hoping the Russians would provide it.

"Gentlemen, please have a seat," Webb said to the twenty-or-so men that filed into the conference room. Most of them were young, late twenties or early thirties, clean-cut and dressed in white short-sleeved dress shirts, and more than a few wore pocket protectors.

"All right, all right, quiet down," Webb scolded. "We have a lot of ground to cover here today."

As each man took a seat, the silence seemed to last longer than was comfortable. Engineers and mathematicians started to look at each other, while Webb sat silently and patiently. Two minutes later, the door opened and four men who were bigger than life glided into the room.

Right on time, thought Webb.

John Glenn, Scott Carpenter, Gus Grissom, and Deke Slayton sauntered into the conference room the way a football team walks back into the locker room after winning the big game. They laughed at an inside joke that would never be shared with the men at the conference table. The whispers began and James Webb let them float through the air.

"That's John Glenn, gee whiz," one said.

"Wait 'till my wife hears this," another one muttered.

"That's really them," a third was heard saying to the man sitting next to him.

"OK, boys take it down a notch," Webb said. "I need all of you to be focused. You've seen these boys in the press, so I don't have to make any introductions. Meet four of the Mercury Seven, our first Americans we intend to put into space."

The room erupted in applause. Several of the engineers stood up to pay their respects.

Webb paused just as he had planned and then slammed his notebook onto the conference table in a thunderous sound that echoed off the walls. Men flinched and froze.

"What are you, schoolgirls?" Webb bellowed. "These four men haven't done a damn thing yet," Webb yelled as he pointed towards the astronauts at the front of the room. "If we are going to reach our objectives than every man in here must be focused on the task at hand. Save your applause until we have earned it."

The room was dead quiet.

Webb took a breath and began, "The four men who stand before you are counting on your abilities with their very lives. At this point, no one has much to celebrate. Alan Shepard is a media darling right now—" Webb started to say, but Deke Slayton interrupted him.

"Yeah, Alan would have been here...but he is at another ticker tape parade."

The room laughed and the ice was broken. Even James Webb had to smile.

Webb continued, "This space race isn't about who does things second, it's about who does them first and does them right. Gentlemen, I don't mind telling you the Russians are kicking our ass, and I want to know why. They put Yuri Gagarin into full orbit a month before we were able to put Shepard into a sub-orbital flight. I just got word this morning John Glenn has been chosen for our first true orbital mission, but it's not scheduled until February of next year. That puts us eleven months behind the Soviet Union."

The three other astronauts looked at John Glenn surprised but said nothing. He was smiling.

Webb focused his attention on John Glenn and asked, "John if we strapped you to a Redstone rocket right now and sent you up into full orbit, what would happen?"

Glenn paused and then spoke, "Well, from what I understand it would be a hell of a ride...and a lot of fun for a little while. We have the propulsion technology to get us into orbit, but your math guys haven't quite figured out how to get my sorry butt back yet."

Webb once again let the words linger in the air. "The Space Race won't be won by space jockeys like Glenn here or any of the other six men chosen for the Mercury or upcoming Gemini programs. It will be earned by men like you by outsmarting the Russians and getting this stuff right. We need the right stuff!" Pull out your slide rules boys, we need to figure out what we know and more importantly what we don't know. We're not leaving this room until we do."

The men in the room who had stood up to applaud the astronauts finally took a seat. Webb walked to the chalkboard. Glenn, Carpenter, Grissom, and Slayton found seats at the corners of the table, effectively splitting the group into fours.

"This will be an open forum gentlemen, no one is taking notes. I want you all to speak freely and give me your honest opinions," Webb said. "What is our issue with re-entry and how is it the Russians seem to have figured it out when we haven't?"

"We have the math," one man said. "The math doesn't change. The problem is in terms of communication. We know the numbers, but we're asking a hell of a lot from our astronauts in the moment...No offense guys."

The man who had spoken was Chris Kraft Jr. Few people know his name today, but he was the first to suggest the theory of a "mission control center." He had been hired by the National Advisory Committee for Aeronautics (NACA) more than a decade before after graduating from Virginia Polytechnic Institute and State University with a degree in aeronautical engineering and was an obvious choice for Webb's new NASA administration.

"Go on," Webb urged the young engineer.

"Re-entry involves hitting a paper-thin window of Earth's atmosphere, at just the right angle, at just the right speed, and doing it in three dimensions," Kraft explained. "You're doing ten things at once; the capsule has to be turned bottom-side-up, so the heat shields become the contact point in the atmosphere. If you miss it, the capsule burns up because of atmospheric friction. It all requires the right velocity, pitch, yaw, angle, roll and trajectory. The on-board mechanical guidance systems can't handle all that information at one time and do the calculations fast enough to make the necessary split-second changes."

Webb urged the young engineer to continue when he paused again.

"Our pilots are the best, but we're asking them to peddle a unicycle, spin plates on sticks, and all the while patting their head and rubbing their bellies...they just don't have enough hands. Space capsules are machines, and we understand machines. But even machines need time to make servo changes or booster ignitions. By the time our ground-based computers can make the necessary re-calculations, we miss our window. No astronaut can do all the calculations and physically maneuver a ship at the same time."

"Okay," Webb said. "So, the communication problem is a computer issue then?"

"It's certainly a big part of it," Kraft said. "Until we have computers fast enough to react to split second changes and then communicate those changes to all the active parts of the ship, well, it just can't be done with any assurance of safety—"

"I think that's bullshit," Gus Grissom interrupted. He looked directly at the other three astronauts in the room and said, "There is no computer in the world that can do what a highly trained and levelheaded pilot can do, and there never will be. Make the equipment do what it is supposed to do, and we will fly it!"

James Webb let the astronaut vent. Failures and delays had plagued the entire Mercury program. Mistakes were not only costly in terms of money, but potentially in the lives of the seven astronauts chosen to fly them.

"Everyone keeps talking about damn computers," Grissom said. "Hell, the first step in all of this is you guys bolting these machines together, so it doesn't blow up the launchpad. We have tested five of your new Atlas rockets in the last four months and three of them failed. That's a sixty percent failure rate on mechanical...if it were your butt on top of that rocket, wouldn't you be asking for better odds?"

Grissom took a deep breath and ran his hands through his military crew cut. He turned towards Kraft and said in a softer tone, "Listen, I know you guys are doing the best you can, but I just think we are over-engineering all of this stuff. I'm a test pilot but I am also a mechanical engineer, and I'm the next guy on the list to launch for yet another sub-orbital flight in July. I flew one hundred missions against Russian MIG's in Korea and I can tell you those guys are in no way, shape, or form, ahead of us. If the Russians even saw an American aircraft, they ran home with their tails between their legs. Just tighten down all the screws and let us do what we do best, please."

A few of the engineers started to rebut the astronaut. Kraft was wise enough to wait and pick his arguments.

Grissom held up one finger to silence them as he continued. "The Redstone rockets have held up just fine. It was your so-called computer issues that kept Alan Shepard from being the first man into space."

Grissom was correct. Technical delays had prevented Alan Shepard from being the first human being in space. The mainframe computer there at Goddard Space Center had malfunctioned nearly a month before Alan Shepard's intended launch of Freedom 7. With additional testing to make sure everything was back online and ready to go, the Russians had swooped in and captured the world's press.

Shepard would have to settle for only being the first American in space...and had done it with wet shorts. The launch of Freedom 7 was delayed at Cape Canaveral five different times due to mechanical or computer malfunctions. On the day of the actual launch, five additional hours of delays tested Shepard's bladder. Shepard's famous quote of, "Let's light this candle," was followed by a quote only those in the Astronaut pool and the engineers would quote later, "And let's do it before I piss myself." The medical team worried he would electrically short out his medical sensors had asked him to "hold it." But Shepard had no choice. Even the simplest biological functions were untried in space and the frustration the astronaut team was feeling was justified. We were making things up as we went, and James Webb wanted to cut the learning curve.

"If you guys just build this stuff so it doesn't fall apart, me and the other fly boys will get the job done," Grissom continued. "I'm still frustrated we shot for second best to begin with. We already have the propulsion to reach full orbit. You guys are damn good with slide rules. Give us pilots the numbers and we will bring her home."

Other engineers at the table, feeling defensive, piped up, "None of this stuff has ever been done before, we're doing the best we can with what we've got."

Another one said, "We're working with what we had yesterday, and we need what hasn't even been invented yet."

"It has been done," Grissom said exasperated. "Yuri Gagarin did it just twenty-three days before Shepard's flight. He reached full orbit, and we are still playing it safe with this sub-orbital stuff. Twenty-three days is not an ass kicking guys, we could have been there first. I launch in a little over three weeks on yet another sub-orbital flight. Hell, that doesn't even make me runner-up to second place. The Russians safely put two dogs into orbital flight almost a year ago!"

Gus Grissom looked at John Glenn. "When is the scheduled launch for your orbital flight?"

Glenn had said very little up to that point. "The flight is scheduled for February 20th of next year," he said.

"Wonderful," said Grissom. "Ten months after Gagarin...Now that's kicking our ass."

Chapter 6

The Meeting at Goddard Continues

After another thirty minutes of heated discussion in which James Webb allowed his engineers and the four astronauts in the room to speak their mind, he once again took control.

He turned to Chris Kraft and said, "Chris, the President's new objective puts your boys under the gun. He wants a man on the moon in less than ninety months. My job is to provide all the necessary infrastructure to make it happen. Your job is to tell me what you think we need."

Kraft thought for several seconds before addressing his new boss. "I still think we need on-board computers capable of calculating telemetry and then communicating the information to the booster engines with ten-to-fifteen calculations per second. We don't even have any on-board computers right now; all our calculations are being done from the ground on a mainframe computer the size of this conference room."

"OK," said Webb. "Rice University is bringing their new

mainframe computer online soon; Northwestern University and M.I.T. are also on board to give us faster speeds and more data transfer by the end of July."

"That's all fine and good, but we need computing power on-board, and the computer has to be small enough to fit in the capsule and not carry a lot of weight," Kraft said. "Extra weight means extra propulsion needed to launch and achieve the needed seven miles per second speed to break free of orbit. We're working with a double edge sword here. Extra weight means extra fuel and fuel has its own weight. The new Atlas rockets we're developing offer a lot more thrust and power and it will help us with payload weights, but we still need to develop smaller faster computers for the capsules."

Webb pushed Chris Kraft for more information. "OK, so we get the new mainframes online with more power...Why can't we handle the computer end of it from the ground then?"

Kraft did not even pause before responding. "Time and distance," he said. "Our first challenge is just an orbital flight, or fifty miles. People drive fifty miles and don't even think about it. We can get that high right now but the Moon is 238,000 miles away; it takes radio waves traveling at the speed of light a full second and a half to get to the moon. A lot can happen in a second and a half. We need on-board computers to make those calculations. Computers that can react with the hardware of a spacecraft fast enough to make those changes. Telemetry must be adjusted from onboard the spacecraft!"

John Glenn spoke up for the first time. "I agree with Chris, we have to engineer the spacecraft proactively. We need to design our hardware in advance of the current technology. We build the equipment with the assumption the computer engineers and technicians can catch up to the needs of the program six months to a year from now."

"That's hoping for a lot there, John," Webb said. "There is no other way to do it, Jim," Glenn said. "President Kennedy is asking for a lot and it's not his ass sitting on top of a rocket. It's the only way we can meet the deadlines; we have to have faith the knowledge will catch up to the needs."

"It sounds a lot like reverse engineering in the wrong direction," Grissom grumbled.

Glenn looked at his fellow astronaut, guessing out of the others in the room, Grissom was probably the most pissed to have heard Glenn would be the first man scheduled for an orbital flight and not himself. "Gus, we're working in unfamiliar territory right now. Hell, the flight engineers don't even know if our eyes will pop out of their sockets in zero G's. The medical staff here at NASA has no idea what a three-day mission to the moon will even require."

Grissom was not one to hold back his thoughts. "The damn doctors have no idea what they're doing anyways John, and you know it. We are test pilots for crying out loud. If our eyes pop out, we will tape 'em back and keep flying. Those doctors are more worried about covering their own asses than they are about us."

Gus Grissom had his reasons for being less than cordial to the NASA medical staff; they had originally disqualified Grissom from the astronaut pool because he suffered from hay fever. That was until Grissom pointed out as far as he knew there seemed to be a lack of ragweed pollen in outer space.

Before more discussion heated the room between Grissom and the engineers, Webb changed the subject. "Alright then, let's answer this question. How is it the Russians had launched twice into outer space and successfully reentered the atmosphere when our best minds can't do it yet? Gagarin is on a world tour right now signing autographs, and Sputnik 5 landed two dogs safely back in August of last year. What do the Russians know or what is it they have on board we can't duplicate at this point?"

Webb looked at the brilliant Chris Kraft again. "Chris?"

Kraft shrugged his shoulders. "Jim, I simply don't know. It doesn't make sense to me. We know Sputnik 5 had to have been controlled from the ground. Those dogs certainly weren't flying the ship. It still doesn't explain how they calculated the numbers for reentry though. Exiting the atmosphere is easy, it's all about brute force and propulsion. Re-entry requires finesse and some serious number crunching. They got Gagarin to the ground, but I can't begin to tell you how they did it. I don't think it is hardware or nuts and bolts—it has to be computers."

Scott Carpenter was one of the astronauts in the room, and usually the silent type. Brains ran in his family. His father, for example, had been a research chemist with a doctorate.

"The Russian's satellite program has me worried," he said. "They are doing the same thing we are in terms of testing flight scenarios. You test a hypothesis with a satellite before you launch a human being into space. On that scorecard, they do seem to be way ahead of us."

Carpenter and the rest of the team assembled that morning were headed towards James Webb's primary objective for having called them together; they just didn't know it yet.

"Go on Scott," Webb urged, "Speak your mind, please."

Carpenter scratched his head. "The Russians launched Sputnik 1 in October of '57; we launched Explorer 1 on January 31st of '58. That's a little over two months later and Explorer 1 used transistors for the first time and is still sending us data. I don't consider two months as, "Kicking our ass," as Gus would say," he explained.

Webb was listening intently.

"Out of nowhere, the Russian satellite program seemed to leap ahead of us in technology. We haven't even come close to the moon, but the Russians have had three of them which have. Luna 1 was supposed to have impacted the moon, missed, and is headed towards the sun. A miss is still important data though and it still tells us they don't have it all down yet. Luna 2 did impact the moon in September of '59. So, they deserve the bragging rights of having gotten there first."

There were some grumbles in the room, they hated having to give the Russians any bragging rights. Carpenter ignored the noises around him as he continued.

"Then Luna 3 circled the moon in orbit and sent back pictures of the back side of the moon. I agree with Chris there is no way they could have controlled it from the ground. Radio transmissions can't travel through the surface of the moon and when the satellite was on the back side, it was outside of radio signals for at least thirty-four minutes. Somehow, they managed to orbit the moon, take those photos, store them, and then transmit them back to Earth after they came back around the moon," Carpenter said. "That part has me totally perplexed. We can't even get to the moon yet and those guys are sending photos back of the dark side. And they did it almost a year and a half ago. That's what has me worried: how did they get such a leap on us? What the hell do they have on board those satellites we haven't figured out yet?"

James Webb smiled for the first time in days. He had the photos of the Luna 3 in his briefcase a certain unnamed CIA operative had taken just two days before. The four astronauts and twenty or so engineers were about to find out why they had been called to Goddard Space Center to begin with.

Chapter 7

London, Twenty-Four Hours Earlier

Gravda Nemiroff parked the Jaguar in the same warehouse she had pulled out of the night before. May in London can be cold and dreary, but not on this day. She felt the warmth of the sun on her bare shoulders and found herself humming as she strolled back to The Shoreditch hotel. She was looking forward to interacting with her male counterparts she had met just two days before.

They seemed nice enough. They were technicians and analysts, and she was sure none of them had ever held a gun before, but they all received their paychecks from the same governmental agency. She had caught all three of them glancing at her legs or looking her way when they thought she wasn't paying attention...she was always paying attention. They were men; she could forgive them for that.

The rotund little pug she had pummeled the night before was a different story. He deserved all he got, and more. Gravda laughed to herself trying to think of what lies he told his buddies at the pub when he showed up battered and bleeding. A pig like him could never let his ego tell the truth of what had happened in the alleyway she had just passed.

She waltzed through the dingy lobby and took the elevator to the third floor. As the doors of the elevator opened, she poked her head out and scanned the hallway from left to right. She was always careful and always on guard. Her habits had kept her alive this long and she wanted to keep it that way. As expected, the hallway was empty. Residents of the Shoreditch hotel were not the type to rise early.

When she reached door number 303, she knocked softly twice, paused, and knocked once more. The door immediately opened, and she glided inside.

"Good morning, Betty," said the man who opened the door for her. "You're looking radiant this morning."

"Why thank you sir," she said twirling in a pirouette as she entered the room, allowing her blue and white polka dot dress with spaghetti straps to whirl up just high enough to silence all three men in the room. "Did you miss me, boys?"

She enjoyed watching the two men in the living room reach up to loosen their thin neckties from their Adam's apples. The three men she had met last night were all CIA personnel but none of them were field agents. One was a photographer tasked to develop her photos and the other two were photo analysts with some background in aerospace engineering or military hardware.

The man who had opened the door said, "The photographs were perfect. Nice work."

"So, did you get what you were looking for?" she asked.

"I do believe we did," said one of the analysts, "but we would still like to ask you a few more questions about your observations though. Things you might have picked up on the photos aren't telling us."

There were fifty-two photographs spread out on the bed and coffee table, and she looked at each one remembering in her mind the view as each was taken. She took her time before finally asking, "What exactly are you looking for?"

"Well first let's start with your assumption this Luna 3 is an actual working backup to the one they launched in '59," said one of the men.

Gravda looked back at the photos and picked up three to pass around.

"There were four armed guards standing next to the satellite," she said. "Not just single guards like the other displays. I know the way Russians think, and it means one of two things. It is either a working model, or the Russians want people to think it is. And I am betting on the first." She reached for another photo on the bed and held it up. She pointed to it and asked, "What is missing in this photo?"

The photo was of another Soviet military personnel. Only this time it was an officer.

"I counted twenty-two guards in the auditorium yesterday," she said. "I can't account for every single one because I never attempted to get behind the scenes or do any surveillance on the loading docks."

The men passed the photo around, looking now at the Soviet military personnel her finger had pointed to.

Finally, the third man said, "No gun."

"That's right," Gravda said, "No gun. Every other Soviet military personal in uniform there yesterday in the space pavilion was armed, but not him. Why? I walked the entire exhibition for two days and the only hall they purposefully chose to have armed guards was their space exhibition. No one was guarding toaster ovens or washing machines. The Soviets want people to think their space program is about superiority in military might. It's why we're here, right? People back home are shitting in their capri pants and Levi's. Look at the epilates on his tunic, three gold bars and a single star. Boys, that is a major. And what is the background color on his epilates?" she asked.

All three men answered in harmony, "They're blue."

"Yes blue. That means he is an Air Force Major, if the background color was red, he would be an Army major."

"That gentleman was the man in charge yesterday, and he spent all day keeping an eye on the Luna 3," she continued. "Those ropes kept spectators ten feet at bay; the Major didn't want anyone looking inside. Every other soldier there was an enlisted man, except for Gagarin himself, and he was in civilian clothing."

"And he was too busy signing autographs," one man said.

"Exactly. When someone tells me I can't look inside of something, it only makes me want to look inside it even more." Gravda was smiling as she said it.

The man who had developed her photos said, "I agree with you, I would love to see what's inside that satellite."

"Well, if you're curious, I have a few ideas on how we can do it..."

"Woah! Uh uh. What's with this we stuff? Our job was to get the photographs, nothing more. Those were armed guards," said one of them. "I'm here to look at photographs, not get shot at!"

"I usually work behind a desk and I'm pretty sure whatever you're thinking is way beyond my pay grade," said the second analyst. "We got the photos, so as far as I'm concerned, we are done here."

Gravda knew each of them only by first name and assumed just like herself, the names were not their own. It didn't matter though; names of any sort just breed familiarity. She knew every trick in the book, while these three had never even seen the book. Her responsibilities, doled out by Allen Dulles personally, were to photograph and gain intel on the Luna 3 capsule, period.

Well, what she was thinking now would still fit into the objective and she saw an opportunity to do much more. Intel was intel, right? All she wanted to do was extend the mission one more evening and she was sure Allen Dulles would understand even if she was adding another paragraph to where Dulles had put the period at the end of his orders. She had found in the past in her line of work asking for forgiveness when providing more than asked for was often easier than asking for permission to do so. She wanted more information, and she knew just how to get it. She would just have to convince the three men around her to help.

As they spoke, there was one loud wrap on the door followed by a long pause and then two more knocks. The photographer glanced her way while the two photo analysts froze. One started to duck down towards the bed.

"Relax, boys," Gravda giggled, "I sent for him."

The three men stood and stared at each other reluctant to move.

"You," she pointed at the photo analyst who had ducked and tried to hide, "Well, go answer the door."

He pointed a finger towards himself hoping he had mis-heard her.

"Yes, you...go open the door."

A nondescript man entered the room and pulled out a United States diplomatic pouch from under his over coat. Gravda gathered up the fifty-two photographs, placed them into the pouch, and sealed it. The man left without speaking a word. The pouch would be delivered to Allen Dulles within the next ten hours; James Webb would have it in his hands two hours later.

Gravda closed the door behind him and noticed all three men taking a deep sigh of relief.

"Guys, relax, I think we can do much more here. We are all here to get information on the satellite and it must be pretty important to someone back home, or I would be on a beach in the Mediterranean in a bikini right now. Give me a little help for just one more night and I'm sure we can give the folks back home more information than they expected. I just want a few more photos of that satellite."

The man who had developed the photos said, "So...what did you have in mind?" Maybe it was the thought of just spending more time with the lovely Gravda Nemiroff that convinced him, especially after she had mentioned the bikini.

"We know the dimensions of the satellite, right?" she asked.

"Yes," all three said at once.

"Therefore, we should be able to figure out the dimension of the crate they would transport it in. I want to know what that crate looks like so I can spot it again," she said.

"Those soldiers have guns," the photo analyst repeated.

"I know," Gravda said appeasing him. "We're going to wait until they put their guns down to photograph it."

All three men looked at her sideways, like a dog who had just heard a whistle.

"The Russians won't trust local civilians here in London to load their exhibit onto trucks, and those trucks won't be driven by locals either. They will all be Soviet enlisted men, and my bet is our Air Force major will supervise the operation. I want photographs of the loading process. Where is the next soviet exhibition?" she asked.

The aerospace engineer had to look at his notes. "Prague, two weeks from now," he said, still looking perplexed.

"The same crate they use tonight will be the same one they use in Prague," she said. "I want to know what the crate looks like." She turned to the photographer who had developed her photos earlier; "Do you have the equipment to photograph at night?"

"Uh, yeah, why?" he asked.

"You boys ever been on a stake out?"

Chapter 8

James Webb Continues His Meeting at Goddard Space Center

James Webb reached for his briefcase and pulled out a folder, filled with fifty-two color photographs. He sorted through them once again, before choosing fourteen of them he was willing to share. He spread them around the conference table for his engineers and astronauts to see.

"What I am about to show you is classified top secret. Is there anyone in this room who needs to be reminded of what that means?"

Each shook his head no.

"That, gentlemen, is the Soviet Luna 3 satellite," Webb said.

Deke Slayton began to ask, "Where did you get these?" But the look on James Webb's face made Slayton answer his own question. "Sorry, I know, don't ask."

No one in the room had actually seen any photos of the

satellite before. The press reels had not been released in American cinemas. President Eisenhower had blocked them, hoping to avert not only another Russian's propaganda coup, but also to avoid more American hysteria over the fact the Russians were ahead in the Space Race. Of course, the photos of the backside of the moon taken by the Russian satellite had been in CIA hands within days of the Russian announcement, but NASA engineers had never seen the satellite.

Chris Kraft was the first to speak up. "That's Luna 3? I am assuming it is a mockup of the satellite then, Jim?"

Webb said, "Let's just say you're looking at a fully functional backup to the original."

"Then this is the real deal then," Kraft said.

"I have the right people telling me it is," Webb answered.

Kraft whistled under his breath.

A younger member of the team asked, "Why would the Russians let us photograph her?" Scott Carpenter looked at the twenty-one-year-old and shook his head. Just because engineers can be brilliant doesn't mean they can't also be naive at the same time. A few others in the room laughed.

"They didn't, numb nuts," said Carpenter, "That's why it's top secret."

"Oh...OH!" the young engineer responded as the message set in.

"The finest minds in America," Gus Grissom added. Grissom was not laughing like the rest of the men in the room.

Adequately shamed, the young scientist held up a hand and said, "Not my finest moment."

"Ok, gentleman we've had our fun," Webb chastised.

"Chris, I want you and your guys to take a look at these and tell me if it answers any questions."

"First, let me ask a few questions," Chris Kraft said. "Do you have any dimensions?"

"It so happens I do," Webb said, reaching for his briefcase again. He pulled out an abridged version of the written report Gravda had prepared.

Kraft picked up four of the photos and looked at each one before commenting, "These all look to have been taken from the same distance. Don't we have any close ups?"

"I can get them," Webb told him. "Look this stuff over and then tell me what you need, and I will make it happen."

Kraft took charge and pulled his most experienced engineers to one table along with the astronauts. "I want to know how you guys would have engineered this thing and then tell me if we missed anything. This thing was built to fly to the moon, take photos, develop those photos, and then send them home. That's impressive, but nothing past what I think we can accomplish ourselves. We just need to figure out how they did it."

One of the engineers spoke up immediately, "The solar cells! They're smaller than I would have thought."

"I agree," said Kraft, "those cells had to power up any batteries needed for electronics, the radio transmitter and receiver as well as whatever they had on board to develop the photos after they were taken. Considering all they had to do, I would have thought the solar cells would have been much larger too."

Deke Slayton added, "Plus they had to have some kind of cooling fans on board. In direct sunlight the metal skin had to heat up to 250 degrees or more. Fans draw a lot of energy."

"It's why we rotate our satellites every few minutes so no one side is exposed for too long to direct sunlight to begin with," one said.

"Yeah, but they couldn't do it that way and still get clear photos unless they put the camera on a gyroscope or some kind of complex gimble," Slayton added. "You can't take good photos from something which is spinning."

"They might have come up with metal alloys we don't know if yet. Dissipates heat better."

"We are getting way ahead of ourselves guys," Kraft said. "Focus on what we know and how we would build it. Let's not guess on 'what-ifs' and conjecture. Jim, refresh my memory. How many photos did the Russians get from the back side of the moon?"

"Twenty-nine as far as we know. They publicized twenty-nine. It is possible they took more and only chose to show off the ones which were clear enough to make out."

"They were on the back side of the moon for thirty-four minutes. We rotate our satellites every three minutes. They could have done the same thing and still have taken all those photos between rotations. You're overthinking this stuff, gentlemen."

"Chris is right," Webb said. "Right now, we are not looking for unicorns and magic metal alloys which haven't been invented yet. They launched this thing over a year and a half ago! Let's go back to basics and analyze what we have in front of us." Webb looked at the photo. "So, we know they have an edge on us on photon charging, what else?"

"There are four antennae on the top and two on the bottom," said someone. "I am assuming the top is for radio reception and the bottom for transmission of the photos."

Kraft interjected, "That's old-school technology, and those are the same antennae they used on Sputnik 1 in October of '57." This seemed to really perplex him.

"Yeah, just bigger," Slayton noted. "A lot bigger."

"With the advent of solid-state electronics, we're now using receivers a tenth of the size than those we had in '58 and '59 when they launched this thing. Why did they need four antennae anyway, and why are they so damn big?" asked another one of the engineers.

"The moon is a long way away," said another. "Maybe they weren't confident in their radio reception?"

Gus Grissom took the photo and said, "The whole satellite is big...and looks heavy too. The whole thing looks to be the size of a phone booth."

"Keep in mind guys," Webb said, "Luna 3 was launched nineteen months ago, technology has come a long way in that period of time...for both sides."

"Yeah, Jim, but you keep asking us to figure out how those guys are beating us," Grissom said. "Kraft is worried about on-board telemetry computers which haven't been developed yet and probably won't be for two more years. I just don't think those guys are that much farther ahead of us," Grissom continued, "I think we're chasing ghosts here."

"Mr. Grissom, how can you say that?" an engineer asked.

Several others looked exasperated at what they thought would just lead into another one of Gus Grissom's rants.

The engineer continued, "The Russians launched Luna 3 and circumnavigated the moon while taking photographs we still can't figure out. We're worried about reentry and the Russians have already done it twice! Sputnik 5 in August of last year with two dogs aboard and recently landed Yuri Gagarin...So, yes, they're ahead of us." The young engineer was respectful but frustrated. "They're not only ahead of us, but they may also be, by your own calculations, two years ahead of us."

"My calculations?" asked Grissom.

"Yes, your calculations!" said the engineer. "You said we won't have on-board active telemetry computers for two more years here in The United States. So how do you explain them launching this thing—" he tapped his finger on the photo, "— and getting it around the back side of the moon without using radio waves?"

Gus Grissom had paused for a while, before finally responding, "...I think they got lucky."

He was not kidding.

The engineer threw his hands in the air.

Grissom explained, "Look at the antennae. Take a good look. They're huge. Those antennae are that big because the Russians were still having troubles with radio reception and transmission. The spacecraft is that big because they are still using cathode ray receivers and not solid-state. Hell, it was 1959 and we're looking at this thing like it is the holy grail to all space travel. I'll tell you why the Russians are beating us. They don't bog themselves down with a myriad of governmental oversight committees and bureaucracy. Risk and reward! They took what they had and did what they needed to do. We should be doing the same thing." Grissom tossed the photo at the engineer who had challenged him.

Several of the engineers in their frustration turned their backs and walked away from the conference table.

John Glenn had not spoken much but stood up and put both palms on the table directing his stare at Grissom. "Gus, you have two kids just like me. You seem more worried about the record books then you are getting home safely to them."

"Yeah, well it's easy for you to say. You're the one who's name will be in those record books."

Grissom walked away to sulk.

Deke Slayton, probably the smartest man in the room, had said little.

James Webb had been standing next to him, and leaned down and whispered in his ear, "What are you thinking, Deke?"

"Well, Gus is a hothead who gets pissed when someone doesn't see his vantage point," Slayton said. "Let him cool off for a while. He is right though; those antennae were already outdated when they launched the damn thing. Other than some really nice engineering on the solar cells, I don't see a lot of innovation here." He added, "It's almost like they were pulling parts off the shelf to get this thing into outer space."

"I've known you a longtime Deke," Webb said, "I'm not used to seeing you looking confused."

"Yeah, well, me either," Slayton laughed. "Gus is a damn good pilot, but his attitude is just, 'Strap me in and light the fuse!' This race is not going to be won by fighter jocks, it will be won by the engineers on the ground." He thought for a moment and added, "We always have our launches on national TV where everyone gets to see how far we still have to go to get it right. The Russians are at least smart enough do it all in secret, then brag about what worked."

"Okay then, just between you and me," Webb said quietly, "What has you so bugged about this satellite?"

"I just can't figure out how they got it around the back side of the moon without on-board telemetry," Slayton said. "Alan Sheppard could have beaten Gagarin into outer space by a few months but without the right equipment, we calculated a fifty-fifty chance of success on re-entry. Gus probably would have taken those odds, but you and I know President Kennedy wouldn't have. Jim, this satellite was the steppingstone to having put Yuri Gagarin into full orbit and returning him safely to the ground, I'm sure of it."

"Maybe Gus is right, maybe they just got lucky," Webb agreed. "Maybe the Russians are ahead simply because they are willing to take those 50/50 odds and we aren't. The Russians have always had a different take on the value of life in general, it's all for the state and not on the individual."

"I don't disagree," Slayton said, "But the Russians aren't stupid either. Both sides have the same objective of getting a man to the moon and getting him home safely, and you can't do it with luck alone. I have to agree with Chris Kraft on this one, to do it safely we need equipment that can chew up data and spit out the right numbers fast enough to make the necessary changes in real time without lag. If this thing made it around the dark side of the moon without radio contact and came out on the other side, then there has to be something on-board we haven't figured out."

James Webb was a master at asking the right questions. It was part of what made him such a good manager of people, engineers in particular. He had a way of redirecting one's thinking to look for alternative solutions.

"Deke, I agree with both you and Chris. We have to make

big strides on computers and telemetry, but you're assuming the Russians have already made those leaps. Let's just say for the sake of discussion that they haven't. We both want to know how they kept the damn satellite from being sucked into the moon's orbit during those thirty-four minutes without radio communications."

"They had something on board controlling the altitude which did not use radio waves and still adjusted the craft with no ground control," Slayton said, thinking. It was phrased more like a question and less of a statement.

"Okay," Webb said, "You mentioned the spacecraft looked, and I quote, 'like they pulled parts off the shelf' to get it into the moon's orbit. What did we have in our inventory back in 1959 which could do the same thing? —And don't answer with 'technology we don't have yet.'"

Slayton scratched his head. "We know the moon's gravitational pull is 83.3% less than here on Earth, or roughly five sixths less. Which means if we ever get a man on the moon an average guy who weighs in at one hundred and fifty pounds will feel like he weighs twenty-four point nine pounds on the surface of the moon. The Russians know those numbers too," he said.

Scott Carpenter had been sitting next to Deke Slayton the whole time and had done his best to listen in on the conversation between Slayton and the newly appointed head of NASA. Carpenter and Slayton had both gone through astronaut training together and had become close friends and both had engineering backgrounds.

Carpenter had said very little the entire time until now.

"So, Deke, what time do you have?"

"What?" Slayton asked as he pulled himself away from his

thoughts to answer. "I'm a little busy here Scott..."

Carpenter looked over Deke Slayton's shoulder and smiled up at James Webb. "Yeah, I know you're busy...so what time yah got?"

"Dammit Scott, I am trying to think here. You're interrupting my train of thought!"

"I know I am buddy. Somebody has to. That train of yours has only been on one set of tracks. You've already decided the logical destination has to be solid state telemetry and on-board computers."

It was James Webb's turn to smile. He was good at asking the right questions, while he left it up to smarter men than himself to come up with the answers.

Carpenter pushed once more. "So, I'll ask you again, what time do you have?"

Slayton gave in and glanced at his watch, "Its twenty minutes after two o'clock. Are you happy now?"

"Not quite yet. How many seconds?"

"You're killing me here Scott," Slayton said, eager to get back to the problem at hand. He looked down at his watch. "It is exactly 2:20 p.m. and thirteen...fourteen...fifteen seconds." Slayton continued to stare at his watch after finishing his sentence. It was now his turn to smile. He watched as the sweep second hand marched in perfect mechanical precision around the watch face.

Carpenter put his hand on his friend's shoulder. "I know the numbers just like you do," he said. "The moon's gravity is constant; it doesn't change. Sometimes the toughest questions have the simplest answers, Deke."

"Son of a bitch," Slayton exclaimed loud enough for John Glenn and Gus Grissom to have heard him.

"What do you have Deke?" both astronauts asked.

"It's not what I have. Scott here figured it out," Slayton said with his head in his hands. "They used...a...mechanical timer."

"What?" asked some of the engineers.

Grissom laughed aloud.

Still, some of the engineers had not yet caught on.

Deke Slayton held his arm up to show James Webb his wristwatch. "They had a mechanical timer attached to the hydrogen peroxide thrusters," Slayton said. "They fired at precise intervals allowing the satellite to stay in orbit and not crash into the surface of the moon. Just enough force to make its way around until radio waves could pick her up again on the front side and guide it towards home."

Gus Grissom laughed again. "They put the damn thing on the back side of the moon with an egg timer, yah got to love those guys. I told you I was right."

John Glen said, "Were never going to hear the end of this, you know that."

"Gentlemen, let me tell you something about myself," Grissom said, looking smug. "I have only been wrong once in my life and it was the one time when I thought I was wrong...but I was mistaken."

Few engineers in the room could tell if Grissom was joking or not.

Deke Slayton stood up and pulled James Webb aside. "I told you earlier this morning I wanted a look inside that satellite to see what they have inside we don't have."

"Yes, I remember," Webb said.

"Well now I want a look inside even more, only this time I want to know what else they *don't* have."

Scott Carpenter joined the two men in the corner just as Webb said, "I know you do Deke, believe me, we're working on it."

Carpenter said, "Jim, I know you have access to intel you can't share with us, and I fully understand, but I just thought of something."

"And what's that?" Webb asked.

"Well, Deke here was counting on Luna 3 as the stepping-stone to telemetry and re-entry, and if we're right about mechanical timers than it pulls one more trick out of the Russian's hat, but it still doesn't tell us how they got Sputnik 5 or Gagarin's Vostock 1 back on the ground safely."

"Okay, I agree Scott, what are you getting at?"

"There are still a lot of unanswered questions, and I've got one of my own. Have you seen any photos or press reels of Gagarin's Vostock 1 capsule...after it landed? I can't remember seeing anything of the capsule itself. I remember seeing photos of Khrushchev and Gagarin together afterwards...but now I am starting to wonder about something."

"If you're thinking conspiracy theories," Webb said, "I can assure you we tracked Gagarin's flight with radar here at Goddard for the entire flight. The Russians even shared their flight plan with us because they were worried one of our own satellites could be in the flight path. I can't tell you everything I know, but I can say Kennedy and Khrushchev have both agreed there will be no sabotage of each other's programs. With all of our delays in getting Shepard into space, the Russians decided to launch a day ahead of schedule, and I don't blame them for doing so. Khrushchev personally phoned the President two hours before launch to inform him they would be going early. There was no fast one pulled on us Scott; Gagarin was the first man into outer space."

"Jim, I know. I was part of the team tracking him; I agree he made it to outer space."

"Then what exactly are you saying then?" Webb asked.

Astronaut and aeronautical engineer Scott Carpenter crossed his arms and said, "Well, Jim...maybe it's time we fired up the radar again..."

Chapter 9

London Just Before Sundown

The day had been warm in London and as the sun started to set, turning the sky into pink and purple parchment. The van felt stifling and cramped. Two of the three men were sweating profusely, more out of nervousness than from the heat.

Gravda turned to them and said, "You boys look like you're going to die."

One of them said, "You told us they would be putting their guns down; I still see a lot of men with guns."

"Relax guys," she said. "They haven't started loading anything yet."

The van was parallel parked across the street from the loading docks of the exhibition hall between a large black Russian sedan and an even larger black Russian limousine. More of a food service truck than anything else, the painted graphics on the side were the same as those used to provide supplies to the several food vendors inside the hall.

Gravda looked at the man who had developed her photographs the night before and asked, "So how come you're not sweating like Twiddle Dee and Twiddle Dum over there?"

"Are you kidding?" he said, "I am enjoying this. Usually my job is boring, this is exciting."

"Hey, which one of us is Twiddle Dee and which one is Twiddle Dum?" asked another.

The woman they knew as Betty Miller enjoyed the company of the three men she was currently working with. They were good men, smart and dedicated. It was refreshing to work with men without some private personal agenda; in her line of work, it was rare. She had noticed early on all three wore wedding rings. But she couldn't fault them for blushing when she flirted. It was a skill she had mastered early in life and one she used often to make sure she was in control of a situation. She envisioned all three of them coming home at the end of a day to an excited dog barking while wagging its tail at the gate of a white picket fence. A doting wife meeting each one wiping her hands on her apron after finishing the evening meal. And she smiled. At the same time, she thought it was a life she could never comprehend for herself.

All three men were naive to some degree, their intelligence and educations would never have prepared them for the things she has had to learn, but at least they were clean. There were times when Gravda felt no matter how many baths she took or how much soap she used, she would always feel dirty.

The objective always comes first, she thought. A tinge of guilt ran through her for just a second. She knew she could take the photos she wanted tonight by herself, but she also knew she would need assistance on the next step of her mission, a mission Allen Dulles had not signed off on yet.

Common sense told her trained operatives would have been a better choice. Those who were skilled in deception would be more prepared, calmer, and more levelheaded in times of stress. There was always stress. These three men knew they were out of their element and yet they had all agreed to come along.

Allen Dulles had provided her with limited bios on all three before their mission together at the Russian showcase, with one syllable codename for each. Dulles had picked her team. All she knew other than from her own observations was their area of expertise and the fact none had been out of Langley before.

The man she only knew as the photo analyst called "Bob" looked like he might just throw up and they had only been sitting there for twenty minutes. All three had agreed with some hesitation to stake out the loading dock.

Tonight, was the easy part of her plan. Simple photographs and a little more information were all she needed. But the next step, if Allen Dulles agreed to it, would destroy all American/Soviet relations if she were caught.

She looked at all three men—the photographer, the photo analyst, and the aerospace engineer; all three were staring back at her...waiting for her direction. Men she barely knew were in a delivery van on the outskirts of London. Against their better judgment, they were there for one simple reason. They trusted her.

A wave of uncommon emotion hit her. Against all common reasoning and everything which made sense to her, she realized why she had convinced them to come along. In a world where a simple mistake or split-second lapse of judgment can get you killed her gut was speaking loud and clear. She trusted them too.

"Let's take some photographs and get the hell out of here, okay?" she said.

The photographer known as "Joe" asked, "What exactly am I looking for?"

"I want to find the crate they packed the satellite into, and I need to know how they transport it. That's the first objective," Gravda explained, "Secondly, I want more photos of the four soldiers who guarded it during the exhibition."

"Okay, why the four guards?" Joe asked. "We already have a few photos of them."

"We only have photos of them while on guard duty," she answered. "You can't tell much of a person's physiological profile when they are standing at attention and a Russian major is five feet away. I want to know those four men. Joe, get me photos of their facial expressions when they think the major isn't looking," she added.

The photo analyst, Bob, asked nervously, "And why do you need to know that Betty?" He turned towards the aerospace engineer who was sitting beside him and muttered, "Oh, dear God Steve, she is up to something."

Gravda smiled and raised one eyebrow. "Of course I am, gentlemen, I am always up to something. Once we know how they ship the satellite and the protocol they use they likely won't be changing it," Gravda said. "I am assuming it is headed to a local railyard and then shipped by rail to Southampton, that's the closest major port. As far as the four guards are concerned, I am looking for a weak link in their chain."

"A weak link in their chain?" asked the man called "Steve."

"Yes, someone who might be disgruntled or doesn't like to take orders, I need to find the man who can be manipulated. I need to find a patsy." She smiled as she added, "You don't expect the four of us to steal the satellite alone, do you?"

"OH, hell no!" the skittish photo analyst started to say, rising to his feet. "Betty, you are going to get us all kill—"

The roof of the van met the top of his skull with a resounding thud. He started to swear from the sparks he felt in his head and his neck. "Son of a..."

Gravda leaned over and punched him in the gut. There was little force behind her strike, but it had the desired effect. As the air rushed out of his lungs, his vocal cords no longer functioned, and he slumped to the floor. Gravda caught him by the shoulders and eased him to the metal floor of the van.

She held one finger to her lips to remind the others to be quiet and then looked at Bob. "Are you okay?"

"Yeah," was all he could grunt as his lungs gasped for air.

"I'm not going to get anyone killed Bob, but you are, if you keep making so much noise and continue doing jumping jacks. After all, the Russians are only fifty feet away."

Bob's eyes rolled back, and he whispered, "Sorry."

Gravda wiped the sweat from his brow and said, "Sorry I had to do that, can you sit up?"

Bob shifted his weight to get on all fours. Gravda thought he looked like a man at a commode who had drank too much earlier in the evening. He forced himself backwards, so his backside slumped to the floor.

Joe had put down his camera but was keeping watch through the one-way glass window on the side of the van. "I think we're okay, I don't think they heard us," he said.

"Betty, please tell us you're kidding," Steve said. "You're

not serious about stealing that thing, are you?"

Bob puffed his cheeks out and fully exhaled. "I'm pretty sure she is not kidding," he said.

"Okay guys, if this makes you feel any better, technically I am not planning on 'stealing' it," she said. "Let's call it...'borrowing it for a little while.' We'll give it back when we're done with it, I promise."

"Oh, well *that's* different," Bob said sarcastically. "For a minute there we were thinking you were going to do something crazy."

"Relax boys, tonight I just want a little more recon. A few photos, a couple of answers and I promise we're done here."

Joe instinctively ducked down as a rumble of twelve British lorries passed by the van and turned into the loading dock.

Gravda looked over her shoulder and out the window. "They're about to start the loading. Joe, is your camera ready?" Gravda turned back to him. "Shoot everything, we can figure out what's good later. I don't want to miss anything."

"I'm on it," Joe said.

"Steve, I need you near this window," she said. "You're the aerospace engineer; tell me when you spot that damn crate."

"What do you want me to do?" the flustered Bob asked.

"Just sit here and be quiet," she said, "We'll let them do the work and you just sit and keep me company."

Bob smiled a half smile; even he thought he could handle that.

Ten minutes rolled by, before Steve said, "There it is!"

With both men blocking the window, Gravda felt no need

to push between them to see for herself. She had faith in Steve's observations.

"Joe, I want to see who is taking charge of the loading process and just how they put it on the truck. Lunch money says it's the major," she said.

"It *is* the major," Joe said. "And they are using a forklift, looks like they will be loading it in an upright position, not laying it down. Damn, the thing must be heavy."

"Keep shooting, she said, "I need to know who will be driving the truck to the freight yard."

A few more minutes passed, as the major barked orders and people jumped to his command.

"Betty come here take a look," Joe said.

As the forklift approached the truck, the Russian major called the British driver out of the cab. The driver walked over to join other British drivers as they stood, smoked, and waited.

The major pointed to one of the four guards who had stood next to the satellite while on display and with a wave of his arm demanded he replace the British driver. He did so with his head down while sauntering towards the cab.

The soldier who ascended onto the running board was an Army corporal; her memory told her the name badge he wore had the last name of Kozlov printed on it. There were no first names on soviet military I.D.s but she knew she could find the information out easily.

The surname Kozlov in Russian is a nickname for 'goat,' and Gravda was hoping an Army corporal did not appreciate being told what to do by and Air Force major. "Come on, come on," she said aloud, "Be my guy...do it."

As the major turned, Kozlov placed the thumb of his right hand between his index finger and middle finger and silently slapped his inner right wrist with his left palm...

"BINGO!" she said aloud.

"Bingo? What did I miss?"

Gravda looked Joe straight in the eye, mimicked the actions of the Russian Corporal, and smiled. She then extended the middle finger of her right hand, while curling the rest of her fingers into a fist for him to see. "It means the same thing in Russian," she explained. "I think we just found our patsy," she said, smiling even brighter.

"Can we go now?" Bob asked.

"Not just yet Bob. You're doing good," Gravda said. "We can't pull out while they're still loading; this van is supposed to be empty remember? Let them finish, we have what we came for...and more."

The British lorries were filled except for the last one in line, and all the tailgates had been slammed shut. The Russian guards and the original British drivers walked to the back of the empty truck and climbed into the back for the ride to the Southampton fright yard. The British drivers would take back their vehicles after they had been unloaded at Southampton.

As all twelve trucks started to pull away, the Russian major, Yuri Gagarin, who had appeared out of nowhere, and four men in black suits started to walk across the street directly towards the van Gravda and the three men had been hiding.

"Oh, damn it, now what?" Steve said.

Gravda peered back through the window and said, "Joe, keep shooting. Those four men are KGB, and when they get to within twenty paces duck down, our windshield is regular glass."

Bob hit the deck immediately. The rest did as they were told.

Gagarin and the Major took seats in the back of the limousine while one of the KGB agents slipped behind the wheel. The other three Russian agents climbed into the car behind them and sped away. After both vehicles rounded the corner and disappeared from sight, the photographer, the Aerospace engineer and Gravda all rose up from the floor. Bob was still laying there with his hands over his head.

"Did you get that, Joe?" Gravda asked.

"Yup, I got photos of all of them," he said.

Gravda laughed as she reached down and patted Bob on the shoulder. "Hey Bob, you want to go back to the hotel now?"

Bob did not get up; he just looked upward and said, "...Yes, please."

Chapter 10

The White House, Oval Office

Allen Dulles relaxed on the sofa and thumbed through a stack of confidential files as he waited for the President. Kennedy was not the type to initiate an "open door" policy to the Oval Office, but then, Dulles and Kennedy had been friends for many years. The CIA director had stopped by unannounced at 8:30 a.m.; he knew the president would be wrapping up his morning briefing by 8:45.

Evelyn Lincoln had been John Fitzgerald Kennedy's personal secretary since his first days as senator and was the unofficial gatekeeper to the President's office. No one got through those doors without having to go through her first.

Born on a farm in Polk County Nebraska, her father had been a member of the United States House of Representatives and she took her responsibilities very seriously. "Good morning Mr. Dulles," she had said, "How may I help you on this fine day?"

"I'd like to see the President when he is finished with his meeting Evelyn," Dulles said.

Looking quickly through her calendar without needing to, she asked, "Do you have an appointment?"

Laughing, Allen Dulles said, "No, but you already know that it will only take a few minutes."

"Mr. Kennedy has a very full agenda and he is a very busy man. After all, he is the President of the United States," she said, smiling.

Allen Dulles smiled too; he had been through this dance before. "I am fully aware of that fact Evelyn, it's why the office you won't let me into is oval shaped."

"Well, what's this impromptu meeting about?" she asked with a smirk, leaning on her elbows in hopes of hearing juicy gossip.

"Evelyn, I am the director for the CIA. I can't tell you that."

"Well then you will just have to bribe me to gain access I guess," she said.

Allen Dulles walked around her desk and gave the austere fifty-two-year-old woman a peck on the cheek. "You know you're a security risk," he said.

"A girl has to do what she has to do for attention around this place," she said. "Do you want coffee, Allen?"

"Yes please, if it's not too much trouble," he said.

"I'll tell Jack you're waiting when he gets back, go have a seat."

*　　*　　*　　*

(Evelyn Lincoln was a true Washington insider. Her dedication to the youngest President of the United States was legendary. Few people know her name, but she walked within a circle of the most powerful men in America. She was in the motorcade two years later when President Kennedy and his wife Jacqueline visited Dallas Texas when a man pointed a rifle out a window of a book depository and ended America's age of Camelot. John Fitzgerald Kennedy would later pay homage to this unknown woman by asking Congress in a will he had drafted back in the first month of his presidency; that she be interred at Arlington National Cemetery at the time of her passing. She resides there to this day. She would outlive her President by thirty-two years and would honor his wishes after succumbing to complications during cancer surgery in 1995. Evelyn made a point of visiting her friend's gravesite every year on the anniversary of his assassination until her own death at the age of eighty-five.)

At 8:47 a.m., Jack Kennedy walked through the door and Evelyn Lincoln followed close behind. In her hands was a small silver tray with two white china cups, a carafe of fresh milk and a crystal bowl of Irish brown sugar. She set it down on the coffee table and returned to her desk.

"Good morning, Mr. President," Dulles said. He rose from the couch and placed a file folder onto the President's desk before walking back to pick up a coffee cup.

Kennedy loosened his tie and reached for the folder without speaking. 'Wonderful,' thought Dulles. 'It is not even 9:00 a.m. yet and already Jack is in a pissy mood.' Either the briefing went badly, or the president was preoccupied; either way, Dulles knew not to make it any worse.

Before opening the file the CIA director had handed him, John Kennedy said, "I received a phone call from the Kremlin last night at 10:30; apparently, Khrushchev plans to launch another rocket less than three months from now."

"And?" Dulles asked.

"Well, we currently have three satellites in orbit, and he asked for the telemetry of each one so, as he put it, "We don't interfere with their launch."

"And what did you tell him?" Dulles asked.

"I told him I would have James Webb provide him with our coordinates later today. I am not out to sabotage the bastards; I just want to beat them. How long until we are scheduled to put John Glenn into full orbit, Allen?" the president asked.

"Not until February of next year," Dulles told him, knowing Kennedy's mood would not improve.

"Damn it, ten months from now is not acceptable, Allen. Can we move the timetable up?"

"Not if we want to do it safely," Dulles answered. "Webb is very much on board with the objectives here, Jack, but he is not willing to take chances on our astronaut's lives. I agree with him. He is not just playing it safe; he is playing it smart."

"I don't like being behind the Russians in anything, Allen," Kennedy said. "Eventually we will outspend them and outthink them, but right now they have the upper hand."

"They may not be as far ahead of us as we thought," Dulles said, raising an eyebrow.

Jack Kennedy smiled for the first time that morning. "Is that what this folder is all about?" he asked.

"It's part of it," Dulles said. "Before you open it though, I must ask you, how deep do you want to be in all this?"

"Meaning?"

"Well, Jack, if you break the seal on that folder, then you lose all deniability on this stuff. As your friend, I am going to recommend you don't. If someday I have to go in front of a Congressional board of inquiry, I would like to be able to honestly say you have never seen its contents."

"Okay Allen," the president said as he tossed the unopened file to his CIA director, "I trust your opinion. Now, tell me what's in the Goddamn file."

Allen Dulles spent the next few minutes informing the president about the meeting held at Goddard Space Center, and the conversations between the engineers and Webb's astronauts. "They think the Russians are still having the same problems we have on re-entry," he said.

Jack Kennedy scratched his head and said, "Okay am I missing something here? Khrushchev has Yuri Gagarin on a worldwide media tour, and I have a damn puppy upstairs who has eaten three pairs of my best slippers. You want to explain to me how they are having problems with re-entry?"

Allen Dulles paused before speaking. "...You said you spoke to Khrushchev last night and he asked you for the telemetry of our satellites, right? It means one of two things; he is either fishing to see if you're full of shit and he already has the information, or they don't have the ability yet to track what we've sent into space. We are able to track all four Russian satellites currently out there because of what James Webb described to me as the 'static radio transmitters' the Russians are still using."

"Let me make sure I am understanding what you're saying. They are not encrypting those signals like we do?" the president asked.

"Not yet they're not," Dulles stated. "Their approach has been, keep it simple and less can go wrong. The transmitters on all their satellites so far have been single frequency without any band change or modulation. Some of Webb's people think the Russians are way behind us on communications hardware and software too. Jack, they may be beating us on propaganda, but they may not be technologically ahead of us at all."

"Allen I must be missing your point here," the president said, "and I'm in no mood for riddles. Please, make your point."

"Jack, we are building an infrastructure for the future with Webb and the upcoming Apollo program. We will consolidate our experts in Houston by August of next year with the new Space Center and we have the brightest minds working on computer advancements. I know the Russians have had the headlines lately, but I think they are tapped out. They may be at the limits of their own technology."

"Allen, thanks for the pep talk, but the Russians still have Gagarin on the ground and photos of the back side of the moon, and we haven't put a man into outer space yet. Please tell me there is something in that file I can use."

Allen Dulles sat back on the couch and put his hands behind his head. "Well, Gagarin is back on the ground Jack...but he didn't get back here inside Vostok 1!"

"What?" Jack Kennedy stammered. "What are you saying? How the hell did we miss that? Are you saying they used a body double for the press conferences?"

"No, not at all Jack. Gagarin is alive and well, we have photos of him at an exhibition in London just a few days ago," Dulles told him. "It's not that we missed it, we just weren't looking for it. If you lose your car keys and then find them on the counter, you don't keep looking in the refrigerator. We tracked Vostok 1 in orbit by radar and with radio transmissions right up until the point of re-entry. One of our destroyers in the Baltic Sea picked up Gagarin's last two radio transmissions. The first was saying he was starting re-entry process at which time we lost radio communications for a full three minutes. I spoke to James Webb at NASA, and he explained this is normal, it has something to do with the ionosphere and magnetic waves blocking the signals—I don't pretend to understand all that stuff."

"For the love of God Allen, please make your point," Kennedy said, irritated.

"I'm getting there, Jack, just bear with me," Dulles said. "The second and last radio transmissions from Gagarin came at an altitude of just over 26,000 feet above sea level, or roughly five miles up. His message was 're-entry granted.' We assumed he was still aboard Vostock 1...but he wasn't."

Allen Dulles decided he was going to enjoy the moment. It's not often the director of the CIA gets to embrace the game of 'I know something you don't.' Especially with the President of the United States.

"The Russians used the same static radio transmission frequency on Vostock 1 for tracking the spacecraft as they did for their communications. It's the same frequency they used on Sputnik and every other launch. The craft sends out a consistent ping at precise intervals every two seconds. It is the same radio frequency they used for Gagarin's communications, and the ping is simply imbedding into the audio like background noise. They did it either to keep things simple or they wanted everyone on Earth with a short-wave radio to hear his communications. We lost the radio reception for three minutes when Gagarin entered the ionosphere, but when we picked up the signal again the pings were separated by only one second for an additional 108 seconds. Then it went back to the usual interval of two seconds apart, 108 seconds. We thought it was an anomaly and ignored it. It wasn't."

Dulles smiled and crossed his legs, making himself more comfortable on the couch and reached for his burl pipe which was ever present in his jacket pocket. He patiently took a gold plated lighter from another and before lighting it he said, "You might want to grab yourself one of those illegal Cuban cigars you keep in your desk once you connect the dots."

The gravity of the CIA director's statement took a few seconds for the president to process. In a thicker-than-usual Boston accent he had worked very hard to eliminate while in front of the cameras he said, "...Two different radio signals separated by time and distance..." He looked at Allen Dulles for confirmation.

All it took was a dry smile and one raised eyebrow from the man sitting on the sofa.

"The son of a bitch ejected from Vostock 1 more than four miles above the Earth, and free fell back to the ground with a parachute? I'll be damned, that is one hell of a ballsy move," he said, impressed.

"I'd say so," Dulles agreed. "They did achieve partial re-entry, but they had no control over the craft. Gagarin must have jumped while the spacecraft was starting to disintegrate around him."

"I'll be damned," Jack Kennedy repeated, softly.

"The radio frequency in his pressurized suit was the same as the Vostock 1 capsule," Dulles explained. "With oxygen tanks on his back, he made it to the ground. The Russians never even tried to attempt to land the spacecraft safely. Our math wizards at NASA did what they did, and figured out the capsule traveled an additional 180 miles before slamming fully back into the atmosphere. It was traveling at 3,600 miles an hour. The heat alone would have most certainly killed him and even if it didn't, the rate of speed would have finished the job when it hit the ground. We had stopped tracking the spacecraft by radar because you don't think to look for something where it shouldn't be," Dulles said.

President Kennedy slapped his knees. "They haven't figured out re-entry!" The president laughed. "You know Allen, there are actual rules to this Space Race. According to the International Aeronautical Federation, unless the spacecraft lands with the person still inside it doesn't count as a space flight."

"I know Jack," Dulles said. "But this is one you should keep in your hip pocket and only pull it out when you really need it."

Kennedy nodded. "I see what you're saying. So, what else do the Russians have us thinking which might be wrong?"

Allen Dulles held up the confidential file he had placed on the president's desk, waving it in the air. "Do you really want to know?" Dulles asked.

The next thirty minutes were spent briefing the president on the field operation from London and the Russian exhibition. No names were mentioned or asked for.

"So, what's your next step?" Kennedy asked.

"I'm going to keep that information to myself, Jack," The CIA director said. "Plausible deniability, remember? I do need your permission to borrow a couple of James Webb's engineers for a few days though."

"Allen, engineers are not field operatives," Kennedy said, "Are you sure you know what you're getting yourself into?"

Dulles shrugged his shoulders. "I know, but I don't have any other choice. If we are going to get a better look at the Luna 3 satellite, I need people who know what the hell they are looking at."

The President of the United States brought both hands up to the side of his head and rubbed his temples. He closed his eyes and said, "Do what you have to do."

The CIA director stood up from his sitting position on the couch prepared to make his exit, knowing there would be one more question coming.

"Allen, wait. So how is it I have a Russian dog upstairs, then?"

"Well, in the words of one of your illustrious Gemini astronauts...They got lucky. Aren't you the fortunate one."

After Allen Dulles left his office, the president poked his head out of the doorway and said, "Evelyn, this meeting never happened, do you understand?"

"Yes Mr. President, I will inform the ambassador your next meeting will be stepped back by a few minutes."

Evelyn Lincoln checked her wristwatch and crossed a few things off the president's daily appointment schedule. In red pen, she wrote, 8:47 to 10:10 a.m. The President...took a nap.

Chapter 11

Prague

The river Vltava makes a big curve in Prague. After passing through the historic centre, below Prague Castle and under Charles Bridge, the river turns 180 degrees, changing direction to flow further to the west.

Gravda Nemiroff stood with one hand on the metal rail and looked out over the wide expanse of the river, watching the swirling water pass beneath her. She caught herself biting the nail of her index finger and stopped herself. Nail biting is a nervous habit, and she was never nervous. Still, she had to ask herself if she might be nervous now. She had been asking herself several questions lately, and none of them were good for her chosen profession.

Looking over the river, she could see the faint outline of Prague Castle in the fading light of evening. She smiled, thinking back to the days when her father called her princess. Her eyes were still open but the image before her disappeared, and she could only see the past.

She saw his walrus mustache and wide grin; she saw the

sparkle in his malachite green eyes, a color she had inherited herself. They were eyes which attracted the right attention when she needed them too. She had not thought of the past in a very long time. She chastised herself for doing so now.

She thought she had not been herself lately, but then laughed aloud at the ridiculousness of the concept. With several aliases and dozens of images she could portray, she wondered if anything about her was real anymore.

All right Gravda, get your head back in the game, there is still work to be done, she thought aloud. She went over her checklist one last time in her mind, making sure the "T's" had been crossed and all the "I's" had their dots.

The latest leg of the Russian exposition had begun three days earlier. Gravda had been a very busy girl, as she had been there two days before that.

She had rented a nondescript Skoda Octavia, using another set of false identity papers and had driven the boxy Czechoslovakian car throughout the streets of Prague learning every pathway. It was never sufficient to have just one escape route. Three were better than one, and six was better than three. She would have preferred an exotic car like the Jaguar she had driven in London, but this was about blending in, not standing out. She now knew virtually every street in Prague and the shortest distances between any two points. Timing would be critical to the operation, and she knew that time would be the biggest enemy.

She had paid for a ticket and walked through the Industrial Palace, Prague's largest exhibit hall, feigning interest in the flower show which preceded the Russians arriving in town. Every square foot of the massive building was memorized along with the loading docks and service entrances.

She had located and secured a salvage yard less than a mile from the Industrial Palace by bribing its owner with 500 Koruns and a promise his black-market dealings would not be revealed to the local authorities. He was happy to oblige the pretty woman, who carried cash—and a gun.

Allen Dulles had provided a safe house per her instructions, and she had seen to it that it was properly prepared. It was a small warehouse within close proximity to the Industrial Palace and the salvage yard. She had made provision making sure it would also soon be outfitted with a temporary dark room, a metal lathe, tools, and supplies. She wasn't sure of everything they might need but she wanted to prepare for the unexpected as best as possible. It had always been her trademark and the reason why Allen Dulles respected her so much.

Her eight-man team would arrive later that night. Some would be strangers which had come highly recommended and three would be the men she had met in London a few weeks earlier. She smiled thinking of how nervous Bob, the photo analyst, had been. Seldom is there comic relief in her line of work. Steve and Joe had both enjoyed the excitement and she found herself looking forward to seeing the three of them again.

She had shopped for groceries earlier in the day, enjoying the task and the feeling of being somewhat normal for a change. She had even purchased flowers to spruce up the dingy space.

The thought alone made for another question which popped into her head. Was she becoming sentimental? *Flowers?* She had never done that before. This was to be just another mission like so many before. In fact, this one involved little or no gunplay if things went according to plan. Of course, few covert operations ever went exactly according to plan, but the goal here was to get in and get out without anyone really knowing they had ever been there. There is always a chance things could go south and there are never any guarantees, but she had done her homework. She always did her homework. So, what was bothering her? She allowed herself a few moments to analyze her own thoughts. *What was different this time out?* she asked herself. *Am I losing my touch?*

Was it not it just twelve weeks before she had stepped up behind a man with a silenced 9MM, placed it at the base of his skull, and pulled the trigger not once, but twice on the streets of Bangkok, Thailand? She had screamed to attract attention and helped him to the ground before disappearing into the newly formed crowd.

She justified herself. The vermin she had terminated had deserved far worse. He had been running one of the largest child sex slavery rings in Asia. Her client, a wealthy businessman from Hong Kong, had suffered the anguish of having his nine-year-old daughter disappear on her way home from school. It had taken Gravda ten months to track her whereabouts. The little girl she returned to her father was not the same little girl he had known before, and never would be again. The first bullet was for her, the second was for herself. Gravda had treated herself to a lavish dinner of pasta and red sauce less than an hour later at the one good Italian restaurant she could find in Bangkok. She had not felt a stitch of regret, then or now.

The hit was not sanctioned by her superiors, and she had no intentions of telling them. There were some things she would keep to herself and that was one of them. Spies have secrets, even from their employers. Her fee was a hundred thousand dollars U.S. Her Asian client had paid it without question. The client had handed her a briefcase with tears in his eyes after hugging his daughter for the first time in almost a year. She assumed he had found the same briefcase in the front seat of his Rolls Royce the next morning, after she had picked the lock and placed it inside. Some things are not about money.

So, what was it that was bothering her? Was she becoming soft? *Hell no,* she thought. She would pull a trigger without any hesitation if she had to. On many occasions, a male opponent had paused for a split second before firing a bullet at a woman. She had never offered the same courtesy in return. Self-preservation was crucial to longevity. It is why she usually chose to work alone when she could. This was her operation and one she had to do a lot of convincing of Allen Dulles to sign off on it. It was to be completely off the books. No congressional sub committees. No political oversights commissions to answer too. It was just Allen Dulles and her who knew the details and it meant if the shit hit the fan, she was the fan.

Shit, she thought. Bob, Steve, and Joe were good people. Good men with families and naive to the world she lived in. It was through her doing all three of them, including the panicky Bob, had signed on to do this job. They were not field operatives, despite all three being CIA employees—they were "desk jockeys" at best. But tomorrow night would definitely not be a desk job. Tomorrow night would be the front lines, and if spies are caught, spies are shot.

Gravda Nemiroff had always known the rules. She had accepted them as just part of the challenge. Those three did not. *On any job, you take upon yourself the necessary risk,* she thought, *you do your best to prepare for the unexpected.*

She had asked for and would receive later tonight two civilian aerospace engineers from Goddard Space Center. It meant five of the eight men she would be meeting at the safe house at 8:00 p.m. were completely out of their league. It also meant their lives were now her responsibility and on her conscience.

She had one more task to complete before meeting them and the rest of her half-assed crew.

"Shit," she said one more time aloud. She found herself once again chewing on her fingernail.

Chapter 12

Prague Continues

Gravda had tracked and kept an eye on Russian Army Corporal Peter Kozlov since the arrival of the Russians three days earlier. The Soviets had booked two hotels to house their contingency of enlisted men and officers that by now had grown bored of babysitting satellites and space hardware. Peter Kozlov was the soldier who had "given the bird" to his commanding officer, Russian Air Force Major Alexander Tkachenko, back in London. He was also the soldier who drove the truck which carried Luna 3 to the freight yard. He was the key to the mission. He just didn't know it yet.

The Russian officers and Yuri Gagarin were staying at the Appian Hotel, with the enlisted men two miles away at the less flamboyant and much less opulent Hotel Prague. Officers do not mingle with enlisted men in the Russian military, and Gravda knew the policy would work to her benefit.

She walked across the Charles Bridge and three more blocks to the Hotel Prague and checked her reflection of the turnstile doors before entering. She had worn her black hair down with a white pillbox hat, which matched her white dress with a short boxy jacket and large buttons. Her stiletto heels added almost two inches to her height and were the current fashion rage. Her hosiery was black, and the seam running up the back encouraged a man who noticed to follow the line to see the curvature of her legs. She tussled her hair just once and decided she was ready.

Gravda walked with purpose through the lobby and headed to the bar. Where else would a bored Russian noncommissioned officer piss away his free time off duty? She waltzed into the bar and stood at the entrance scanning the crowd of twenty-five or so men and women seated at the bar itself or the chairs and tables situated around the room.

Peter Kozlov was seated at the bar as she hoped he would be. Two buddies, one on each of his sides, were men she recognized from earlier photos, talking and drinking. Kozlov's back was to her, but her memory recognized him immediately. She stood there waiting for the inevitable. It usually did not take long.

One of the three men spotted her and patted Kozlov on the shoulder saying something in his ear.

Peter Kozlov had been sitting with his head down, far away from family and home. His slumped shoulders told Gravda he was indeed the perfect "goat" for the next step in her plan.

She had not heard the Russian soldier's utterance but by reading his lips and being Russian herself, she knew the phrase... "Take a look at that," he had said.

The twenty-three-year-old corporal turned and looked her way. She made sure to make eye contact as he turned her way, raised an eyebrow, and smiled a bright white smile his way.

The smile was not to allure him. For Russians, smiles are

kept for friends and family alone. There is an Old Russian saying, "To smile with no reason, is a sign of a fool."

Her smile was perfect.

Kozlov turned back to his friend and whispered into his ear. She could not hear them, but it did not matter. Either he had told him she was gorgeous, or that she was naive, and either way she had accomplished what she had come there for. With his back turned she had backed out of the bar and bar and headed directly to the safe house. She had planted the seed; she would harvest it later tonight.

Chapter 13

The Safehouse

Gravda arrived at ten minutes 'til eight, and her crew would start filtering in at any moment. She used the time to go over her preparations one last time.

The warehouse was small, but it would do. Two roll-up doors led to a quiet alleyway to the side of the building and would allow them access without being noticed. The fresh oil stains on the concrete floor told her the building had recently been occupied, and probably would be again after they had left.

Maybe it was an automotive repair garage or machine shop, she did not know. Workbenches lined one wall with greasy hand tools and metal fabrication equipment. Gravda had parked the rented Skoda deep in one of the bays earlier in the day and had traveled on foot. She did not want anyone to connect her with the vehicle just in case things did not go as planned. The lathe she had requested had been shipped from Goddard Space Center and was still in its crate; there would be plenty of time to open it later. A large chalkboard took up the center of the room and she had placed chairs in front of it so she could explain each man's responsibilities for the next night's activities.

A child's bicycle was leaned up against the wall by the service entrance; she had purchased the bicycle on her first day in Prague. They would need it.

The office area was now a makeshift kitchen and the refrigerator, which looked like it was made prior to World War II, was now stocked with meats, cheeses, and fruits. The flowers she had purchased were sitting on the little table along with a tablecloth and real china. Gravda chuckled; maybe she was becoming domesticated after all.

She climbed the stairs to an overhead loft which would be used for the temporary dark room and tables were set up to analyze the photos they would need.

Cots had also been set up for sleeping arrangements, but she understood tonight she would probably not be sleeping there. Tonight, she would be in a hotel room which was not her own and she would not be sleeping at all. It was just part of the plan and part of the job.

Gravda turned a circle taking everything in, she was ready. She hoped the eight men who would soon be joining her were ready as well.

At exactly 8:00 p.m., a horn honked twice in quick taps. She took a deep breath and negotiated the steep stairs in her stiletto heels to pull the chain on one of the roll-up doors. A nondescript van backed into the workshop, and she closed the door behind it.

From inside the van the two side doors opened, and three men stepped out. Two of them were dressed identically in white shirts, skinny black ties, and very short haircuts. She assumed she was about to meet her engineers from Goddard

Space Center. Both looked a little tired and bewildered but carried an air of confidence as well.

The third man who stepped out of the van was the exact opposite of the two engineers in appearance and in attitude. His shaggy hair and beard and wire-rimmed glasses made him look more like a radical college professor than the photojournalist he was. Gravda had asked for him by name, his real name.

At forty-one years of age, he was the oldest member of her crew and had seen more through the lenses of his camera than most soldiers will see from behind the barrel of their guns. At twenty-one he had enlisted in the Marine Corp as a "conscientious objector," standing steadfast on his decision of never carrying a gun. He had landed on the beach at Normandy in the first wave of infantry. His camera caught images of the front lines during the battle of the bulge. His camera had also filmed the grizzly release of what few survivors there were at Auschwitz and Treblinka. Wounded seven times, he had refused the stack of purple hearts presented to him saying, "Medals are for soldiers, and I would never be a soldier." A year and a half ago, Brad Ray had walked through the doors of CIA headquarters in Langley Virginia and had asked for Allen Dulles by name.

There was a fourth man in the van, and it had taken him awhile to extricate himself from behind the wheel. Gravda knew of him only by reputation and by his alias. He appeared to live up to both.

When the man finally freed himself, the van rose noticeably by two inches. Standing six feet seven inches and every bit of three hundred pounds, Big Tony wore a black leather trench coat that must have cost several cows their lives to produce. His bald head was covered by a newsboy cap which appeared to be two sizes too small.

"You must be Big Tony," Gravda said.

The big man pointed to himself before saying, "Nope, you must mean him," as he pointed to the much shorter of the two engineers.

Gravda smiled and so did Big Tony. She already liked the man.

"Welcome to Prague, gentlemen," she said. "Once everyone is here you will be informed of what's required of each one of you. Until then, feel free to unpack your personal belongings. You will find cots upstairs; they're first come first serve, so settle in."

"How much gear do you have, Tony?" she asked.

He said, "The van is pretty much full. Brad brought all the equipment he needs for developing film and the NASA guys brought a boat load of tech stuff too."

"Do you need help unloading?" she asked.

Tony laughed. "You're kidding right"?

As the macroscopic Tony pulled large metal trunks out of the van and set them aside with ease she asked him, "How did you guys get in?"

Tony responded while working, "I flew into Zurich the day before yesterday and secured the van. From there I drove to Vienna where I picked up your NASA boys. We crossed over the border into Czechoslovakia earlier this morning. I have to tell you—" he started to say before he caught himself. "By the way, what name are you using on this one?"

"I have four more men coming and all are CIA. Three of them I worked with in London a few weeks back, and they know me as Betty Miller, so let's keep it simple, okay?"

"Okay then, Betty Miller it is," Big Tony laughed. "Nice name. Shouldn't you have a bow in your hair?"

"Maybe later," she quipped. "What were you going to say?"

"I was about to say your NASA boys seem bright enough, but I like working with pros, not civilians. Are you expecting any fireworks on this one?"

"Not if everything goes according to plan," she told him. "This one should be down and dirty, in and out as quickly as possible. You should know though, three of the other CIA boys. They're backstage boys, not field operatives..."

She let her words hang in the air.

"Well, that's just wonderful," Big Tony said, "Who's the fourth guy?"

"You'll see, I think you two know each other," she told him.

As they spoke, there was a polite knock on the service entrance door; Tony reached under his trench coat reaching for his sidearm. Gravda reached over and pulled his massive arm down and away. "Relax," she said.

She walked to the door, unlocked it, and opened it. Standing outside was Bob, Steve, and Joe. "Come on in," she said, "Welcome to the party."

All three walked into the warehouse, looking dazed but happy to see her.

There was no need to inquire about the three men's travel arrangements because she had set them up herself. Allen Dulles had flown then directly into Prague from London on false diplomatic passports, where a United States consulate employee met them and drove them to a hotel they checked into but never intended to stay at. Czechoslovakia was an independent nation but fell steeply under Soviet domination. Sometimes the best way to hide someone was not to hide them at all. They had taken a taxi from the hotel to within two blocks of the garage and walked the rest of the way.

Gravda greeted the three like long lost friends and introduced them to Tony. The other men made their way downstairs and said their hellos with a brief description of their own expertise. They were now just waiting for one more man.

Four loud bangs on the service door startled Bob, Steve, and one of the NASA engineers. The always-nervous Bob subconsciously stepped behind Gravda.

A gruff voice bellowed, "Open the fucking door."

Big Tony had once again started to reach for his sidearm but slipped it back into its holster when he heard the voice. "Really?" he said, glancing at Gravda. "Please tell me you're shitting me?"

"Nope," she said smiling. "He is the best at what he does, and you know it." She pointed to the door. "Tony, you may have the honors."

Tony's massive shoulders slumped as he walked slowly to the door like a troubled student on his way to the principal's office. His hulking frame blocked every inch of the doorway as he opened it and said, "Get in here you little piece of shit before you wake the neighbors." Tony did not step aside.

The last member of her handpicked team walked into the warehouse by waddling directly underneath Big Tony's legs.

Hank was an inside legend within the CIA. Born in Romania in 1935, he had spent the first twenty or so years of his life as an acrobat and circus strong man. The only man in the room who could out bench press him was Big Tony, and Big Tony was more than twice his height. He was dressed in American Levi's rolled up at the hem and a black Cossack shirt, a half-smoked cigarette dangled from his lips. The newsboy cap he wore was identical to Big Tony's.

"What's the problem Hank?" Tony asked, "Couldn't you reach the doorknob yah little shit?"

Hank waited until Tony had turned around and reached up and popped him with a straight shot to the groin.

Tony grunted but did not flinch. "Ugh, is that any way to treat an old friend? Come here," Tony said as he picked Hank up off the ground until his feet were dangling five feet off the ground. "Give me a hug yah little bastard."

Hank reached down with his small hands and sausage fingers, clasped both sides of Tony's massive skull, and kissed him on both cheeks. "Now put me down, you massive gorilla, you're making me look bad in front of the hot chick," Hank said, starting to squirm.

Tony set him down and looked seriously at Gravda. "This is your team? Three desk jockeys from Langley, two slide rule boys from Goddard, a conscientious objector..." and pointing almost to the ground he added, "And this guy?"

"Yup," Gravda said, smiling.

"Wonderful," Big Tony said sarcastically. "What could possibly go wrong?"

Gravda took charge as she walked to the chalkboard. "Yes Tony, this is the team, and they are all here for a reason. Gentleman, please have a seat," she said.

Hank crawled up into his chair and sat next to Tony; the rest took the first chair available.

"We are here to steal a Russian satellite," Gravda began. "We will have roughly twelve hours to secure it, dismantle it, photograph it, analyze the photographs, and then reassemble it and get it back to the Russians before they find it missing. Timetables will be critical on this operation, and everything needs to be timed to the minute if we can. The Russians have it on display at the Crystal Palace less than a mile from a salvage yard I've obtained so we can do what we need to undercover. At the salvage yard, Big Tony will act as look out—and you will also drive the truck to and from. Alright?"

Tony simply said, "All right."

Gravda listed his name on the chalkboard along with his responsibilities.

She turned to Steve, the CIA Aerospace engineer she had come to know from London. "You and one of our NASA boys will be on site to dismantle the satellite and get it back together." She looked at both NASA engineers. She had never asked their names and did not want to know. "One of you will stay here for any fabrication work we might need. I'll leave the decision up to you two as to who does what. Give me your answer in the morning."

The photographer she had met in London, Joe, was next. "Joe, I want you on sight at the salvage yard to photograph every part of the satellite. Brad has experience in the field and is used to working under pressure, but I need those photos developed as fast as possible and your work in London took a little time. So, Joe you shoot 'em and Brad, you develop them. Got it?"

Both men agreed.

"Hank, you're going to do what you're best at. You will shuttle film and questions between the salvage yard and here at the safe house. I even bought you a special gift to help you out." Gravda pointed to the child's bicycle in the corner.

Hank turned to look at the bike and mentioned, "The pink basket is a nice touch lady. Hey, when do we get to meet the boss in this operation?"

Big Tony reached down and punched Hank on the shoulder, "She is the boss, numb nuts. This is her operation."

Hank looked up at Big Tony with a look of surprise. "We're working for a dame?" he asked. "You're shitting me, what's the world coming too?"

Tony just nodded.

Hank paused and said, "Well okay then toots, you bark the orders, and I will peddle the bike, gee whiz."

Nervous Bob was the only one present without his name on the chalkboard. "Betty, what about me?"

"You'll stay here out of harm's way and tell us everything you can about the photos Joe takes and Brad develops. Is that all right with you?"

"Oh, thank you God," Bob said aloud.

The briefing was almost complete when Big Tony stood up and asked, "Do you have an inside man on this job? How the hell are we going to secure the satellite?"

"That is my responsibility," Gravda said. "I have a patsy and I will let you know later tonight. You let me worry about those details. We all have our own talents here," she added.

"Get all your equipment and gear ready, gentlemen!" Gravda said, "I want to be ready by 7:00 a.m. tomorrow."

As the men went their separate ways to uncrate the lathe and check their equipment, Gravda pulled Joe aside. "Do you have the handbag I requested from Langley?" she said.

"Yes, it's in my bag," he told her. "When you close the latch, it will activate the camera, it will take a photo every fifteen seconds until you run out of film."

"How many photos and how much time?"

Joe scratched his head. "Sixty photos at fifteen second intervals. Fifteen minutes," he said.

"Good, it should be more than enough," Gravda told him. "I will be back here by 2:00 a.m.; I want you to personally develop and make prints of what I bring back. Understood?"

"Sure, Betty, whatever you need," Joe said, looking hesitant because of the tone of her voice.

"Joe, I am trusting you," Gravda said. "If you show any of those prints to a single member of this team, I will slit your throat and then gut you. I'll drop your carcass off the Charles Bridge. Do I make myself clear?"

Joe gulped, "You're serious."

"Yes, I am serious. I need someone who I can trust."

"I promise Betty, I swear it."

"Good," Gravda...Betty said. "Now go get me the purse...I have work to do."

Chapter 14

No One Enjoys Working the Night Shift

She had left the safe house ten minutes after 9:00 p.m. Gravda's walk took her back to the Hotel Prague and she arrived at the front doors by 9:30. The night was still young, and she assumed she would find Peter Kozlov still at the bar; after all, he was Russian. She had run through the soldier's dossier in her head and worried about only one thing. What would she do if he didn't take the bait? Would tonight be the night she found out at twenty-nine she had lost her touch? She didn't have a plan "B," but then again plan "A," had never failed her before.

Peter Kozlov was a corporal in the Russian Army. He had been passed up twice for promotion for dereliction of duty—once for falling asleep while on guard duty, and another for not saluting a senior officer. His wife Maria was expecting their second child back home, a home Peter had not seen in over six weeks. Peter would never be a career soldier or military man; he lacked the discipline and the ambition to do so. But both factors were what led him to be in the military to begin with.

In a strange twist of fate, it turns out the Russian Air Force major young Peter had flipped off at the loading docks of the London Exhibition Hall was also his father-in-law. Gravda safely assumed the major held considerable contempt for the slacker who had married his precious daughter.

Peter Kozlov had a year and a half of art classes from the University of Moscow but had dropped out at just about the same time his new bride had become pregnant for the first time. Gravda could read between the lines. A doting father-in-law whose life was all about discipline with a daughter married to a "dead end" liberal with no future. The military was not Peter Kozlov's choosing and it appeared daddy pulled the strings in Peter's life now. The entire mission rested on her being correct.

The fact Kozlov was Army and not Air Force was Major Alexander Tkachenko's way of telling the boy he was not up to his father in law's standards. Major Tkachenko had the young man stationed under his watch so he could keep an eye on him and maybe whip him into shape before his second grandchild was born. She assumed it wasn't going well.

Peter Kozlov had spent most of his basic training in the motor pool and Gravda knew that fact would help her in her plan. *Poor bastard*, she thought. Well, maybe at least he would enjoy the night, because in the morning his life would never be the same.

Gravda walked through the doors of the Prague Hotel and once again walked straight to the bar area.

Peter Kozlov was on the same barstool as before and this time he was alone. He sat with his head down with several small plates of food partially untouched nearby.

Gravda knew the routine. Kozlov had set in for a long night

at the bar. This might be even easier than she had hoped.

She took a seat two barstools away from her patsy, set her purse upon the bar, and ordered a fruity drink. She did not look his way; she did not attempt to make conversation. When fishing, you drop the bait and wait. It took less than five minutes.

Peter Kozlov looked up from the depths of his glass and turned her way. He leaned her way with one elbow on the bar and said, "You were here before."

"Scusa," Gravda said in Italian.

Kozlov did what most people would do when confronted with a different language. He repeated himself much slower and pantomimed his meaning with hand gestures of pointing to her, then to the bar and then to his watch.

"OH! Si," she answered again in Italian. "You are Russian," she said in Russian, but broken by an Italian accent. She spoke her next words slowly as if to have to think, "Ya N'emnoga gavar'us perusski." She had phrased it as a question but had said, "I speak a little Russian."

Peter Kozlov smiled; his teeth were not straight but they were white.

Gravda pretended to struggle though another phrase. "It was too crowded earlier, I don't like crowds," she said.

"Nyet," he said. "No, me either, people are a pain in the nonka."

Gravda laughed, "Nonka, what mean nonka?"

Peter Kozlov blushed, as he pointed to her backside.

She looked down the barstool at her own figure and then looked back to Peter making sure she had made eye contact. Putting her manicured hand on her backside, she laughed again. "Oh, nonka."

Peter blushed again. "Ser," he said smiling, "Yes, nonka."

Gravda grabbed her drink and her purse and moved over to the empty bar stool next to Peter. Peter did not complain. Fish on.

They spent the better part of an hour chatting. She had introduced herself as Bianca Verti, just another alias, just another name. He had been truthful when he told her his name was Peter but had caught him in his first lie when he had told her he was a lieutenant and not just a corporal in the Russian Army. A man lying to a pretty woman in a bar in hopes of impressing her. *Well, that was a first,* she told herself.

He was, "on special assignment," he told her, but could not tell her anymore because of the "secrecy" involved.

She could have responded with the same words but instead told her own lie, that she was on vacation by herself, and she had always wanted to see how beautiful Prague was.

Peter drank throughout their conversation while pausing to take small bites of the plates on the bar. He enjoyed teaching the Italian woman who spoke some Russian the proper way to toast before he drank another shot of vodka. He had started with "To your health." Four or five more shots later, he had the courage to progress to, "To your beauty, or to your eyes."

It was time for Gravda to start reeling in her fish. "Teach me how to swear in Russian," she asked smiling.

Peter was more than happy to oblige. His first attempts were innocent enough and he was honest with his answers. She would repeat his words purposely making mistakes and pat his knee when he said something funny. When she leaned into talk to him, she would catch him looking at her cleavage.

Two shots of vodka later his innocence was gone. His last phrase he told her was supposedly "go screw yourself" in Russian. It was not, and she knew it. The young corporal had just told her exactly what he would love to do if her body was his own. It was time for Bianca Verti to land her fish.

She stood up from her barstool and smoothed the non-existing wrinkles from her skirt. She paused as both her hands came to rest on her backside. She raised an eyebrow and said, "Nonka....correct?"

Peter's glassy eyes grew wide, "Ser... yes," he said.

Gravda slowly ran her hands from back to front and starting at her pelvis, she ran her hands up her body until both hands clutched her chest. "And these?" she asked.

Peter Kozlov gulped, "RpyAb."

"I saw you looking," she told him.

This time Peter did not blush.

"Do you like?" she asked, in broken Russian.

"Ser," was all he could say.

Gravda opened her purse, took out a small stack of Koruns, and laid them on the bar to pay the corporal's tab. "Show me how much you like," she said. She grabbed her purse in one hand and grabbed Peter's hand with the other and guided him off the barstool and led him out of the bar. *Who needs a plan 'B' when plan 'A' works so well,* she thought to herself.

Chapter 15

A Room on the Fourth Floor

Peter Kozlov stumbled twice on the way to his room. He reeked of Vodka and pickled herring, and twice he had rested his hand on the wall to steady himself. Bianca kept him moving. When they got to his room, he fumbled for the key, and she knew his fumbling had only begun. As he turned to attempt to unlock the door for the third time, her mind started to wander back into her past, much farther into her past, to a time when she was just fourteen. She shook the memory from her head, grabbed the key from him, and opened the door.

Turning on the light, Bianca surveyed the room quickly and placed her purse on the dresser, making sure it was angled just right so the bed was in full view. She snapped the metal closure to the closed position and gently pushed Kozlov onto the edge of the bed. He sat there, wide-eyed and greedy. She counted to ten, slipped off her jacket, and tossed it on the bed next to him.

His eyes grew wider.

He started to get up, but she pushed him back into a seated position, this time she was not as gentle. She was in charge and Peter needed to know it. Bianca Verti reached back with both hands to the nape of her neck and flipped her onyx hair off her shoulders. She paused again, counting, ten, eleven, twelve. She reached with one hand and slowly slid the zipper of her dress downward to the small of her back.

Kozlov started to speak, but she silenced him by placing her index finger to his lips. While leaning forward she allowed her dress to fall forward as it slipped from her shoulders. Kozlov's stare became spell bound and she thought to herself, *If this Cossack has a heart attack now, the game is over before it began.* She stepped backwards, making sure she was in frame and her Russian predator was clearly visible. Knowing the cadence of the concealed camera in her purse, she slid her dress off her arms and let it drape in a petite pile on the floor, as it hit the carpet surrounding her stiletto heels. The tan lines of an earlier vacation in the Mediterranean highlighted her bare backside to the camera, framed by garters which held up her black stockings.

Peter Kozlov rose to meet her, and she did not object. He had seen exactly what he had desired. *The rest will be easy*, she thought. As he embraced her, she leaned into his ear and whispered in broken Russian, "Be gentle."

He wasn't.

The next twenty minutes were filled with grunts and groans in Russian and an occasional false moan from a beautiful woman who wished to be almost anywhere than where she was. She waited until she felt sure he had fallen asleep, gathered up her clothing, and dressed. At almost 1:00 a.m., she grabbed her purse and made her departure.

As Bianca—Gravda, made her way back to the safe house she thought how the Russian corporal must have been dreaming of how his luck had just changed for the better. In just a few hours she was determined to make sure he couldn't have been more wrong.

Chapter 16

Late Night Shadows

The streets of Prague at 1:00 a.m. are a lonely place, not because of the lack of people at that hour but for the lack of souls. Most large cities have the same feeling of desolation long after dark. The blackness devours not only the night sky but also the people who ply their trade while decent people sleep at home in their beds. Gravda did not think of herself as judgmental, she had been through too much in her life to think badly of others for the things she had done herself, but tonight she felt her first pangs of remorse.

Is an individual to be judged by their actions alone or weighed upon a scale of the motivations as well? She passed a young streetwalker trying to stay warm with what little she wore on what the clock said was a morning in early June but still felt like night. Gravda asked herself if she fit in to these surroundings. Her Chanel dress said she did not, but she was still here in the moment, just like the rest of them.

Darkness has its own set of rules, and she understood them well, knowing those rules had kept her safe and alive over the years and she had learned them at what should have been a tender age. Gravda wanted to reach into her purse and hand the younger woman enough kurons to send her home for the night but knew she couldn't. Maybe she had a little one at home needing food on the table in the morning and this was how the woman provided. Maybe that child would wake up later crying and there would be no one to hold them and comfort them; mom was at work, doing what she could.

If Gravda had stopped, spoken, or even made eye contact then the silent rules would have been broken. Any act of kindness was condescending and confrontational, even if not meant to be. Especially if not meant to be...

So, Gravda continued walking.

When she rounded the corner to the safehouse, she felt like she was coming home. It wasn't home, and she knew it, but she was happy to escape the outside world. As she put the key into the lock of the service door, she paused to reflect but only for a second. "I don't even know what home feels like," she whispered to herself and turned the key.

Big Tony was sitting in the office and makeshift kitchen, lit by the single dim bulb that cast strange shadows on the greasy garage through its glass window. He rose to his full height as she stepped inside.

She turned, closed the door, and re-locked it as Tony stepped to meet her. "Everyone else asleep?" she asked.

Tony just nodded in the affirmative.

"Did you wait up for me big guy?" she said, smiling.

Tony smiled back, raised his palms to the air, and grunted, "Yeah, well, I was also working on my third sandwich."

"Well, thank you," she told him, being sincere. "I will need you at 7:00 a.m.," she told him. "Maybe you should get some rest too."

"How did it go?" Tony asked, not knowing or asking for the full details of what had happened.

"We have our patsy," she said, not needing to explain any more than that. "Tony, do me a favor would you please? Wake up Joe and ask him to meet me in the kitchen if you don't mind. I need a drink."

"Sure Betty, whatever you need," Tony said. "Maybe you should get some rest for yourself, you look tired."

"Thanks again, Tony," she said as the hulking man turned to climb the stairs to the loft.

Gravda walked into the kitchen and found herself a glass. She had hidden a bottle of the finest Russian Vodka in the back of the freezer, pulled the cork, and poured herself three stiff fingers. She sat and sipped. *How was it possible that something so cold could burn so good,* she thought. She rested with one elbow on the table with a glass in her hand, with the other hand on her forehead as she leaned across the table. She felt the fire in her gullet as the alcohol tricked down her throat, and her mind went blank to the memory of earlier.

Joe came into the kitchen wiping away eyeball buggers and pillow scars. "Sorry to wake you," she said. "Have a seat."

"Ah, it's no big deal. I was surprised I fell asleep at all. Hank snores like he is three times bigger than Tony," he joked. "How was your night?"

"That's what you're about to find out," Gravda said. "Do you remember our deal?"

"Yeah, something about gutting me and dropping me in the Vltava River over the Charles Bridge as I recall," he said.

"Yes, something like that," she said smiling. "I need you to develop these photos tonight. Did you and Brad get the dark room set up?"

"Yeah, it's ready to go," Joe told her.

"Good," she said pushing the purse across the table to him. "I'll need prints in duplicate and in 8 X 10, and I will need them by 7:00 a.m. Split them into two separate envelopes if you don't mind."

"Okay, will do," Joe said. He started to get up from the table and paused to sit back down. "Betty, can I ask you a personal question? You don't have to answer me, and it is none of my business, but still...Why do you do what you do?"

She drained her glass before asking, "What do you mean, Joe?"

"This, all of this," he waved his hand in the air to encompass the garage, the kitchen, Prague, and life in general. "Why do you take all the risks?" Before she could answer he added, "Betty, you're smart—you're talented, you're gorgeous, you could do anything you want...why this?"

Gravda had been thinking too much lately, and his question was one she had been starting to ask herself. The problem is questions make you stop and think, and it is hesitation like that that gets people in her line of work killed. It was always better to not think of things, better to just react in the moment.

She could have said, "It is none of your business, go do your job," but she didn't. Instead, she bit the nail on her index finger of her right hand and answered his question with another. "We both work for the CIA, why do you do what you do?"

"Betty, I don't do what you do," he said. "I am a photographer, and that's it. I don't crave excitement. I don't usually look for drama. I am just good 'ol boring Joe. Two years ago, I was in a shithole town in Florida shooting weddings and family portraits. You know...the type of photos where everyone in the family gets dressed up in matching white shirts and blue jeans while laying barefoot on the front lawn. I'm no spy."

"You didn't answer my question."

"What, why am I with the CIA?"

"Yeah, what's wrong with family photos and weddings?" she asked. "It sounds nice, tame but nice," she added.

For the first time, Gravda noticed Joe was not wearing the wedding ring he had worn in London.

"Betty, I am a pay grade five. My life is still boring usually. I work in a dark room in Langley where people like you send photos for people like me to develop. The stakeout in London was my first time ever in the field and it scared the shit out of me."

"But you enjoyed it," she said.

Joe, stammered, paused, and groped for words. "Well, uh, it—was exciting."

Gravda, just as Joe had said, was a smart woman. She had to be, and her next question pinned him into a corner which would require him to reflect on his own motivations. "So, the excitement you felt, was that for you, or to prove someone else wrong?"

Joe paused again as Gravda interrupted his thought. "Can you develop those photos with a shot of vodka in you?"

"Probably not," he told her honestly.

"Okay then, you keep talking. I need one more drink," she said, standing up to reach for the freezer one last time. "Was it you who told yourself you were boring, or someone else? Who planted that seed in your head?"

Joe laughed, "How did this become a therapy session, Betty?"

"You started it," she told him. "So, let's cut to the chase, how long ago did she leave you and who was it she found more exciting than you?"

"Jesus, Betty, is all this in a file somewhere?"

"No, Joe, but if you pay attention long enough most people are an open book. What happened?" she asked. "Who's the other guy?"

"Is it that obvious?" he asked. "Geez, he's a professional water skier in some stupid show at Busch Gardens in Tampa."

Gravda didn't mean to laugh. "And that's more exciting than you are? How long ago did all this happen?"

"Two years ago," he told her.

"And you have been wearing your wedding ring all this time? Were you hoping a life in the CIA would drive her back into your arms?"

Joe looked sheepish and a little foolish. "No...well yeah, something like that I guess."

"Why would you want to be with someone who tells you that you're less than you are? You're not wearing it now. What changed?" she asked.

I haven't worn it since London," he admitted. "I think all this time I was hoping just being a CIA employee would make me seem more interesting. More exciting. But I'm still just a photographer. London reminded me of that." He sighed and chuckled. Almost to himself he said, "Sometimes...I would walk into a bar after work making sure my laminated CIA employee badge was still clipped to my lapel... hoping someone noticed."

"Someone attractive?"

"Well yeah. I work for the CIA I wasn't hoping to go home with some ugly chick." He smiled.

She laughed. "So how did that work out for you?" she asked.

"Hey, I never got a ten like you, but I got my fair share of sixes and sevens."

Again, there was laughter, and she took a pause to take another sip.

He finally added, "In London I realized I was tired of pretending. Tired of trying to be something I'm not. Sitting in that van, exciting as it was, told me I'm not cut out for this spy shit."

She sat back down with only one finger of vodka left in her glass. "And what's wrong with who you really are? Boring can be really nice sometimes, especially when the world seems filled with way too much drama." She patted his hand.

"Thank you," he said, "but you never answered *my* question."

Gravda took a long sip and drained her glass. "Same reason you joined. Trying to forget the past. You know, when I spoke to Allen Dulles and requested you for this assignment, you could have said no. It's out of your pay grade and both he and I would have understood. Why did you take it?"

"I guess I didn't want to let you down," he told her. "Why *did* you ask for me on this, when you know my limitations?"

"I work every day in a circle of professional liars, Joe. I wanted someone I felt I could trust."

"Thanks Betty. I didn't mean to pry," he told her.

"Well, me either. But that's what we CIA people do, right?"

They both chuckled and headed up the stairs to the loft.

"Betty, why don't you get some sleep? You can sack out on my cot. I will be up the rest of the night developing these photos. If you want, you can change in the darkroom."

"That's a good idea Joe, thanks, I'm tired."

As they reached the top of the stairs, he whispered, "Betty, I am still really nervous about later tonight. I'm not sure I am ready for this."

"You'll be ready, and I'll watch your back, I promise. Right now, you only have one thing to worry about."

"Let me guess," he asked, smiling, "you gutting me and throwing me into the river?"

"Yeah, something like that," she said, returning the smile.

Joe spent the rest of the night developing photos while Gravda fell asleep. At just after 4:30 a.m. Joe stepped out of the darkroom to take a five-minute break and stretch his eyes.

He softly stepped over to the cot on which Gravda was fast asleep, and gently pulled her blanket up to her chin.

Her instincts woke her before his fingers had even touched the blanket. She did not move or open her eyes.

His whisper was so faint she could barely hear him as he said, "I don't know who you are lady, but you are amazing!" He finished tucking her in and quietly walked away.

Only then did she open her eyes...and smile.

Chapter 17

The Sun Rises in Prague

At 6:30 a.m. Gravda was up and sitting in the kitchen in bare feet, shorts, and a white tank top. Last night she had praised her people for the wonderful invention of vodka, but this morning she was much keener on anyone who was Columbian and the mass marketing of coffee.

Joe wandered in from upstairs and without making eye contact said, "The pictures are done."

"How did they turn out," she asked, "Did we get everything?"

Joe stammered, "Uh, yeah, I would say we got everything." He had two large manila envelopes in his hand and laid them on the table.

"Good. Would you like some coffee?" she asked, getting up to pour a cup from the pot she had just made. She turned her back to him while at the counter and Joe caught himself looking at her slender frame and averted his eyes. When she turned, she noticed him looking at the floor and said, "I was doing my job, Joe."

"Oh, I know Betty, I am not judging you, I am just trying to be a gentleman. This is all new to me, alright?"

"You are a gentleman Joe, and I appreciate it. But sooner or later you're going to have to make some eye contact with me. I am not always proud of what I have to do but I get the job done, and later today we have a bigger job to focus on."

As they spoke, Big Tony plodded down the steps with an echo that resounded on each tread of the stairs. He entered the kitchen dressed all in black with his signature trench coat and asked, "Okay Betty, what's the plan?"

"Let me get dressed, then you and I are going to stroll over to the Hotel Prague and make sure our fish is deeply hooked. I think we are about to ruin someone's day."

"Does your fish deserve to have his day ruined?" Tony asked.

"Does it matter?"

"Not to me."

"Hell, we might even be doing him a favor in the long run."

"Oh, goodie," Tony said, "You know how I love to do charity work."

Gravda bent over and whispered into Joe's ear, "Put those photos out of your head Joe. We still have a job to do here, okay."

"You're right, and I'm sorry," Joe whispered back. "I will get my head out of my ass."

Gravda Nemiroff giggled and whispered, "Joe, it's definitely not your ass you're thinking about."

Joe blushed and Gravda patted his cheek as they made eye contact for the first time that morning. In that moment, they both knew they would be fine.

Chapter 18

Time to Hook a Patsy

At 7:20 a.m., Gravda was standing near the revolving door of the Prague Hotel with a manila envelope in her hand. Big Tony stood just across the street on the fringe of an alleyway with a similar envelope.

Twenty minutes later, Peter Kozlov emerged, in uniform, with one of same men he had been seated next too at the bar much earlier yesterday evening. Deep in conversation, she heard Kozlov say, "No really, I'm telling you the truth, it really happened." She waited until he had almost bumped into her.

"Good morning, Peter," she said.

Peter Kozlov was taken back but tried to recover by asking his friend to give him a minute. Gravda led him to the corner of the building and out of sight of his associates.

"How did you sleep Peter?" she asked, only this time her Russian was crisp and clear.

He paused. "I slept fine—you disappeared," he said.

"I got everything I needed," she told him, again in fluent Russian, holding up the envelope for him to see.

Kozlov started to smile thinking of his own sexual prowess...but paused when he registered that her Italian accent was now missing. Perplexed, he just stammered, "Wait, I thought—"

"Well, you thought wrong Peter," she said.

She handed him the envelope, which he then opened. He slid the first photo partially from inside and his eyes grew wide.

"You've been a very bad boy Peter," she scolded.

His expression told her he was no longer thinking of lust, but instead fear. He looked at the second photo and then at her. "How did you get these?" he asked.

Gravda snatched the envelope back from Kozlov and said, "The important question is how your wife's daddy will react to seeing his little girl shamed by a womanizer?"

Peter reached for the envelope again and she pulled them just out of his reach. "Don't be stupid Peter. Do you think these are the only copies?" She pointed across the street where Big Tony stepped out of the shadows just long enough to wave a similar envelope for him to see.

Peter Kozlov's shoulders slumped. In a weak attempt to show bravado, he said, "You bitch, what do you want—money? I am a simple soldier. I don't have much money."

"Oh, I know, Lieutenant—oh wait, it's actually Corporal Kozlov, isn't it?" she said smugly. "I know everything about you Peter, and you don't know anything about me. That puts you at a decisive disadvantage, doesn't it? We both know Major Tkachenko thinks his son-in-law is a buffoon and a loser, and sadly these photos won't do much to change his opinion of you. You have created quite a scandal here Peter." She was rubbing it in.

Peter's hands started to shake. "Okay, what do you want, please?"

"You're going to help me with something Peter," she told him.

"I can't help you," he stammered.

"Well then, maybe you can help yourself," she said now in a softer tone of voice.

"I don't understand," he said frustrated.

"I know you don't Peter, let me explain it to you. These photos will end your military career and probably your marriage as well. Daddy will have been right, and you will have been wrong, but you can most likely live past all that. The big problem comes when Major Alexander Tkachenko finds out the woman you spent last night with, in your hotel room, is an American agent. I haven't been home to the Motherland for a long time Peter. Tell me, do we still use firing squads?"

The air rushed out of Peter Kozlov's lungs as if he had been kicked in the groin. He bent over thinking that he would be sick.

Gravda put her hand on his shoulder and said, "You're not a bad guy Peter, and I really don't want to hurt you. But I will if I have to. You're going to do a few favors for me today and in return, I will burn these photos and any copies of them. If you're smart enough to keep your mouth shut, then it will be like last night never happened. Do you understand?"

"Yes," Peter said weakly. "What do I have to do?"

"You're going to do what you usually do. Go to work and act like nothing is different. You won't say anything to anyone out of the ordinary, or if you do, I will know it and you will hang. Do I make myself clear?" Gravda told him.

Peter still looked ill but nodded.

"At lunchtime, I want you to pull one of the sparkplug wires on the truck you will be driving later to the freight yard. You spent time in the motor pool, you know how to do that right?" she asked.

Again, he nodded.

"You are going to make sure your truck is the last one to leave the exhibition hall with the satellite you have been guarding on board. You won't leave until all the other trucks have headed to the freight yard. Take your normal route. One of my men will meet you a few blocks away, you will bring that truck to me."

"What...You're going to steal the satellite? Are you insane? You are going to get me shot! When it shows up missing the major is going to know I was the one who took it!"

Gravda once again put her hand on his shoulder to calm him. "No Peter, we are not going to steal it. Let's just say that we are going to borrow it for a little while. All you have to do is drive the truck, that's it. Give me a few hours with the satellite and we will return it long before your father-in-law ever knows that it was gone."

"It won't work," Peter said, starting to panic. "Oh, God. He is going to kill me."

"You really hate the bastard, don't you?"

"Yes, I really do," Peter spat. "He has been making my life a living hell from the first day I met him."

"Well then, this is your chance to get back at him," Gravda said softly.

"By getting shot!"

"No one is going to get shot, and no one is going to get caught if you do your part, Peter. I'm sorry, you're a convenient cog in a wheel and this wheel has been in motion for a long time now. I need a look at that satellite, and you are going to help me get it."

"Why me?" he pleaded.

"Why not you?" she asked in return. "You made it easy Peter, after all, you were more than willing last night. Besides, I know everything about you, your background, your family, your second child on the way. I do my research, it's what I do."

"Lady you're crazy, your plan won't work."

"Yes, it will Peter, I've had my eye on that satellite for a long time. There are four more cities on the exhibition tour, and no one pays attention when it's not in the exhibition hall and after it's loaded. I know how Russians think, we're creatures of habit. It will work, and my plan is perfect."

Kozlov wanted to believe her. He spun on his heels while slapping his cap off his head in a fist and running his free hand fiercely through his hair from front to back and then once again from back to front. He looked like he still needed some convincing.

"Peter, you spend your whole day standing with your back to the Luna 3. You're there to keep an eye on the people around you, not the satellite. The major does the same thing, and so do the other guards. The only time anyone pays any attention is when it is being loaded or unloaded and, in both cases, there are deadlines to meet. All we are going to do is take a few photographs, and every nail in that crate will be put back exactly the way it was, and nothing will be out of the ordinary."

"It won't work...please," Kozlov pleaded once more.

"It will work," Gravda told him, "And you need this to work Peter. You're already in this. You don't have a choice. I am your only way out of this situation Peter. Doing what I ask of you is the only way you will ever see your family again."

"So, all I have to do is drive the truck like I usually do," he asked, looking for hope.

"Yes, that's all you have to do. You will have to sit for a few hours as my team does what they need to do, but you will have it back in place at the freight yard before the major or anyone else finds it missing."

"But what if someone notices something is different?"

"You're missing the best part, Peter," she told him. "It would take an engineer to discover any sort of tampering, and my engineers are every bit as good as yours are. No one is going to be looking that closely at it until it gets back to Russia, and that won't be until late August. I could change every screw on the satellite, and no one would even know it for months or maybe even years to come. You're a soldier, not an engineer. If anyone finally does suspect anything, who would they blame?"

Peter looked confused.

"By the time the Luna 3 gets back to Moscow it will have been in cities all over the globe, several different ships, rail-yards, and exhibitions. They won't track anything back to Prague and today. Peter, there are too many scenarios to count. There is one thing though which has always remained constant. Who oversaw the overall security of the satellite on this entire voyage? Who would they think to blame: a low-level Army corporal, or the Air Force major who was in command? If or when the ruse is discovered, who will the major's superiors hold responsible?"

Peter smiled a devious smile as he let the thought ponder in his head. "The major," he said.

"Yes, the major. I told you I was not out to hurt you, Peter. Would you like me to leave just one screw un-tightened to be sure?"

"No, you better not," he told her, wondering if she was kidding or not.

"Just drive the truck and do as you're told, and after tonight, your life will be yours again."

Peter took a deep breath, weighing his non-existing options. "Okay," he said. "Where do I need to bring the truck?"

"You will pull out of the exhibition hall using your regular route," she told him. "At Glossten Street you will turn left instead of right, and one of my men will meet you there and direct you the rest of the way."

"How will I know who he is?" Peter asked.

"You'll know," she said. "Look for the unordinary."

"What does that mean?"

"Just trust me Peter, you'll know."

"Okay," he said, still confused.

"Peter, just one more thing," Gravda said. "Don't go getting all brave on me. If you say anything about this to anyone, or double cross me in any way, it will not save your *nonka*. I still have the photographs, and if my plan blows up because you suddenly decided to become a loyal soldier, I will personally tell the K.G.B the whole plan was yours to begin with. That would make your father-in-law very happy, wouldn't it?"

"Yeah, yes it would," Peter grunted.

"I'm the only friend you have in the world right now Peter, and the last thing I want to do is make the Major happy. Now go do your job," she told him as she patted him on the rearend to get him moving.

Chapter 19

Hooked and Landed

Big Tony walked across the street from the hotel and met Gravda at the street corner. They strolled in the opposite direction of the young corporal.

"Is your fish fried?" he asked.

"I would say he was well done," Gravda told him.

"Yeah, but can you count on him?" Tony asked. "Listen, this is none of my business and I know this project is yours to run. I don't usually question authority, but..." He let his last syllable hang in the air.

"Tony if you have something to say then just say it," she told him firmly.

"Betty, you and I are professionals, but you have a lot of rookies on this team, and I don't like rookies. You, me, and Hank are the only ones who have ever had any field experience and now we're counting on a Russian soldier to make this come together? I am not a big fan of surprises, and so far, that's all this mission has been."

"Tony, I picked everyone on this team personally and for

individual reasons. There is no 'field expertise' for stealing a Russian satellite. We don't have a book to go by on this one, big guy. Playing outside the norm is what is going to make this work, okay? Don't worry about our Russian soldier, our 'fish' will do what he's told," she said. "Besides, he wasn't given any choice in the matter."

They walked a little further before she added, "Russians think differently than most people. They are survivalists, and no one is better at saving their own ass when need be. Our soldier will be there tonight."

"You sound pretty sure of yourself," Tony said.

"Well, I should be..." She let her words linger this time.

Big Tony stopped in mid-stride. "Wait, you? You're a ruskie, a red, a commie, a pinko, a chotch...a Russian?"

His list of euphemisms was just long enough to make her laugh instead of being offended.

The smile on his wide face told her he had meant no harm, but he was surprised.

"Yup, born and raised," she told him. "And you forgot 'beet eater,' that's always a good one. By the way, ' Ruskie' means 'a type of hat,' dumbass. It is actually called an 'ushanka' in Russian. It's the type of hat with fur flaps worn over the ears when it's cold outside. It's a stupid insult."

"Well, you learn something new every day," Tony grunted.

"Speaking of stupid hats, what's the story on the one you're wearing, and why does Hank have the very same one?"

"Hank earned his," Tony said." He took a bullet for me five years ago, on a bad night in Egypt when we had too many rookies and not enough professionals."

"Hank walked in front of a bullet meant for you?" Gravda asked, truly concerned.

"No, actually he leapt—leaped, hell I don't know. Anyway, you know how tall the little bastard is, so you can figure out where the bullet was headed. If I ever have any kids, I have to name them after Hank."

Gravda laughed, "And if you ever have a daughter?"

"Well then, my daughter 'Hank' will get a lot of ribbing on the playground, and she will learn at an early age that life can be tough."

"So, you gave him your hat?"

"Yeah," Tony said, "It's all he asked for, I told him I could never repay him, and he told me, 'Yes, you can, give me your fucking hat,' and what was I supposed to do? Now every time I see the little shit, he punches me in the nut sack to remind me."

Gravda had to stop walking to laugh. It took a while, but even Big Tony joined in.

When the moment was over, Tony reached into his black overcoat and pulled out the manila envelope. "Betty, are you going to let me keep these and see what's inside?" he asked.

"Nope," she said, grabbing the envelope from his hand.

"Yah know what Betty, this job just doesn't have any perks anymore."

Chapter 20

Preparations at the Safe House

The rest of the morning and into the late afternoon Gravda pushed her team to prepare for what was coming later that night. The lathe was set up and her Goddard engineer had set up workstations to prepare for any unexpected delays in reassembling the satellite. Big Tony had driven the van, with all the necessary tools to do the job, to the salvage yard and had walked back to the safe house.

Nervous Bob had asked her several times to go over his role once again.

"You will analyze the photos Joe takes at the salvage yard. Brad will develop them, and you will take your notes. Even the smallest of details may become important later," she informed him, "So be thorough and don't miss anything. One of the NASA boys will be onsite, but he will be busy taking things apart and making sure they go back together. He won't have much time for analysis."

Big Tony had pulled her aside and asked, "Shouldn't one of

us be keeping an eye on your corporal?"

"No need, Tony," she said. "He will either show up or he won't, and I am betting on the first one. If he doesn't show up, we pack up and disappear."

"Betty, he has seen both of us and I am a little easier to spot in a crowd than you are."

Gravda put her hand on her hip and tossed her hair, pouting her lips to look provocative, and jokingly said, "So you think so, huh?"

"Okay, so maybe you're right," Tony agreed. "But what if he shows up with the cavalry behind him?"

"He won't, he doesn't have the balls for it," she said. "Even if he tried to be the hero, he knows those photos would hang him anyway. His father-in-law is the Air Force major in charge of security, and 'Daddy' and the corporal don't exactly get along. The kid isn't that bright, but he is not completely stupid. He knows daddy would take the credit and his ass would still be toast. He won't say a word."

"Ouch, you have this guy hooked from both ends," Tony said, looking impressed.

The question would not come up again.

At twenty minutes to six, she gathered her team one last time to fill in any blanks. Everyone grabbed a chair and sat in front of the chalkboard again.

"Hank, you're going to meet our truck at the corner of Glossten Street and Mayfair in about a half hour," she told him. "If the truck is not alone, ignore it and get back here by back alleys. The driver does not know what you look like, but I told him to look for the unexpected."

"By unexpected, you obviously meant extremely handsome and in prime physical condition, right?" Hank asked.

"Yeah, something like that," Tony chided.

Hank looked up at his hulking friend he always seemed to sit next to and grunted, "Fuck you."

"Nice hat," Tony said smiling.

"Why thank you," Hank retorted.

"Are you two done?" Gravda asked.

"What? Oh, yeah sure lady," Hank grunted again, "Sorry, keep going."

"If the corporal is alone, then wave him down, stay on your bicycle and lead him two streets up and turn left. Tony, you will meet them there and take command of the vehicle and bring it to the salvage yard. The field team will meet you there."

"Okay," Tony simply said.

"Hank, you're going to get your exercise tonight. Your job is to shuttle film and information between the salvage yard and here at the safehouse. You're the runner, and any parts or questions will be your responsibility to relay between the two points."

Nervous Joe piped up, "Isn't someone going to notice him?"

"What the hell is that supposed to mean?" Hank asked, preparing himself to stand up in his chair.

"I know what you mean," Gravda said, motioning Hank to sit down. "Sometimes the best place to hide is in plain sight. Hank, make sure you look a little disheveled, and people will get used to seeing you riding back and forth. There won't be any problems."

She took the time to look each member in the eye and ask, "Are you ready? If we botch this, there could be huge international repercussions, so stay focused. One more thing, gentlemen. Steve, Joe, and you," she had pointed to the unnamed engineer who was going to be at the salvage yard, "I need your wallets and your passports. There's no reason for anyone to know who any of us are or even know we have ever been here. Just leave them on the table over there and you will get them back when we return. It's go time!" she told them.

Hank walked over, grabbed his bicycle, and headed out as Gravda and Joe followed him out the door. Big Tony followed Steve and one of the NASA aerospace engineers James Webb had suggested.

They left Nervous Bob, Brad Ray, and another NASA engineer who was ready to fabricate and supply needed parts at the safe house ready for their queues.

At exactly 6:00 p.m., it was indeed, game on.

Chapter 21

Noon, Washington D.C. – The Oval Office

Allen Dulles had asked to speak to President Kennedy at noon, or as close as the President's schedule would allow. Evelyn Lincoln had ushered him into the Oval Office without her usual social engagement and teasing, where the President was waiting.

Dulles did not carry any files with him—what he was about to report would not be 'official' business.

"What do you have for me, Allen?" the President asked.

"Jack, it is 6:00 p.m. in Prague, and my team should be on the move. They have less than twelve hours to secure what we need, but I won't hear anything until the operation is complete."

"What are our chances at success?" the president asked.

"I would say sixty-forty in our favor," Dulles told him. "We have some 'newbies' in the field, but I trust my operative and provided exactly what that individual asked me for."

"Damn it Allen, if you screw this one up it will make the Bay of Pigs look like an Easter egg hunt. I don't need Khrushchev catching our hand in the cookie jar."

"I fully understand what you're saying Jack, but right now your cookie jar should be in route, and I will keep you informed as best as I can," Dulles told him.

President Kennedy rubbed his temples. "Call me on my private line and let me know how things shake out—this is going to be a long night."

"Aren't they all? Mr. President, I will call you sometime around midnight," Allen Dulles said.

The President of the United States did not even respond. The Director of the CIA turned and walked out of the Oval Office with nothing else to say. Things were now out of his hands.

The meeting had lasted less than three minutes.

Chapter 22

Prague

At 6:14 p.m., Hank was at the designated corner and less than four minutes later, a lone Russian lorry pulled around the corner. Hank looked past the vehicle and seeing no one tailing, he put two fingers in his mouth and whistled a shrill whistle as if calling for a cab.

Peter Kozlov looked nervously at the little man on the bicycle and slowed down, pointed a finger at his own chest asking silently, *do you mean me?*

Hank put his head in his hand. *Who else would I mean, dumbass?* Hank thought to himself. Hank spoke no Russian, but the internationally understood hand gesture of one finger in the air, followed by him waving his arm over his shoulder meaning to follow, was understood.

Kozlov was hard on the accelerator trying to keep pace with the strong man peddling ahead of him while grinding through the slow and cumbersome gears of a five-ton Russian lorry loaded with freight. When Hank reached the second intersection, he turned a sharp left into a tight alleyway and Kozlov found himself now hard on the brakes. Blocking his way was a wall. A wall wearing a black leather over coat and strangely enough a matching cap as the little man on the bicycle.

Tony wasted no time in climbing onto the running board, opened the driver's door, and pushed the young corporal across the bench seat to the passenger side. An icy stare told the soldier there would be no attempt at conversation on the short route to the rented salvage yard.

Hank peddled fast and Tony meshed through the notoriously finicky gears of the Russian Army truck without grinding a single one. There was nothing Tony could not drive. In most places, the sight of a little man on a bicycle followed by a Russian military vehicle would have aroused suspicions or at least raised an eyebrow from any locals who might have seen the small parade pass by. But this part of town was crowded with soot-covered buildings and dank puddles, and people tended not to ask questions. The air smelled thick from a paper mill a few blocks away and even with the evening sunlight of June, the streets seemed dark and foreboding. Shadows seemed to stretch farther. This side of town was waiting for sunset to cover its misery.

Hank only slowed when reaching the tall wooden gates of "The Kotchak Brothers Salvage." The white paint indicating the location on the nearly rotten wooden boards was faded and matched its surroundings. Hank whistled again and Gravda, along with the assistance of Joe, opened the doors wide to the alleyway. Big Tony muscled the truck past the opening and backed the truck into the yard.

The fence and gates were ten feet tall, with wooden planking which had seen much better days, but the place would do. There was no cover; they would be working in the open air. A small cinderblock building served as an office and there were several small tool sheds scattered across the yard, but nothing big enough in which to drive the lorry. Old, rusted engine blocks and fenders littered the grounds dropped where they had been removed and left to decay.

Gravda greeted Big Tony as he stepped from the truck. "Well, so far so good," she said. "How's our passenger?"

"Numb," Tony responded.

Peter Kozlov sat in the truck still staring out of the windshield of the unmoving vehicle.

Gravda leaned into the open cab and said in Russian, "Peter, it's okay, you can come out."

Peter slid across the seat and exited on her side. This morning she had been 'the bitch' that was out to destroy him, but now she was the only familiar face, and he was happy to see her.

"Nice work," she told him, trying to help him to relax. *The day must have been difficult for him,* she thought. This boy was no soldier; he had dreamed of becoming an artist and artists are notoriously sensitive. He must have spent the entire day inside his own head, thinking of scenarios where he was the victim and crapped on like a statue by pigeons in a park. "How did it go?" she asked.

"I think it went well," Peter said. "I don't think anyone is on to us."

Gravda caught the word "us" in his comment. She also considered her own internal thought of referring to him as a "boy." *This is a twenty-three-year-old Army corporal, with a wife at home and a second baby on the way. Well, a man is defined by his life experiences, not his chronological age,* she thought. Peter Kozlov was scared. Almost overwhelmed by the changes she had forced into his life in such a short period of time, he didn't want to feel alone. He had said "us" for this simple reason.

"How did you dismantle the truck?" she asked. "Did you pull a sparkplug wire?"

"No," he responded almost from a distance, as if he had to re-trace his actions before speaking. "Diesel engines don't have sparkplugs. I loosened a wire to the starter, so the engine would crank but not fire."

"Good thinking," she told him, chastising herself for not knowing the details of a diesel motor or for even knowing the truck was diesel at all. *What other factors might she have forgotten?* "How did the major take the delay?"

"His usual," the corporal told her. "The man yells for a living and enjoys his work, especially when it is directed at me. I told him I had it and would have the truck back on the road as soon as possible. He told me to get it fixed and get my ass to the freight yard as soon as possible, and that he would be taking Major Gagarin to the airport."

"Any chance someone will acquire a new-found sense of dedication and double back to the exhibition hall to check up on your progress?" Gravda asked.

"I doubt it," the corporal stated, "Today was pay day."

Gravda being Russian understood his meaning. The rank and file of the Soviet military is paid once a month. Tonight, at the Hotel Prague, there would be rubles on the bar top and the vodka would pour freely.

Gravda breathed a sigh of relief. This was her first operation where she was not only in charge, but she was also responsible for others. Most times, she was utilized as someone who could get a job done and then disappear. The first objective ingrained in her was lone survival; she did not take unnecessary risks. When you work alone, you control most of the factors that can endanger you; when you work with others, you can't.

That fact gnawed at her. It had from the moment she had convinced the three CIA agents in London to assist her on a mission even Allen Dulles had told her was ridiculously risky considering the consequences if caught. She was still asking herself why she had pushed so hard for the operation.

"You did well, Peter," she told him, and he smiled.

"So, now what?" he asked.

"Now you sit and wait," she told him.

"Can I help?"

"No Peter, you've done your part."

Peter found a rusted truck seat and sat down on the springs with his knees close to his chin. The look on his face was once again distant.

Gravda turned towards Tony and said, "Okay, let's get moving. I want Hank on his bike with the first test photos in thirty minutes. I want the crate marked before we begin. Every screw needs to be in the same place when we're done."

Hank waddled up to the back of the truck with a roll of masking tape in his hand. Tony picked him up like a pillow and plopped him down on the wooden planks of the truck bed, still standing on his feet. Hank pulled strips of tape from the roll and marked the location of the lower fasteners which held the crate together.

"Nails, not screws," Hank yelled back. "We need a crowbar."

Tony joined him in the back of the truck, along with Steve. He had a crowbar and a block of wood, while Steve had his own roll of masking tape, his ledger, and a pen. Using the block of wood for leverage, Tony pulled each nail from the bottom of the crate and handed it to Steve who labeled it and set it aside. Each hole was marked with a similar piece of tape corresponding to the writing Steve had just added to each nail. A-1, A-2, A-3, etc.

"Pull them out as straight as you can Tony, so they have to go back in the same way," Steve told him.

The crate stood at an impressive eight feet high, and even Big Tony needed a ladder to reach the nails on the top section. Twenty minutes later, the evening sun was reflecting off the metallic surface of the Luna 3 satellite.

Both Steve and the NASA engineers whistled in harmony. Steve turned to Gravda and said, "It's the real deal all right. It is missing its engine, but I am sure this is the back-up to the one they launched."

The bed of the truck was getting crowded as each one wanted to see their first Russian satellite up close.

Joe burned his first roll of 35mm film as the engineers crawled under and over their newly uncovered prize. It was still early, and Gravda knew it was too soon to get excited. When Joe had finished, he popped the back of his camera open and dropped the film into a canister he had waiting in his vest pocket. "Hank it's time for you to do some peddling," he said.

Hank snatched the canister of film and looked at Tony. "Elevator please, my good man."

Tony lumbered down off the truck, picked Hank up by his waist, and gently placed him on the ground.

Hank faked a punch to Tony's groin making the big man flinch, then tipped his hat and was off to the safe house a few blocks away.

Luna 3 stood within a steel framework of metal tubing, purposefully built to support its weight and size for display. The stand was nearly three feet tall.

The satellite nestled within the metal stand was big by usual standards, standing over five feet if you included the four antennae on top and the two underneath. The cylindrical midsection was roughly four feet in diameter at its widest point, and housed the double row of solar cells which powered the internal batteries.

Steve pointed out micrometeoroid detectors on the underside and the added cosmic ray detectors to his list of things to be impressed by. "Joe, get a few photos of this stuff, would you please."

Working from the bottom and going up, Joe started snapping more photos. They would have to wait for Hank's return to know the first roll was acceptable, but Joe was confident his skills were up to par.

Brad, back at the safehouse, could develop a roll of film in thirty minutes, but it would take longer to make prints. However, he would have all night to catch up. They had roughly twelve hours to dismantle the satellite, photograph everything they could and get it re-assembled and then get it to the freight yard.

Joe had four cameras with him, and he trusted each one. If a roll came back as unsuitable, he would have to re-shoot earlier photos with another camera. He was not waiting for Hank to return to get a head start on what would be a pressing task.

Steve and the NASA engineer scoured the satellite for more details on the satellite's construction. Steve had never asked the other engineer his name, and the same was true for the Goddard engineer back at the safehouse who was standing by to fabricate any parts needed throughout the night. Gravda had made it clear in their first team meeting, "We have two civilians on this team. I don't want to know your names, and no one will ask you. When this is said and done, plausible deniability is your best defense. Don't throw it away by talking too much." So far, neither man had done so.

As the two engineers lay on their backs looking up at Luna 3, the first looked at Steve and said, "Those are photoelectric cells. My guess is they are for maintaining orientation to the sun and the moon. One of the questions they are asking back home is if they could have used them to automate the camera's timing."

"It's possible," Steve said, admiring the bank of twelve cells surrounding the bottom of the craft. "You might have something there. Cells like these are used to draw energy from the sun and then translate it into electrical current. I'm sure they used them to drive the cooling fans and charge the batteries. They could have used them to trip an electrical switch as well. We don't have an electrical schematic on the damn thing, so I won't be able to tell until we crack it open, and hand trace some wires."

Steve continued writing more notes in his ledger. The other engineer rested his head on the wooden planks of the lorry and closed his eyes. Long enough for Steve to nudge him with his elbow and said, "Hey buddy, this is no time for a nap. We're just getting started here!"

"I'm not napping, I'm thinking." He was thinking of what Chris Craft back at Goddard had asked him to verify. If the craft was controlled by radio waves from back on Earth, and radio waves can't bend around the surface of the moon, how did the satellite know when to take its photos? There had been talk of a possible timer inside the craft and it was a plausible enough explanation, but it still didn't answer the big question of how the timer itself was triggered while on the back side of the moon. But what if...*they used the photocells themselves as a timer?*"

The engineer got back up, pausing before speaking again. "Get a better look at those photocells, would yah?"

The photocells were rectangular pieces of blackened Lexan glass, similar to the material used in the cockpit glass of fighter jets. Black absorbs heat, and the sun's rays create heat.

Luna 3 had taken photos of what civilians called "the dark side of the moon," but when the photos were taken it would have been when the craft was between the sun and the moon's surface. The moon was illuminated.

"...What if they oriented the craft when it first got into lunar orbit so only one side faced the moon? They could have done it with radio waves before it reached the backside. The side facing the Earth would have been dark, right? They could have used the photocells to trigger the camera's aperture to start taking the photos when it came around the moon and picked up sunlight again."

Steve thought about it for a moment and said, "Well yes, but there are two problems there. First is the heat buildup. If they don't rotate the craft every few minutes, those temperatures would have fried the electronics. The second is it's a 240,000-mile trip and it took almost four days to get there. Which means for half the trip the photocells are in direct sunlight. A little thing we aerospace engineers like to call daytime and nighttime. If they used sunlight to open the aperture and take the photos, every time the spacecraft was in sunlight, it would have triggered the electrical switch on the camera and the photos would have been taken prematurely."

The unnamed engineer was used to sarcasm, but he worked at NASA. He did not appreciate a desk analyst from Langley busting his chops.

"Are you done?" he asked. "Before you tell me more stuff I already know, how about doing what I ask and taking a better look at those panels. If what I am thinking is correct than at least one of them is going to be different than the rest!"

Photocells were not a new idea; they had been around since the late 1940's. They take in light energy and convert it to electricity and even kids played with them in Heathkits using a sixty-watt light bulb to spin small square-bladed propellers, and they only work in direct light. Move the light bulb away from the photocell and the spinning slows down. Remove it and they stop.

If Luna 3 was oriented with only one side of the craft facing the moon when the photographs were taken, then his premise would work. If the engineer was correct, it wasn't the primary cells used to trigger the camera. It would have to be the ones which were facing the moon on the side of the craft which would currently be in the craft's own shadow using only re-flected sunlight from the moon's surface itself. Luna 3 orbited the moon at 6200 kilometers or roughly 3800 miles from the surface. There was only one problem: the limited amount of sunlight reflected off the surface from so many miles away would require a solar concentrator, and he knew the Russians did not have that technology. On the other hand...*maybe they did.*

"Well, what am I looking for?" Steve asked.

"A trademark or copyright. Look in the lower right-hand

corner of each panel."

Steve crawled deeper under the satellite and had checked four of the twelve when he exclaimed, "What the hell is that? Joe, do you have a macro lens, how close up can you get of something?"

Joe looked at Steve with almost a hurt look on his face. "You're kidding me. This is what I do, of course I have a macro lens. What do you need?"

"Sorry, Joe, take a look at the lower right-hand corner of all of those twelve photoelectric cells, please."

Both engineers crawled out from under to give Joe some room to work in the limited space. Steve looked the other engineer in the eye and patted his shoulder. It was a sign of respect and a silent apology for earlier. "Betty, you might want to come over here!"

Gravda had been working on helping Tony set up portable tables neatly organized with tools, and various equipment for when they may be needed. She had just reached the back of the truck when Joe blurted out, "How is that possible?"

"What is it, Joe?"

It wasn't Joe who responded. It was the NASA engineer.

"Corning Glass Works, Corning, N.Y. I helped to develop those panels back in '58 at Corning's research and development facility. How many panels have those markings?"

Joe continued looking at each panel through the close-up lens of his camera while snapping photos. "Just these two," Joe said pointing to panels mounted next to each other.

"When we crack this thing open you will find four wires from each panel running directly to the aperture on the top of the satellite. Two of those wires sent a signal to the electric servos to open the top of the satellite when it came out of darkness and felt heat from the reflection of the sun on the moon's surface. The other two are wired from the aperture to the camera, telling it to start shooting photographs."

"It makes sense," Steve said. "That is slick."

"Yes, it is," The engineer said. "Those sneaky Russians."

The implications were not lost on Gravda. What was to be a risky mission of stealing a Russian satellite without being detected, and returning it before being caught, was now becoming a much bigger issue.

Steve turned her way and whispered, "Betty, if those solar panels are highly classified as top-secret, and they partially built this damn thing out of American parts..." He went on to add, in case she had not come to the same conclusion, "You know what that means?"

She did.

"It means James Webb has a leak at Goddard," she stated.

"The question is, how big a leak?" Steve responded.

"We won't know until you crack into this satellite," she said. "But we're about to find out."

Chapter 23

Their Work Continues

When Hank returned from the safe house, he pounded on the weathered boards of the gates to the Kotchak Brother's Salvage yard and bellowed, "Avon calling...Fuller Brush...anybody want to buy a Kirby vacuum cleaner?"

All of Gravda's team was in the back of the truck when he returned and heard Hank's thumping on the well-worn boards.

Before any of them could react, Peter Kozlov got up from his rusted seat and walked to the gate. Sliding the latch to open it, Hank slipped between the cracks and said, "Hey 'Ruskie,' yah want to buy some Girl Scout cookies?"

The language barrier was enough that Peter just looked perplexed, closed the gate behind him and silently walked back to his dilapidated truck seat and sat down.

"Wow, tough room," Hank said, as he walked to the truck. "Big red has no sense of humor."

"Are the photos good?" Joe asked Hank.

"Yeah, they're fine, you get to keep your day job," Hank responded.

Steve and the engineer had completed their assessment of the outside of the satellite. It was time to find out what was inside. The engineer had done his counting and said, from the top of a ladder, "There are seventy-five bolts holding the aperture with the camera lenses and the nose cone to the top of the satellite. I'm going to need some help, or we are going to be here all night."

"I'm not worried about being here all night, I am worried about still being here after daybreak," Big Tony said.

Gravda had caught herself looking at her watch several times. She was starting to think the same thing. "Okay Steve, it is time to break out the scaffolding," she said.

"Sure thing, Betty," Steve said. "It will take me about ten minutes to set it up though."

Gravda had tried to think of everything in terms of speed and efficiency. There was only one ladder, but she had prepared for this scenario. In the back of the van were eight-foot tubular reinforced aluminum supports, pre-drilled with quick release pins to stretch across the top of the side supports of the truck bed and clamp into place. She had requisitioned them to be built at the same time she had asked Allen Dulles for the metal lathe and other equipment.

Big Tony, not willing to wait or waste the ten minutes, called out, "Hank, get your ass over here!"

Hank waddled to the back of the truck and Tony reached down and pulled him up with his outstretched arms. In one fluid motion, he raised his own arms above his head, resting Hank upon his shoulders standing feet first. "Give the little guy a wrench," Tony said.

While Steve and Gravda assembled the scaffolding, Hank

and the other engineer got to work. On several occasions, Hank needed to stand with one foot on top of Tony's head and balance himself on top of his human platform as he reached for the uppermost bolts. *It always helps to have at least one acrobat on your team,* Gravda thought.

The new metal rails went up quickly and soon there were two supports for the men to stand on, one in the front of the satellite and one behind. Sunlight was starting to fade, and there were a few more things to accomplish before darkness fell.

Gravda plugged two work lights into extension cords, ran them to the cinder block office, and plugged them in. She handed two more additional aluminum tubes up onto the truck's bed and instructed Tony to attach them to the metal hoops designed on military vehicles to support a waxed coated tarp canopy which kept the bed or occupants dry during inclement weather.

"Tony when you get a minute," Gravda said, "Unroll the tarp and get it over the satellite, I want to block as much light as possible." The tarp was attached to one end of the back of the cab.

Tony flipped the loose end of the canvas over the Luna 3 and then pushed the new supports skyward, making the back of the truck appear to be tent-like. He clamped them down and moved the work lights inside. It would be cramped working quarters for the rest of the night, flashbulbs and work lights created attention, and it was the last thing they needed. Gravda's team was now ready for the dismantling of the Luna 3.

It would take Steve and the engineer over an hour to remove all the rest of the restrictions keeping them outside of their goal. Each bolt was marked and recorded in Steve's ledger and then sealed in plastic bags. As the NASA engineer climbed down from the scaffolding to place the bolts with the other parts already removed, Steve called Tony and Joe up onto the scaffolding and said, "The nose cone will be the heaviest part we need to disassemble. Tony, can you hold it while I disconnect the wires and Joe gets some more photos?"

Working together, they pried and twisted the uppermost portion of the satellite from the rest of the cylindrical body. The nose cone housed the four radio antennae, the camera with two lenses, and the solar reflectors which charged the chemical batteries which drove the film processing equipment inside.

The nose cone assembly weighed almost seventy pounds and Tony was required to lift it almost over his head in order to allow Steve and Joe enough room to work. Gravda who had been standing on the ground at the back of the truck lifted the tarp when she heard Tony complaining, "Man this thing ways a ton. How long do I have to hold it?"

"Until Steve tells you to put it down. Stop your whining big guy. You weren't chosen for this job because of your good looks."

Hank who was standing next to her piped up, "Yeah, that's my job. I already got it covered."

Just as Steve started to disconnect the first wire and at exactly 9:30 p.m., there was a loud electrical 'snap,' and the entire salvage yard was bathed in light. Everyone froze. Those who were not on the truck bed and covered by the tarp found themselves casting elongated shadows fully exposed. There was nothing they could do and nowhere to run. The engineer standing next to Gravda threw his hands in the air with his eyes closed, not willing himself to see what was coming next. Peter Kozlov who had been sitting alone, staring numbly off into space came out of his thoughts and dove to the ground covering his head while exclaiming, "*Kakoro yepta*!" or, 'What the hell?" Hank was simply gone.

They waited for the loud voices of Russian soldiers, gunshots, or the sound of weathered boards on the fences or gates being smashed, as commandos stormed the salvage yard. Gravda's heart skipped two beats, but her eyes scanned the perimeter of the yard at the same time. *No exits, just the front gates,* she thought. For the first time in years, her mind set was not of self-preservation, but of regret for risking other people, good people, in order to get a job done. "Damn it," she said aloud, still scanning the yard hoping to find a way to get her team to safety.

There was none.

The gunshots never came.

The sound of splintered wood did not happen.

In fact, the silence was more deafening than the expectation of chaos. There was only silence. It took Gravda a few seconds to realize what had happened and she reached over and gently pulled the unknown-named engineer's arms down to his side. She walked over to Peter Kozlov, who was sure everything he ever knew of his life was about to be over, and said, "It's just flood lights on a timer, Peter, you're fine, everything is going to be okay."

Peter raised his head but remained on the ground, unable to move.

Big Tony flipped back a corner of the tarp and asked, "Betty, what's going on?!" Tony had his hand on his sidearm.

Gravda waved her hand in the air. "Put that away, it was a false alarm! The spotlights are on a timer."

Tony asked with one eyebrow raised, "Did you know about that?"

Gravda looked up and mouthed the word, "No."

His disapproving look was well deserved, and she knew it. What else had slipped through the cracks of her usual attention?

"Let's get this over with before there are any more surprises," Tony said.

Steve and Joe were still under the tarp and Joe called out, "Hey Tony, this is getting heavy."

"I'll be there in a second—Hey, where is Hank?" he asked.

Gravda did not want to admit once again to not knowing the answer to one of Tony's questions. The little guy had just been standing right next to her. She bent down to look under the truck and Tony jumped down just as there were three softened taps on the front gates from the outside.

Tony positioned himself between the gate and Gravda and drew his sidearm, cocked and ready.

The moment once again intensified until Gravda laughed.

Tony spun his massive head her way, about to chastise her once more, when she said, reaching for his arm, "Bad guys don't knock."

Tony's shoulders slumped realizing she was correct.

Tony slowly walked to the gates, his weapon still drawn and at the ready. "Hank, is that you?"

"Yeah, you gorilla. Open the gate!"

Still worried about the unexpected he asked, "Are you alone?"

"No, Marilyn Monroe is with me, and I promised her she could see a Russian satellite. Open the damn gate!"

"I'm not kidding Hank," Tony told him. "If we have visitors then say the 'word', and then lay low."

"Big guy, I'm good, I'm good," he repeated.

Big Tony started to unlatch the gate and paused. "Okay, I am going to open the gate, but I swear to God, if you punch me in the nuts, I will shoot you. I'm not kidding!"

Tony opened the gate and Hank slipped in with abrasions on his forehead and a bent but still lit cigarette in his mouth. His hat was on sideways.

"Are you okay?" Tony asked with true concern.

"Me, yeah, I'm fine. Things were just starting to get interesting."

As they both walked back towards the truck Tony asked, "How the hell did you get outside?"

"I don't know, those damn lights came on and I figured it was every man for himself." Hank pointed to the top of the fence and pantomimed with his little arms how he had scaled it and flopped over the top.

Even Peter with his language barrier laughed. Then so did Gravda, and then so did Tony.

"That fence is ten feet high!" Tony said.

"Yeah, I know it now. And by the way, there is a sticker bush on the other side, right about there," Hank said pointing.

The tension of the moment had been broken. "So, you're admitting you abandoned me," Tony said, chiding his little friend.

"Nah, I would have come back and saved your ass like I always do," Hank said looking stoic. "By the way, I almost lost my hat," he added, looking for unneeded sympathy.

Chapter 24

Prague Continues

The two engineers worked hard for the next forty minutes until they ran into their first real roadblocks. The first was a threaded aluminum rod rising out of the top of a large stainless-steel box which was bolted to the base of the satellite. It had been designed to support and stabilize the weight of the canopy and camera equipment. The box housed the photo processing equipment and additional electronics as well as the batteries which were needed to power the satellite. The rod was threaded at both ends allowing the nose cone to be spun into place at one end and the other in order to attach it to the photo processing housing. The nose cone had come off easily enough, but the threads had stripped inside of the mounting hardware on the top of the photo developer making it impossible to remove.

"Crap, I can't get the rod out," Steve called out.

"What's the situation, Steve?" Gravda asked as she climbed into the truck and slid under the canopy.

Steve looked down from the scaffolding and said, "I have a three-foot-long threaded rod and it won't unthread from its base. If I force it, we will never get this rod back into place during re-assembly."

"Okay, what is it mounted to?"

"It is mounted to the top of the photo processor."

"Can you unbolt the mounting hardware to the fixture and pull the rod out that way?"

"No, that's the problem. The bracket is bolted through the top of the processor from the inside," he explained. "The only way to get the top of the processor off is to unbolt it and turn it sideways. Otherwise, it won't fit through the hole in the opening for the nose cone. I can't turn it on its side with a three-foot rod attached."

"Okay," Gravda said. "How thick is the rod, what's the diameter?"

"Approximately one inch," Steve told her.

Gravda did the equation in her head: one-inch equals two point five four centimeters. She paused while thinking. "Cut it," she said.

"What?" Steve protested.

"I said cut it," she said sternly. "Take measurements of how much of the rod is exposed outside of the threading in the nose cone and the bracket on the processor. Hank needs to run more photos back to the safe house; he can take the rod back with him and let the NASA engineer make a new rod."

"Okay, I understand, but it is only half the problem," Steve told her.

"Great, what's the other half?"

"The photo processor has a plastic seal attached to a wire

running through the main screw holding the top of the film processor to its sub chassis. I can't read Russian, but it is probably an inspection seal of some kind. We can't get the processor open without cutting the seal."

"Let me take a look," she said, climbing onto the bed of the truck and scaling the scaffolding.

Steve handed her his flashlight and pointed.

The seal was circular, flat like a coin, and black in color. One side displaying the Russian symbol for the hammer and sickle. The other was a serial number or inspection number and the reproduction of the signature of Russia's chief aeronautical engineer: Sergei Korolev. Gravda did not recognize the name, but then again Korolev's name had never been released to the western press.

"Joe, get photos of every angle of this seal, record the dimensions as well," she said.

Steve looked at her almost shaking his head, "You're going to tell me to cut that too, aren't you?"

"Yup."

"Betty, if the engineer back at the safehouse can't replicate that seal, we're as good as caught. You know that, right?"

"I know," she said. "The Russians are not going to be opening this satellite any time soon, but I understand the political ramifications. Let's hope our guy can pull off a miracle in less than six hours."

Hank was back on his bike ten minutes later with several rolls of film, the threaded rod, and what were now two pieces of black Russian plastic, which had snapped in half while trying to remove it.

As Steve and his engineer continued to remove wires and label them while Joe took photos, there was little for Tony to do. He walked over to the truck seat Peter had claimed as his own and sat down. Reaching into the pocket of his overcoat, he pulled out a paper bag and removed a thick sandwich of cheese and meat. Before taking a bite, he turned to the Russian and without words offered him half.

At first Peter declined but Tony pushed the sandwich towards him once again.

Peter took it saying, "Spasibo."

"You're welcome," Tony replied, assuming he had said thank you.

They sat quietly and ate as Hank peddled furiously through the back streets of Prague headed to what everyone in the salvage yard was hoping would be answers to their current problems. It was reaching eleven o'clock and they had not yet reached what they had all come there for. Time was running out.

Chapter 25

The Safehouse

Sliding to a halt just outside the roll of door of the safe hours, Hank leaned his bicycle against the wall and caught his breath before knocking three times on the entry door. He had made the distance of just under a mile in less than seven minutes. He was immediately allowed access. The three men inside had been waiting for him. Brad, who had been tasked with developing the photographs, chastised the little man.

"What the hell took you so long? If I am going to get these photos printed by dawn, I will need a little more lead time Hank."

"Well, we ran into a few little snags," Hank said unapologetically while reaching into his pockets to pull out six more canisters of film and handing them over. "Which one of you two is the NASA guy?" Hank asked, looking at Bob and the other engineer.

"I am," the man replied.

"Okay we have two problems, and it's your job to fix them!" Hank handed him the section of threaded rod. "We had to cut it. It wouldn't come out of the base it was threaded into. You need to make another rod to fit the nose cone and make all of that stuff go back together."

The engineer took the rod and walked over to a workbench. "The rod won't be a problem, I can mill it to fit both ends, but do you have all the dimensions?"

Hank patted his pockets before retrieving a piece of paper Steve had written notes on. Looking over the notes, the engineer said, "You don't have the dimension of how far the rod is threaded into the bracket, Hank."

"The other part of the rod is still in the damn bracket, college boy," Hank said. "We couldn't get it out. It's why we cut it. The bracket holding it is bolted from the underside on a big box. You need to make another rod to fit the nose cone and the bracket, or the hunk of tin doesn't go back together."

"I will have to make some assumptions on how deep the rod is threaded into the bracket, but I can make this work. There is one issue though, and I can't make the call on this one. Hank, you might be back on your bike sooner than you thought. If the threads on the original rod are stripped, the only way to remove it will be to cut it flush with the bracket and then bore the rod out. When they drill it out it will widen the bore on the bracket. If they use a tap they can reset the threads, but it means I will have to use a thicker rod. Do you understand?"

"I'm short, not stupid, asshole. Yeah, I get it," Hank said. "How much bigger will the bore be?"

The engineer put calipers to the rod and said, "This rod is two point five centimeters. If I use a one-inch threaded rod, I can cut down on our manufacture time by a lot."

"How much of a difference are we talking about?" Hank asked.

"Less than one and one-half hundredths of an inch," the engineer replied.

"Can that be seen with the naked eye?"

"No, but any Russian engineer who puts calipers to it will spot it immediately." the engineer told him. "It's an imperial measurement, or American, the Russians only use metric."

"I'm not the boss on this one. It's the dames' call, but for right now I would say do it until you hear anything different from me and her, okay?"

"I can shave off four millimeters off the top of the rod and re-thread it so it will thread back into the nose cone. What's the other problem?" the engineer asked.

"This," Hank said, reaching into his pocket, pulling out the two pieces of black plastic. "This either needs to go back into one piece or your need to make another one just like it. It was some kind of seal they ran through the main access bolt on a piece of steel wire. We had to cut the wire, but then the damn thing broke in half."

Taking the pieces, the engineer again walked to the workbench and put it under some magnification. The seal was thin and brittle on purpose. It had served its purpose well. The engineer muttered under his breath, "Is this the only seal you found?"

"I don't know," Hank said, "It's the only one I know about so far, why?"

"Because if they find more than this one and they cut it or have to break it, then the satellite won't be put back together before sunrise. I think I can reproduce this one, but I'll have to make a mold of each side, and I'll have to guess how the front and back snapped together. I won't know until I take it all apart."

"Wonderful," Hank said sarcastically. "How long will it take?"

The engineer looked at the seal again. "Twenty minutes to make the rubber molds, and half an hour or so for them to set up, then maybe thirty to forty minutes additional curing time for the plastic. I need a telephone."

"Who the hell are you going to call?" Hank asked.

The engineer ignored the comment, walked into the kitchen, and unplugged an old phone from the wall. Returning to his workbench, he cut the cord to the handset and unscrewed the earpiece. He began cutting pieces of the black plastic and placing them in a crucible above an un-lit Bunsen burner.

"What the hell are you doing?" Hank asked.

"I need the plastic," the engineer told him. "This seal is Bakelite; it doesn't conduct electricity, is heat resistant, and just happens to be twenty-year-old plastic technology. Telephones are about the only thing still made from the stuff and I didn't happen to bring any with me. Did they build this thing out of spare parts? It will take a while to melt this stuff, and there is no guarantee this will work."

"It better work. Without that seal we're as good as busted," Hank said. "I would hate to think World War III started because you couldn't melt a phone."

"I will make it work! Now go," the engineer said. "Get back here in an hour and a half, and I will have two halves of the seal and the rod waiting for you." The engineer looked at his watch. "Hank, when you get back here make sure you have the last rolls of film on you. Tell the team to remember how things went together on whatever they take apart from now on. Brad will give you the photos he printed earlier and the rolls you just gave him, but he won't have time to develop any new ones and get them back to you before daybreak. The team will have to re-assemble it from memory or notes from here on out."

"Wonderful," Hank said sarcastically as he walked to the door and headed to his bicycle. "'Come to Prague,' the dame says, 'you'll get to work with Big Tony again' she says, 'it will be fun,' she says. Shit, who is this woman?"

The engineer had already turned and hurriedly walked to his work bench.

It didn't matter though. He had spoken the words only for himself.

Chapter 26

Kotchak Brother's Salvage Yard

At twenty minutes until midnight, the team was still struggling to remove the cowling from the photographic processing equipment. It was tight quarters with Joe, his camera gear, and the unknown engineer vying for space inside the cramped satellite. In the nearly six hours they had been working, few radical discoveries had been made which might support Soviet supremacy. In fact, more had been learned of how the Soviet scientists had borrowed technology instead of developing it. Peter Kozlov was asleep on his truck seat when Hank knocked on the wooden doors of the salvage yard. Big Tony opened the gate and Hank slipped in with his bicycle.

"How's it going Hank?" asked.

"Slow," Tony responded. "Everything good at the safe house?"

"Yeah, so far. The engineer is going to mill a new rod for the nose cone and make a new seal, so I think we're okay. He told me if we find another seal, he won't have time to duplicate it before we run out of time."

"It seems to be the only seal," Tony said. "But we are cutting this close on time, little buddy."

"Yeah, I want to be long gone before daybreak," Hank said. "I am not a big fan of the Russian army."

As Hank and Tony walked back to the Russian lorry, Hank reached up and pulled Tony's pant leg. "Who exactly is this Betty Miller chick?" he asked.

"Your guess is as good as mine," Tony told him. "This operation is definitely her own though, it was her idea, and the top brass didn't waste any time signing off on it."

"So why is this hunk of tin so damn important anyway?" Hank asked.

Gravda had walked around the front of the truck and was standing behind them when Hank continued, "And do you think this dame is up to pulling this off without getting our asses locked up in a Russian gulag somewhere?"

"I think she is capable of just about anything," Tony told him. "She is a lot tougher than she might look. I know I wouldn't want to screw with her."

"Hell, I would," Hank said suggestively. "You see the legs on that girl? I would climb her like a tree fort."

Big Tony laughed, and Hank latched onto his leg, humping him like a small dog. Tony tried to kick him free while still laughing at his smaller friend. "Knock it off!" Hank curled his legs around Tony's and hung on for the ride.

Gravda did her best not to laugh and coughed. "Hmm, you boys about done, or should I leave you two alone for a while?"

Hank was startled and Big Tony laughed even louder. Hank

released his grip on Tony's leg and plopped to the ground on his backside. "We were just playing around," Hank said, rather embarrassed.

"No one is going to a Russian gulag, Hank," Gravda told him. "I have seen what it does to good people and it's not going to happen again on my watch. The hunk of tin you referred to is what the Russians are hoping will bring their own domination to the world and I am going to make sure it doesn't happen. We have one more step in dismantling this damn thing and I need your help, Hank. I didn't just pick you for your bike riding skills. You're the only one who will fit inside the satellite without totally dismantling it. Are you ready to play, sardine?"

Hank looked up at Tony, and Tony looked at Gravda. She had indeed thought out her plan well.

"What's the word from the safehouse?" she asked.

"Your NASA guy is working on reproducing the seal but said if there is another one, we won't make the deadline," Hank told her. "Your guys will need to cut and drill out what's left of the rod and then re-bore the threads in the bracket to one inch. The problem is if the Russians measure it then someone will figure out it was tampered with."

Gravda thought for a moment. "By then we'll be out of here, and it will take them months or maybe even years to discover the difference. Let's do what we came for and by then, it won't matter. Besides, there are times when leaving a calling card in espionage garners respect not animosity. Now, you're on deck Hank. Are you ready?"

"Let's do it," Hank said, as they walked back to the Russian truck.

*　　*　　*　　*

Thirty-one years after Neil Armstrong first stepped foot on the moon with the words "One small step for man, one giant leap for mankind," an unknown soviet engineer tasked with the responsibility of dismantling antiquated Soviet hardware raised an eyebrow and took a pair of calipers to a rod supporting the nose cone to the interior of the now ancient back up to the Luna 3 satellite. Nikita Khrushchev had died 29 years ago, and so had the Russians' dream of reaching the moon before the Americans. The Russians would not report the tampering for another four years.

In 2004 President George W. Bush was contacted directly by Russian Incumbent President Vladimir Putin as the Russian leader was seeking a second four-year term. In the angry phone call, Putin demanded The United States admit to the world the theft and dismantling of a Soviet spacecraft. George Bush's father had been the forty-first president, and before that the director of the CIA, and happened to be standing in the oval office with his son when the call came in. Bush Senior took the phone and told Putin if he would admit Yuri Gagarin had parachuted back to Earth instead of riding in Vostock 1, and thereby officially had not been the first man into space, he would then be happy to acknowledge not just one but two examples of American superiority in the now dead Space Race. Putin hung up the phone angrily and the topic was never discussed again by either world leaders.

Chapter 27

Washington D.C.

Allen Dulles paced in front of his desk. He would not be hearing from his team in Prague for another five hours, but his patience was growing thin. There was a lot riding on this one and he had already had to eat crow over the Cuban mishap weeks earlier. Espionage is a game of one-upmanship, and this was a round he could not afford to lose. His faith in Gravda Nemiroff was well placed, even if the team she had selected was completely unorthodox. He had more engineers with pocket protectors than spies on this one, and it made him nervous.

All he could do was wait. But what Allen Dulles did not know was, there was another man in the game he had not counted on.

Less than four blocks away sat a nerdy man in a booth of McMillan's tavern. He too was waiting.

Robert Lawson was one of James Webb's engineers. He had also been a "computer." The term computer to most people means a machine capable of calculations, and today the assumption would still be correct. What most people do not know is it was also a job classification for those smart enough to do those equations in their heads before solid-state technology had even been dreamed up. The job description was most impressively used during World War II when women with math degrees were utilized to do the complex math required by the U.S. Navy to determine projectile trajectories and distance during the D-Day invasion of Normandy. Any naval gunner thanked his lucky stars for their "gunnery tables" which saved countless Marines on the beaches on June 6th of 1944. With so many men having been drafted, it was a team of six women who had done the calculations. All six women would then transfer to the Manhattan Project and when machinery finally caught up with their own brilliance, they would become the world's first "computer programmers."

Robert Lawson had been selected to work on the same team purely for his ability to do massive calculations in his head. He had been passed up for the draft in 1942 due to his asthma. He had actually been dismissed from the responsibility because all six women had reported him to be "creepy," unbeknownst to him. Dwight D. Eisenhower would acknowledge all six women after the war, with America's highest civilian award, the President's Medal of Honor. Robert Lawson would get nothing.

Lawson was the oldest man on Webb's team at age forty-seven. He had worked for the NACA, the predecessor to NASA, for the last twenty-two years and would retire in another year or two. He just needed a little more money. So, for the past four years, Robert Lawson had been selling classified information to the Russians.

Robert Lawson had no friends, as his intellect prevented him from the usual conversations most people have. He lived alone in a small one-story house outside of Arlington Virginia, where his neighbors referred to him as, "the strange man on the corner." Most nights found him in his basement indulging himself in his two hobbies—model rail-roading and taxidermy of stray cats he found in the alleyway behind his home. *The extra $150 a month would come in handy one day,* he thought.

Lawson had been in the conference room the day James Webb had called his finest into the room to discuss the Luna 3 and he thought his buddy, Alex, who was soon to meet him, might like to hear of the conversation. It was Robert Lawson who had first told Alex about the Corning solar cells way back in '59 after hearing about them while eavesdropping at the water cooler at the NACA. Alex appreciated his input. He was always complimenting him on his brilliance and his ability to provide him with just the right information. Maybe one day Alex would invite him to a barbeque, no one had ever invited him to a barbeque before. Lawson thought to himself, *now that would be nice.*

Alex, or Aleksey Baryshev, detested Robert Lawson. His monthly meeting with the "weirdo" was just part of the job as a KGB handler and he dreaded it every time. As he sat down in the farthest booth from the bar, he handed an envelope to Lawson under the table.

Lawson slipped it into his trousers and pushed it far below his belt.

"What do you have for me?" Alex asked, hoping to make this visit as short as possible.

"I don't know if it means anything, but there was a meeting at Goddard and there was some discussion on the Luna 3 satellite," Lawson told him.

Alex paused before asking his question, knowing the man who sat across from him. "We launched that satellite almost two years ago, why the sudden interest in it now?" Alex prepared himself for a very long answer.

Lawson spent the next twenty minutes telling the Russian everything he knew about satellite telemetry in general, more than Alex really cared to hear. Lawson tended to talk at length simply to have someone to talk to.

Alex finally interrupted and reigned him in by saying, "So the meeting at Goddard, what was discussed?"

"Not much, really. James Webb seemed curious about how you tracked it around the moon, and there was some real interest in knowing what equipment you had on board. He pointed out the meeting was top secret, so it must have been important."

"Anything else?" the Russian asked.

"Only that I heard one of the engineers mention he would like to see what was on the inside and Webb said he 'was working on it.' I'm worried they could trace those darn solar cells back to me somehow and I might be in trouble."

"You worry too much," Alex said, "Besides, how could you Americans ever get your hands on a Russian satellite?"

"Apparently, there is a mockup of the one you sent into space and Webb and the rest of the engineers would really like to get a look at it if they can. Is there a second Luna 3 somewhere someone could get their hands on?" Lawson asked.

"Hell, I don't know. But again, I think you're worrying too much."

"Yeah, you're probably right," Lawson said. "Oh, by the way, they moved up the first orbital flight to February of next year and they picked John Glenn to pilot it. Hey, do you think next time we meet can it be at the zoo? Have you ever seen the big cat exhibit?"

"We will see, Robert. Wait ten minutes, then go home," Alex told him. "There is no need for you and me to be seen together any more than necessary." Alex grabbed his hat and slid out of the booth.

"Maybe we could catch a movie sometime," Lawson called after him. Alex did not respond and continued towards the door and the Washington sunset.

Chapter 28

Prague

Big Tony stood on the scaffolding and slowly lowered Hank into the satellite. When Hank's feet came to rest on top of the photo developing equipment, he let go.

"Okay, I'm in," Hank said, "Now what?"

"The stainless-steel shroud you're standing on covers the photo processing equipment," Steve said. "We need you to unscrew it from the floor, so we can pull it out. There should be four screws on each corner, and we will need them for later when you put it all back together. Here is a plastic bag for the screws and a screwdriver. Label everything."

Hank flipped on to his belly and slid over the edge of the shroud catching the tops of his feet on the edge. Working upside down, he got the first twelve screws out, and yelled back up, "Is this how they built this thing?"

"No, Hank." It was Betty's voice he heard. "They put everything in place and then skinned the satellite. We are trying to minimize any evidence of tampering from the outside."

He removed all the rest of the screws and then pulled himself back up to sit atop the processing equipment. He was drenched in sweat. "Okay, now what?" he called up to the others.

Steve asked, "Can you wedge yourself between the photo equipment and the side wall of the satellite?"

Hank slithered off the side and wiggled his rearend until his feet were resting on the floor of the Luna 3. Once again Hank called up and said, "All right, now what?"

"Can you still reach what's left of the rod we cut earlier?" Steve asked.

"Yeah," Hank told him.

Steve lowered one end of rope down and told Hank to tie it off to the rod. "Tony will help pull out the shroud, just hang on."

Five minutes later Hank was looking at what they had all come there for.

The photo developing equipment was the only part of the Luna 3 which truly impressed Steve and the other engineer. The cameras in the nose cone had been triggered by the reflection of light off the surface of the moon using the stolen U.S. solar collectors and had taken thirty low-resolution photos. The film was stored in two canisters holding fifteen shots each. The stolen photon collectors had tripped a mechanical switch opening the camera's aperture and allowed light to follow from the nose cone to a series of mirrors reflecting the images to a window in the top of the shroud covering. As each photo was taken, a conveyor dragged it into a dry processor to develop the pictures. From there they proceeded into a scanner, which reproduced the image electronically line by line to be later transmitted back to Earth by radio waves. What impressed the NASA engineers was not the complexity of the unit, but the brilliance in its simplicity.

After tracing the wires, they also discovered the same solar panels were also attached to two very small hydrogen peroxide thrusters mounted to the side of the satellite at 180 degrees. A relay switch dictated where the electrical impulses would be sent periodically, spinning the craft to rotate in three-minute intervals pausing the photography. A super wide-angle lens in panoramic mode meant each subsequent photo overlapped the previous one to some degree, allowing the spacecraft to film almost the entire surface while still staying cool.

"Man, I hate giving credit to the opposition, but you have to admit it is one slick piece of engineering of using what yah got to get the job done," Steve said.

"True, I am just happy it's not slicker than we thought it might be," said the other engineer. "We had some folks at Goddard worried it was built out of magic beans and unicorn dust. At least our two main concerns have been answered: how they got the camera to function without radio waves and then how they kept it from incinerating itself while doing it."

"Okay you two, enough with the congratulations. Climb on out and let Joe in there to take some photos. We're not done here yet and we still need to put it back together!"

"Sorry Betty," Steve said, as they extricated themselves from the cramped confines. "It's just hard not to admire their handiwork."

When they were free, Tony helped lower Joe into the tight quarters so he could photograph the equipment.

"Get what you can Joe," Gravda said, "And then let's get

this thing back together and get out of here."

As Joe started taking shots, he focused his camera on the two film canisters mounted into the satellite. As he zoomed in to grab closer details he stopped and laughed. "You have got to be kidding me," he said.

Gravda, hearing him, leaned over the edge of the opening and asked, "What is it, Joe?"

"Hey Steve, did Eastman Kodak ever make 35mm film for the U.S. Air Force?" Joe asked.

Steve popped his head up next to Gravda. "Yeah, they still do, why?"

"These canisters are American, not Russian," Joe said. "They're not yellow like the film I use. The canisters are brown and have a U.S. government number on them." Looking back through the lens of his camera and readjusting focus he added, "There is some fine print here. It says, 'radiation resistant'...in English."

Steve thought for a moment and asked, "And you say the canisters are brown?"

"Well, they're actually beige I guess, like a brown paper bag at a grocery store. The printing is in black ink."

"Hell, we haven't used film like that since just after the war," Steve said. "It was designed for high altitude spy balloons we launched in Alaska to get a better look at the Soviet Union. Back then, we didn't know if putting a balloon into the iono-sphere would affect film, so Kodak came up with radiation re-sistant canisters. All they are, are paper rolls with black and white film lined on the inside with aluminum foil. We haven't used that stuff since 1949."

"Well, I have two of them sitting here in the backup to the

Luna 3 satellite," Joe told him.

Steve looked at Gravda and said, "Someone back at home will be happy to hear about this. Hell, they didn't just build this thing from parts off the shelf, they built it from parts off *our* shelf."

The time in Prague was exactly 1:00 a.m.

Chapter 29

Washington D.C. - 7:00 P.M.

Aleksey Baryshev walked out of McMillan's Tavern and walked hurriedly to a phone booth. He dropped a coin into the slot and dialed the Soviet embassy in Washington.

Wiretapping and the recording of phone conversations date all the way back to the 1890s with the invention of the telephone recorder. But as the term "wiretapping" implies, it required authorities physically attaching a separate wire to a phone line to intercept phone conversations. The Soviet agent knew full well in order to do so required manpower and technicians far outweighing the government's ability to "tap" what were several hundred pay phones in Washington D.C.

His call was immediately connected and his conversation with his superior went unheard by anyone other than the two of them. If the call had been intercepted, then Allen Dulles would have pulled Gravda Nemiroff and her team out of a dilapidated salvage yard in Prague immediately. The problem was Dulles was in the dark, with no way to contact his beautiful spy in Czechoslovakia, even if he wanted to. A single phone call had the potential to unravel what little timeline Gravda had to complete the mission and get the satellite to a freight yard a few miles away. Yet neither man on the phone; one a Russian agent, the other his superior, had no idea just how important the phone call was to be.

Bureaucracy usually moves at a snail's pace, especially Russian bureaucracy, but tonight pieces of an unknown jig-saw puzzle would fall into place more by coincidence than anything else. Protocol in the Soviet Union is not unlike our own government. Our CIA keeps secrets from J. Edgar Hoover and his FBI, and Hoover keeps secrets from everybody. Communication spills freely only when both parties benefit from the equation. The Russian K.G.B. does not go out of its way to discuss matters with the military unless the need arises to do so.

Aleksey Baryshev's boss was closing in on his retirement. He had served the Motherland faithfully at Stalingrad during the war and had been promoted to Red Army Colonel by the war's end. His just reward was a cushy desk job in Washington, overseeing the twenty-seven Soviet spies currently under his command. Most often it felt more like babysitting then intelligence gathering, and he spent most of his days filtering through worthless information garnered by frightened men hoping to please their master. There was little excitement, and it was just how he liked it. He filled out the required report on what his agent had told him and stuffed it into a diplomatic pouch to be sent to Moscow the following day. But right now, he had better things to think about. At 8:00 p.m. he was to attend a cocktail party there at the Russian embassy. The guest of honor was an old friend and one he had not seen in many years.

Anton Petrov had recently been promoted to Major General in the Russian Air Force. It meant his old friend now out-ranked him, and Alex's handler was sure he would enjoy showing off the one star on his epaulet and rubbing it in. He would take the ribbing but would remember to remind the new general if not for him he would never have met his wife. In Russian life, just like in America, wives still outrank generals at home, he would tell him. He gathered up his work and reached for his jacket.

Chapter 30

Kotchak Brother's Salvage Yard

"Steve, do you have everything you need? Joe, is there anything else you need to photograph?" Gravda asked. "I want to get this thing buttoned up and get the heck out of here."

Both Steve and Joe looked at each other and said in unison, "I think we have it."

"Good. Start rewiring it. Hank, get on your bike and go get the new rod and the seal. When you get back, we will be ready to reassemble this thing."

Joe unloaded the last film canisters he had shot and handed them to Hank, saying, "Brad can develop them later once were back home, but I think we have everything."

"Hank, it's 2:00 a.m., and we have to have this to the freight yard by 6:00 a.m. We're going to be cutting this one close, so pedal fast, okay?" Gravda said.

Hank grabbed his bicycle and as he ran it to the wooden gates to the alleyway which now led to dark and tired streets.

He saw Peter Kozlov, sound asleep on the rusted truck seat which had become his solace and last place of solitude.

As Hank peddled the little girl's bicycle with the pink basket attached to the handlebars, Big Tony and the two engineers began the laborious process of cutting the remainder of the rod and then boring out the bracket on top of the processor with a tap and die. The work had to be done by hand because of the softness of the aluminum which made up the bracket. Power tools would run the risk of boring the hole too wide, and even a small fraction of an inch in difference would have made reassembly impossible. The air had turned cold as the darkness of the Prague night waited for faint rays of sunlight to return to warm the air. Gravda was starting to worry those beams of light over the horizon may come too soon.

Hank skidded to a stop outside the dented rollup doors of the safehouse. The unknown engineer had the side door open for him before he could climb off the bike. "What the hell took you so long?" he asked. "I said to be back here in an hour and a half, and it's been two."

"It was a bitch to get apart," Hank retorted, not happy at being snapped at by a college boy.

"Well, if you think it was tough to disassemble, wait 'till you try to put it back together. By my calculations, it will take almost twice as long."

"How often are you wrong?"

The engineer did not understand the question. He paused and then said, "I'm paid to be right, so I'm usually correct."

"Well, let's just hope tonight you got paid to be wrong, 'cause we've got less than four hours to get it all done and get it to the freight yard. If you don't hear from me, Tony, or the dame by 6:00 a.m., get your asses out of here and disappear."

Nervous Bob had overheard Hank's remarks. "Disappear, what do you mean by disappear?" he yelped.

Hank pointed to the Skoda Octavia Gravda had parked in the back of the garage earlier. "I mean, leave your shit, get in the car, and drive. Leave everything behind, tools, equipment, everything. Drive due west to Bonn. It's roughly five hundred kilometers, or what is that—" Hank stopped, trying to do the calculation in his head. "...three hundred or so miles from here? When yah get there, find the U.S. Embassy and tell 'em you need to talk to Allen Dulles."

Brad Ray had walked out of his impromptu photo developing room and had walked down the steps to find out what the commotion was.

Bob was almost apoplectic. "Oh my God, we're going to get caught and spend the rest of our lives in a Russian jail cell."

"No one is going to jail, Bob," Brad said, trying to calm the panicky photo analyst.

"If we get caught, we will," Bob protested.

"Nah, The Russians don't jail spies, they shoot 'em," Hank said, pouring gasoline on the fire with a smile.

Brad swatted at Hank and said, "That's not funny. No one is going to get caught either."

Brad had seen more than his share of combat situations and had done it all without a weapon. His composure was rock solid and even though Hank did not know the full details of Brad Ray's background, Hank liked the way he carried himself.

"Tell him you're kidding, Hank," Brad said sternly.

Hank said nothing.

Brad thumped him in the back with his knee. "I said, tell him you're just kidding,"

Hank shrugged his shoulders and said, "Okay, I'm kidding, don't get your panties in a knot."

Brad pulled Hank off to a corner and looked over his shoulder, calling out, "We're fine Bob, we're just fine..." Then, looking down sternly at Hank, he whispered, "Why the hell do you do that stuff, Hank? The guy's nervous enough already."

"Because I wasn't kidding. We're really cutting this close on time and if we can't get that bird back together, the turd is going to hit the propeller. If you don't hear from us in the next four hours, get out of here and head to Bonn West Germany. Make sure what's left of that old Russian seal is melted, and what's left of the old rod is buried somewhere where no one can find it, yah got it?"

"Why drive all the way to Bonn when there is a U.S. consulate here in Prague?"

"Because if things turn sour it will be the first place the reds would look, and we need to distance ourselves from any involvement in this shit. This could be boom, boom, bye, bye, stuff, if we get caught."

"I see your point," Brad said.

"Do you?" Hank asked. "Because I'm talking mushroom clouds. I know those bastards. If the Russians think the CIA came into their sandbox and stole that hunk of tin, then there are going to be a lot of embarrassed red, white, and blue faces with no good answers. The Russians have the bomb too, and Khrushchev's finger is itchy on the button. I don't want us to be the reason he decides to push it!"

"Okay, you made your point, Hank."

"Good. You're the only one in this garage who has ever seen combat, which means you're now in charge of babysitting. Those guys are scientists and desk jockeys Brad. They're not equipped for this stuff."

Brad did not like the sound of his last comment.

"Hey, lab coat," Hank said, referring to the NASA engineer who had been working on replacing the rod and seal. "You got the stuff done for me yet? I have some place I need to be."

"It's finished," the engineer said as went to retrieve the needed parts off the work bench.

Brad whispered, "When you said I was in charge, what exactly does that mean?"

Hank held up a tiny finger as if to say, 'Just wait and I will tell you.'

"Do you have more film for me?"

"Yeah, these are the last rolls," Hank told him, reaching into his pockets. He then whispered, "If you think anyone is on to us, torch the photos and the negatives, okay?"

"I will," Brad said.

Hank had waited until the engineer was out of earshot. "I'm starting to get a bad feeling about this," Hank said honestly. "You got nothing but pocket protectors and slide rules here. Get those boys out of here if you need to."

The engineer returned, handing Hank the new length of aluminum rod and two halves of a Russian seal, with one half attached to a wire thread. "Don't snap those two halves back together until it is exactly where you want it. If you do, you will never get it apart again without breaking it."

Hank nodded and headed back towards the door. Brad followed him outside and as Hank climbed on the little bike, Brad asked, "What about the team at the salvage yard? If this goes south, then what?"

Hank lit yet another cigarette and paused. He had been hoping this was a conversation he wouldn't need to have. "I'm not worried about Tony, he can get out of anything, and the broad seems much tougher than those pretty legs might make yah think."

"...And what about you?" Brad asked.

Hank laughed just to ease the tension. "I'm small, I can hide in places no one ever thought to look in."

"...And what about the NASA boys...?"

"Yeah, the NASA boys..." Hank sighed. "Tony and I were told no gunplay towards *any* Russians. Dulles is worried about international relationships and cold war diplomacy, and this one is way off the books."

"So...what about the NASA boys?" Brad repeated.

Hank paused again, but only for a second. "Tony has his sidearm. If shit goes south the CIA considers them to be...expendable in the name of secrecy."

Brad's usual composure changed; his stance now filled with shock. "Does Betty know about this?"

Hank didn't like the truth, but he was hired for reasons other than just riding a bicycle with a cute little pink basket. "Dammit Brad, you've played this game before. I don't set the rules, and you know as well as I do that someone is always paid to watch the boss."

"Oh shit," was all that Brad could think of saying.

"Yeah, shit," Hank responded.

"So, what did you mean by 'I am in charge?'" Brad asked.

This time Hank paused much longer, before he reached inside his Cossack shirt and pulled out a small vial, shaking it until three small pills fell into his tiny hand. "They're not aspirin, but they do make other people's headaches disappear. If your guys get caught, they'll talk..." He handed the pills to Brad who reluctantly took them and slid them into his own pocket.

"Which makes us Allen Dulles' headache."

"Let's hope this dame can pull this off and you and I never had to have to finish this conversation." Hank stepped onto the peddles and disappeared into the grimy night, leaving Brad there to stare off into the darkness.

What no one in Prague knew was at the same time two old Russian friends, 4,284 miles away in Washington D.C., were currently talking about them. Yet even they were not aware of it.

Chapter 31

Washington D.C. - 8:50 P.M.

There are emotions and expressions of gratitude which transcend all cultures and foreign differences. One of which is seeing a dear friend, time and responsibilities have separated you from. We are not all so different from one another, no matter where we grew up. The cocktail party was small in relationship to usual embassy events with forty or so people in attendance.

The Russian embassy, built for American railroad tycoon George Pullman's widow in 1912, was Washington's most expensive private home at the time of its construction. Residing at 1125 16th Street, N.W., it was built for the pricey sum of $360,00. George Pullman had passed away in October 1897 after having amassed tremendous wealth with his introduction of the Pullman sleeping car which transformed rail travel for the wealthy. After President Abraham Lincoln was assassinated, it was a Pullman sleeper which transported his lifeless body from Washington to Springfield Illinois. Hundreds of thousands of distraught Americans lined the route in homage and whether it be advertising or national grief, the orders of Pullman cars began to pour into his company. At the time of Pullman's death, his net worth was valued at $17.5 million, and his grieving spouse Hattie was out to spend as much of it as she could. She never spent a single solitary night in the massive three-story mansion, stating its grand size and the echoes made her pain for the loss of her passed husband. The property was sold less than a year later to Russian Emperor Nicholas II at a loss of $10,000. The average American's income in that year was $800, meaning the loss on the sale of the home was equal to almost thirteen years' salary for most people. The building had stood as the home of the Russian embassy ever since.

Colonel Dmitry Ivanov was emotional about seeing his oldest friend, the newly appointed Air Force major general Anton Petrov. It had been almost five years since they had hugged and toasted to one another's health. Both were career officers, but with much different career trajectories. Both men had known since childhood Anton Petrov would one day make general. The Army colonel cared little for rank in his own life. He had risen to his command more by longevity than by ambition, and his white hair and bushy eyebrows were a physical sign of his pending retirement. He was looking forward to a little house on the lake in Adler on the Black Sea Coast where he would garden and pass the long summer days relaxing in the sun. Anton Petrov was seven years his junior, and the pair would have been unlikely friends, had they not grown up together in the same village just outside of Leningrad. Their age difference meant little in their youth and even less now, but Petrov had always thought of his friend as a mentor and big brother. They had even married a pair of sisters—one of course much younger than the other.

Ivanov had become a widower just two years before and

was his sole reason for accepting the position in Washington and transferring on loan to the KGB. He had never felt the joy of fathering children himself since his wife had been found to be infertile right after their marriage. He had replaced the loss with the elation which came from being the godfather to all nine of Anton Petrov's children.

The two ignored most others in the room and spoke of older days and childhood memories. "How is Sasha...And the children? Do you still have that damn wolfhound? That dog was a beast!" Tonight, was not about work, it was about catching up and reliving past memories together. A simple comment or a loan question in passing could very well ignite a spark which, if it took flame, would burn Gravda Nemiroff and her entire team.

As the evening wound down and the older of the two decided to take his leave and say goodnight, the younger man who enjoyed chiding his friend asked if the life of a spy handler was offering him any excitement. "With Nadia gone now for so long, maybe you are sleeping with young blonde American women to gain secrets for the Motherland."

Both laughed.

"It is not so exciting," he said, "It is mostly a kindergarten, and I am the teacher. I am not a spy, I just push papers around and hope no one does anything so stupid it reflects badly on myself."

"Oh, as married man with a fat wife at home, I was hoping to hear some juicy gossip," Anton joked.

"So sorry to disappoint you, Anton," he said smiling. "On most days, it is just another boring job, and one I am soon hoping to say *dasvidaniya* too." With his mind somewhat back on his work, he paused and asked, "Anton, tell me, is there such a thing as a backup of the Luna 3 satellite?"

The general smiled while raising an eyebrow. "An obscure question my friend, but dah, of course we do. Why would you ask?"

"One of my agents made a reference to it earlier this evening. Apparently, NASA would like to 'get their hands on it,' or so he says."

The new General's eyebrow raised higher. "What exactly did your man say?"

"He said there was a meeting at Goddard Space Center recently, and their engineers would 'like to get a look inside.' And my man's contact told him 'they were working on doing so.' It's all I know. I put the information in my report tonight and it will be in Moscow tomorrow. I just thought I might ask."

"Interesting," the general said, stroking his chin.

"There is no way the Americans could actually get to it, surely it must be hidden away," the handler said.

The general laughed. "Only if you consider public exhibitions a safe place to hide such a thing. The whole world knows where it is."

The handler truly looked perplexed. American newspapers had been banned from printing any news of the hugely popular exhibitions the Russians had been staging around the globe. President Kennedy did not want free advertising for the "Soviet way of life," nor wished to glamorize Soviet accomplishments when the U.S. space program had been fraught with mistakes and failures.

Several late arrivers at the party had sauntered over to the new major general wishing to pay their respects, and the moment was no longer private. The general held them at bay by holding up one finger and leaned in to say, "You need to get out of your basement office more often, my friend. We have been showing the Luna 3 all over Europe, and in two weeks it will be shown again in Mexico City, along with Major Gagarin and other great victories of the Motherland. I do not believe in co-incidences my friend; your contact may be onto something. I will look into it personally." The moment passed and both gave each other another round of hugs and kisses on the cheek.

General Major Anton Petrov slapped his friend on the back and said, "I am in Washington for a few more nights. One of those evenings we are to have dinner, just the two of us! Promise me."

A promise was made for an upcoming evening, and Dmitry Ivanov took his leave. The general went back to being congratulated and the party picked up its pace once more.

Chapter 32

Prague

Even in the dank cold air, Hank broke a sweat riding back to Kotchak Brother's Salvage Yard. He told himself it was from the exertion of trying to make up time, but he knew differently. Joe had taken up position by the wooden gates awaiting Hank's return. Peering through the weathered slats of wood, he opened the gate allowing Hank to ride in at full speed. The time was ten minutes before 3:00 a.m.

"Yah got everything little buddy?" Tony asked, seeing Hank park his bike next to the Russian lorry.

"Yeah, I got it, where are we at?" Hank asked.

"You got here just in time," Gravda told him. "We have drilled out the bracket and replaced the shroud on the processor. We need you to squeeze back in there and bolt it back to the floor of the satellite."

Hank looked up onto the bed of the truck and pointed to the still unnamed engineer, "Hey you, whatever your name is, come here." As Hank reached out to hand him the length of rod and the seal the man said, "Roger."

"What?"

"You asked me my name. It's Roger."

"What? NO, I didn't! There are rules here, this ain't the water cooler back home. Cheese and rice Tony did you hear this guy?"

"Yeah, I heard him. Forget about it, we have more important things to focus on right now." But Hank would not forget and every time someone asked a question, another answered in the affirmative Hank would say, "Okay, got it, over and out. Roger that!" It would become a running joke to break the tension on a timeline which was starting to feel short on time.

"Okay, fun time is over. Let's get back to work," Gravda chastised.

Hank had only to raise his arms up for Big Tony to hoist him up onto the back of the truck. Tony then lumbered up onto the back of the truck and Hank handed him the length of the new aluminum rod, and then passed the two sides of the newly fabricated seal gingerly to Roger while saying, "Be careful with it. It's the only one we have!"

As he climbed the ladder to the scaffolding, he waited until his diminutive height reached ear level of his much taller friend, and whispered, "We need to talk..."

Tony whispered back, "No we don't. We're gonna make it. Just do what you do best."

Hank paused on the ladder, understanding Tony had the same information but confused by his comment.

Hank threw Big Tony a silent look of, 'What the hell does that mean?'

Tony smiled and said aloud, "Screw fast little buddy, screw fast."

Hank smiled for the first time in several hours and allowed Tony to haul him up over the edge of the Luna 3, lowering him onto the top of the processor shroud. The bag of sixteen bolts was already there, along with the driver needed to coax them into the pre-threaded holes in the sub-frame. He dropped the bag over the edge and flipped himself onto his belly until he could slither upside down into the narrow space. Hanging once again by his feet, he replaced all sixteen screws in less than fifteen minutes.

While he worked, Roger also crawled inside of the satellite, and Tony started the process of threading the new three-foot rod on to the top of the processor shroud. Tony turned the rod by hand from above as the engineer guided it into the recently bored out bracket from on top of the processor.

"Go slowly," he called out, as Tony tried to lessen his brute strength. The milling was perfect, and the threads took.

Hank hoisted himself back onto the processor into a seated position and called back up, "Okay, what's next?"

Roger who was still crouched on top of the shroud reached into two separate pockets and handed Hank both sides of the Russian seal. "Hank, you need to thread the wire back through the shackle and then, *carefully*, snap both sides together. We only get one chance at this, and let's hope it goes together."

Hank once again flipped onto his belly and reached down, doing exactly what he was told. Each end of the thin steel wire was connected to a tiny ball bearing. Each side of the seal had small cups in which to hold those ball bearings. Hank lined them up and pressed both parts together.

...Nothing.

He pressed only a little harder, worried the fragile Bakelite would fracture. A small bead of sweat formed at the front of the headband of his newsboy cap and continued to grow until it grew sufficiently enough to escape its confines, only to roll down his forehead and onto the bridge of his nose. He pressed a little harder as the bead of sweat reached the edge of his nose.

With just a little more pressure there was a resounding snap, which made not only Hank, but everyone close by freeze. In the silence of the late-night air, it was like a rifle shot. Hank refused to release his grip on the seal, worried it had crumbled in his fingertips. Slowly, very slowly, he opened his tiny hands, hoping not to find pieces of delicate plastic in his palms.

His hands were empty. He sighed a long sigh of relief and scrubbed his little hands down the length of his face wiping away the sweat and worry. He laid there for a while, exhausted.

"Tell me we're good," Gravda said, peering over the edge of the capsule.

Hank finally rolled over and said, "...We're good.

"Okay Steve, now what?" Gravda asked.

"Well, Betty, now we re-wire the processor to the cameras in the nose cone, button it up, re-crate the damn thing, and get out of here."

"How long?"

Steve looked at her and grimaced. "An hour and a half."

"Make it an hour," she said.

"And how am I—"

Gravda interrupted him by softly saying, "Just make it happen."

Steve could see the mounting concern in her eyes and simply nodded. "Let's get Hank out of this shoe box," he said. "And get me those wire ties...*now!*"

Big Tony extracted Hank by his usual method of reaching down and hauling him out.

Roger was on the scaffolding moments later with twenty or so labeled plastic bags containing braided nylon cords which had been coated in wax. "Steve, I think I need you to squeeze in here with me, there is no way I can tie all these knots by myself and get this done in time." As Steve slid himself over the top of the satellite and wedged himself in to the tight confines, he said, "The damn Russians seem to have stolen most of this technology from us, why the hell couldn't they steal a few Ty-Raps along with it?"

The process of cable lacing, or wrapping wires to keep them secure, dates back to the earliest days of electricity. It is referred to as "grooming," and the methods used by naval and aerospace engineers before 1958 required tying small cords of string dipped in wax around wires to secure them together. It was tedious and taxing work which often resulted in cut fingers and abrasions. In 1958 Maurus Logan, an engineer working for the Thomas and Belt's Company, designed a plastic band that would thread through a series of notches and grip securely. The product was patented on June 24, 1958, and would go on to revolutionize the way in which American airplane manufacturers, the military, and later aerospace engineers would assemble their crafts. The product would be come to be known as "Zip Ties" to the general public in the early 1980s, but NASA had been using them since their earliest development. The Thomas and Belt's company has become a multi-billion dollar a year conglomerate and still manufactures Ty-Raps today.

"Help me secure these wires to the threaded rod," Roger told Steve.

Both men started the mundane job to tie down each wire together and then secure it to the treaded rod. Each cord was about a foot in length and was first tied in a series of running lockstitches, then finished off with a figure eight knot at the ends. Each wire had been marked with masking tape to indicate the start and finish lines where the Russians engineers had first done the same job. Even the number of stitches was replicated so as not to make it look any different under close examination. Steve had been told, "One hour," but they had missed their deadline by ten minutes. The time was now exactly 4:25 a.m. in Prague. The upper half of the hourglass was starting to empty, and the sand was running thin...and they all knew it.

Chapter 33

Washington D.C. – 10:25 P.M.

Major General Anton Petrov was growing tired. It had been a long, yet eventful, day. Had he been a few years younger, he would have enjoyed staying up late and toasting to his own success, but his better judgement told him it was time for some rest. Russian parties are known for dragging late into the wee hours, and after his flight from Moscow earlier that day, it was clean sheets and cold water on his face he wanted most. He turned towards his aide and gave him 'the look.'

The general's aide knew exactly what was expected. "Gentlemen, the major general is most assuredly tired from his travels and needs his rest," he said. The one reward of being in command was you could have someone else make your escape for you. As the general made his leave, he once again thought of how nice it was to have seen his old friend once again, and their prior conversation came to mind. He turned to his aide and said, "Have the switchboard phone Major Alexander Tkachenko in Prague, and then have the call transferred to my room. He is staying at the Appian Hotel."

The pieces of the puzzle were falling into place, purely by coincidence. Major General Anton Petrov was the man Nikita Khrushchev had put in charge of overseeing the world-wide exhibitions, which included the now world-famous Luna 3 and everything surrounding it.

"But General, it is almost..." he paused doing the time difference in his head, "4:30 a.m."

"I am fully aware of what time it is. I gave you an order, now do what you are told."

The aide scampered off to find the switchboard operator and apologized with a salute and a "Yes sir, right away sir," called back over his shoulder.

The general smiled to himself. Maybe there was more than just one reward to being in charge.

Chapter 34

Prague

"Just hold it there if you can, and we will make the connections," Steve said to Tony. Tony was currently holding the entire top assembly to the Luna 3 satellite, while Steve and Roger were struggling to reconnect the wiring. The four antennae had been remounted, so the top assembly again weighed in at almost seventy pounds.

"I got it," Tony told them. "Just get it done."

The wiring took another ten minutes, then Roger looked at Steve. "We're good, let's get out of this thing and button it up."

Climbing out of the satellite and back onto the scaffolding, Steve told Tony, "The nose cone and the cameras have to be treaded to the new rod. Be careful, and for God's sake, don't strip those threads. Line it up and spin it slowly until it grabs."

As the other engineer extracted himself out of the confined space, Tony hoisted the top of the satellite above his head and gently lowered it onto the newly fabricated rod. Both engineers peered between the gap of the top and the housing, and guided Tony to line it up exactly to where it needed to go.

"You're good to go Tony," Steve said. "Now go slowly."

The upper-most portion of the Luna 3 satellite threaded perfectly to the rod assembly and Tony spun it lower and lower until the mounting holes lined up with the original holes of the center section. Each opening had been labeled with tape and numbered to match the seventy-five bolts that held the camera lenses and the apertures on the top of the Luna 3 to the main housing.

It took Gravda, Big Tony, and both engineers just over thirty minutes to accomplish the task. Earlier in the evening, it had taken more than twice the length of time to remove it.

Peter Kozlov had awoken and was now starting to worry. He paced back and forth along the truck as the others finished with the much-needed assembly. He had said very little throughout the night, but he finally called up to Gravda and asked, "How much longer?"

In perfect Russian, which surprised almost everyone but Tony, she looked over the edge of the truck and responded, "Just a few more minutes Peter, we just have to crate it back up and you will be on your way."

Peter Kozlov did not look well. He was pale and exhausted, and even with some scattered moments of sleep, he looked like he had not rested in days. His hand shook as he looked at his watch for the twelfth time in less than ten minutes. "Maybe we could all just run," he said. "I really do not want to go back there."

Big Tony helped her down from the truck and she walked to the tables her engineer had set up earlier to lay parts out. She reached for her oversized Louis Vuitton bag and pulled out two large manila envelopes and walked over to where Peter was standing. With her free hand, she gently took Peter's hand in hers. "We can't do that, and you know it, Peter. If you don't go back, then you will be a hunted man. You'll never see your lovely wife or your newborn child. Believe me," she said, "you're not cut out for being a man on the run. We have to finish what we started, and then maybe one day you can stand up to your father-in-law and create the artwork you love so much."

Peter lowered his head, knowing she was telling him the truth.

"Maybe this will help," Gravda said. "Give me your lighter."

Peter broke his grasp and reached into his pocket.

Gravda opened the first envelope and pulled out all sixty photos. She fanned them so he could see they were what he remembered.

He blushed.

Gravda did not. She struck a flame and ignited the corner of the photographs, tipping them upwards so all would catch. She let them burn in her hand until the heat had started to consume his sins completely, dropping the smoldering pages to the ground. "You're not a soldier Peter," she said. "Go home and become an artist."

"And what about the other set?" Peter asked.

"In due time, Peter. I'm not out to hurt you in any way, and I always keep my promises. You still have one more thing to do and when I know your part is completed, they will turn to ashes, just like those."

"And what if the major finds out?"

"No one knows we're here Peter. The freight yard foreman at the railroad station leaves the yard every night at 7:00 p.m., and he returns at 7:00 a.m. every day. No one ever thought to add additional security to the freight yard because no one in their right mind would try to steal a Russian satellite. All you have do to is drive the truck and park it and wait. When your father-in-law arrives, you did your job. You did what you were told to do. You will have delivered the satellite and even spent the night in the truck, making sure it was safe and sound. Tonight, you have been a good soldier."

"You don't know the major," Peter said. "I hate the son of a bitch."

"I know him even better than you do, Peter," Gravda said. "I have spent my entire life dealing with men just like him. Just get the truck to the rail station and you will be fine."

Peter exhaled, feeling better. "I hope you're right," he said.

"I am always right," Gravda told him. "My life depends on it."

"So does mine," Peter told her. "Again, I just hope you're right." Corporal Peter Kozlov walked away as the team did their best to reassemble the crate. As each nail was carefully and gingerly tapped back into its original and marked hole, Peter Kozlov once again took his place on the rusted truck seat and contemplated his future.

At the same time Gravda and Peter were talking, a phone rang in a room at the Appian Hotel. A groggy Major Alexander Tkachenko reached for the phone, wondering who would be calling at such a late hour. Calls at this time of night were never good news.

Chapter 35

Prague

"Yes, hello," The major said, answering the phone while rubbing his eyes. He looked at his watch.

"Major Tkachenko, Major General Petrov wishes to speak to you, please hold the line."

Shit, now what? the major thought to himself.

It took a good five minutes before the call was transferred to the general's suite at the Russian' embassy in Washington.

"Major Tkachenko, forgive the late-night intrusion," the general said.

The fact the general had apologized made the major relax somewhat. *Generals seldom apologize for anything*, he thought.

"How may I be of service, Major General?" Tkachenko asked.

"Major, I would not have bothered you at such an hour, but I have it on strong authority your Luna 3 satellite has become much coveted by the Americans and my sources tell me they may very well be making an attempt at getting a better look at it soon."

"When you say soon, General, may I ask...how soon?" The Major asked.

"I do not think they would have the balls to attempt anything while you are in Prague, only fools would attempt such a thing on Soviet soil. But the satellite will be in Mexico City in two weeks and that is too close for comfort," He added, "You were chosen for this duty because of your eye for details, Major. I am not one who believes in coincidences, and Mexico City is less than a two-hour flight time from the American border. I want you to step up your security. That satellite is to be guarded around the clock. Do I make myself clear, Major?"

"Of course, General," the major said. "When would you like me to make additional changes to the security protocol?"

"I didn't call you at such an hour for you to make a decision later in the day, Major," the General barked. "Do it NOW!"

"Yes General, I understand. I will see to it myself," the major answered. It was the general's next question which made Major Alexander Tkachenko sit up in bed.

"Where is the satellite currently, Major?"

SHIT, thought the Major to himself. "It is at a freight yard here in Prague, ready for our return to Moscow later this afternoon. We will be leaving at 7:30."

"Keep an eye on it Major," the general said. "There are things in that satellite I never want the Americans to see. I am counting on you."

"Yes General," the Major said, but the line had already gone dead.

Chapter 36

Prague, Kotchak Brother's Salvage Yard

"How many more nails before this thing is crated back up and we can get out of here?" Gravda asked.

"Maybe twelve more," Steve told her.

"Well let's go," she urged. "Be careful though, it will be daylight soon."

There was no telling how close the Russians would examine what they had undone and put back together, but Gravda had taken as many precautions as possible to eliminate suspicion.

Big Tony had started pulling down the scaffolding, had rewrapped the tarp, and tied it once again to the back of the cab of the truck. Joe had stepped in and had put most of the tools back into the van, while Peter Kozlov had stood watching, pacing nervously.

Gravda, who had been standing at the back of the truck, walked over to Peter and said, "Okay, all you need to do is drive the truck to the freight yard. Again, the station master always leaves at exactly 7:00 p.m. to return home, so if anyone asks, you spent the night there doing your duty. Got it?"

"But what if..." Peter started nervously.

"There are no what ifs. That is your story, and you stick to it!" Gravda said, squeezing his arm. "It will take you less than ten minutes to get there, and I will time it. Thirty minutes after you leave, I give you my word, the other photos will be burned, and your life is yours once again. What you do with your life from here on out is your choice, Peter."

"You promise?" Peter asked.

"Yes, Peter, I promise," Gravda told him. "You'll be fine, just use your wits and remember this: *Little thieves are hanged, but great ones escape.*" It was a commonly used phrase in Russian that even children use. Peter had heard it many times before, but at ten minutes until five, it had never made more sense.

Chapter 37

The Appian Hotel, Prague

Only a fool would attempt such a thing on Soviet soil, the major repeated in his mind. He had told the major general the Lunik 3 was in the freight yard. But in fact, he was only speculating. He had not seen it since last evening with his own eyes...Could Peter be *that* foolish? Even the general had said it would take balls to tamper with it here in Prague, and he knew his son-in-law had no balls at all.

But...

The major reached for the phone and dialed the room of his aide who was just down the hall.

The phone rang only once, and before the voice at the other end could speak, the major said, "Get up, I want you to drive to The Prague Hotel. Bring me Corporal Kozlov, bring him to my room. Leave immediately." He slammed the phone down and sat on the edge of the bed, deep in thought. Like the general, he was a man who did not believe in coincidences.

He ran his fingers down his stubbled chin and thought out loud, "I know Peter has disdain for me and feels like I bully him, but damn it, it is the only way a young man like him will every learn discipline. He has no respect for authority."

The major rose and walked to his bathroom and looked into the mirror. He wondered if maybe he had been too rough on the young man his daughter had been foolish enough to fall in love with. As he reached for his razor to shave, he had another thought. If Peter Kozlov was somehow involved in a conspiracy to discredit him, well, he was then saddened by the thought of his grandchildren growing up without a father.

*   *   *   *

The Hotel Prague is just two miles from the Appian Hotel and the major's aide, at this late hour, had made the drive in under five minutes. Dressing had taken another three but leaving the large black sedan at the curb had saved additional time. He was now standing in front of Corporal Kozlov's door and banging on it. Then he banged again. And then a third time.

There was no answer.

The aide rushed back down to the lobby, and when he saw the man at the desk, he demanded a pass key for room 312. The tired lobby attendant hesitated, so the aide reached down and unsnapped the holster for his sidearm. Room key 312 was in his hand just moments later.

Again, taking the lift to the third floor, the aide paused, exhaled, and turned the key. "Corporal Kozlov? The major has requested I bring you to him immediate—" as he spoke, he had flipped the light switch on the wall by the door and saw there was no need to finish his sentence. The room was empty and Corporal Peter Kozlov was nowhere to be found. The bed was freshly made and unslept in. Kozlov's clothes were not packed and ready to go for the 6:30 a.m. roll call. Peter Kozlov had not been there all night. "Shit," the aide said loudly, knowing the major and how he hated not having his demands met. He spun in a circle and then once more.

Low ranking military did not have the extreme luxury of a phone in their rooms. A call home was not to be paid for by the government, but by the soldier himself at a payphone in the lobby. *Do I call the major and inform him or drive back to the hotel to inform him in person?* he thought to himself. "Shit," he stammered again. *Better to get it over with*, he figured. He would rather get his assed chewed on the phone than see the Major's face redden in person.

At the front desk, he walked around the counter and picked up the phone without confrontation, as the desk clerk had seen him coming and had made plenty of room. He paused before dialing, but only for a moment.

*   *   *   *

The major had shaved and dressed in a freshly starched uniform. He had packed the night before and his two suitcases stood just inside his door. He had pondered the possibilities of the general's call and would wait to talk to Peter before making any rash decisions. *He was not a bad kid, just misguided,* he thought.

The one thing he was sure of was Peter Kozlov was not cut out to be an American plant. He did, however, think he was more than capable of being a patsy, and it was that thought alone that he was currently worried about. The general had referred to Mexico City. He knew the Americans had barred the display of Russian space hardware from their own country and even understood the reasoning behind the decision. No one likes having their nose rubbed in someone else's superiority. If the Americans wanted a look at the Luna 3, then Mexico City would be the logical place to try to get closer to it. *Spies work in a world of inequities*, he thought to himself. They don't do what would be considered by most as the logical choice simply because is it just that, logical. The unexpected and the audacious move is the one most would not think of, and stealing a Russian satellite here in Prague was as audacious as it could ever be. He stared to pace the floor, waiting for Peter Kozlov to be delivered to him.

Chapter 38

The Salvage Yard

The gear had been stowed in the van. The scaffolding had been removed and dismantled, and the team was working on loading it as well. The time was now 5:20 a.m. Gravda was pleased they had finished just ahead of schedule. All that was left was for Tony to grab the work lights from the cinder block office and make one last cursory check of the grounds to make sure nothing would be left behind. "Hank, pick up those cigarette butts and find a place to bury them. There is no reason to advertise we were here," Gravda told him.

Good thinking, Hank thought. He only smoked a particular brand, and they weren't Czechoslovakian, they were Romanian. He purchased them by the box load, twenty-five cartons at a time, and had them shipped to his current home in Italy. *No sense in leaving any calling cards,* Hank thought to himself. *Maybe this Betty Miller did have things in order.*

Tony unplugged the lamps and found the timer which had activated the flood lights which had surprised them earlier in the evening and turned it to the off position. The salvage yard was once again comfortable in its blackness. As their eyes adjusted to the dark, the faintest tinge of pink had appeared off to the East. Roger looked up and said, "That was cutting it close. We're lucky today is Monday and not Wednesday."

Both Tony and Gravda looked at him perplexed.

"The Summer Solstice," the engineer explained. "We gain two minutes and eight seconds of daylight each day until Wednesday, then the days get shorter again. If this were Wednesday, the sun would be coming up sixty-eight seconds earlier."

Tony turned to Gravda and said, "Wonderful. You do know how to keep things exciting."

Hank joined the conversation and said, "Sixty-eighty seconds is enough time for us to get the hell out of here. Let's move."

"Tony, get everyone into the van. I'll get Peter on his way."

Gravda walked over to the young Corporal and touched his shoulder. "It's time, Peter."

The look in his eyes was weary, exhausted, and frightened.

"Just drive the truck, it's all you have left to do."

"What if the major starts asking me a lot of questions?" Peter asked.

"Then you lie to him. It's that simple. There is no way that anyone is on to all of this. This plan was too audacious, and no one could ever expect it. So. The truck broke down, you fixed it, and delivered the satellite just like you said you would. Nothing more, nothing less."

"Sometimes I feel like my whole life is a lie," Peter told her.

"I understand that feeling more than you could ever understand," she told him. "Sometimes finding the half-truths in each lie makes it a little easier to swallow. You need to go now, Peter...go."

Peter climbed up onto the running board and opened the driver's door of the Russian lorry. His rifle was still leaning up against the passenger door like it had been all night long. He turned before climbing in and said, "This may sound strange to say but somehow...thank you."

"After this night is through, make your life your own, Peter," Gravda said, "*Dasvidaniya*."

She walked ahead of the truck and opened the gates to the Kotchak Brother's Salvage Yard. Peter fired up the diesel motor and deftly wheeled the lumbersome truck through the opening and turned a hard left. As he got to the corner he turned right and disappeared into the last moments of night. Gravda stood there for a moment thinking of her own words of advice. *Maybe I should start listening to myself,* she thought.

Hank joined her by her side and said, "He could still blow this for us. You know that, right?"

"He won't," she said. "He's Russian." She paused for a moment, then added, "But let's play this safe just to be sure. Hank, there's one last thing I want you to do. Get on your bike and follow him. I just want to make sure he gets there without any problems. Stay well clear and out of sight. Be my eyes on this. I need to know we accomplished what we came here to do. When everything is complete, get back to the safehouse. We should have everything packed up by then and we can get the hell out of Prague."

"Betty, for you, anything," he told her while walking back to get his bike. As Hank sped past her and disappeared into the faint rays of day light, she whispered as loudly as possible to Tony, "Let's go!"

As Tony edged the van through the gates, Gravda closed them behind her for the last time and climbed into the van in the front seat. He turned and said, "I don't know about you, but I have had enough excitement for one night. That was cutting it close."

...None of them knew just how close.

Chapter 39

Appian Hotel

"What the hell do you mean he isn't there?!" the major barked.

"He isn't here," the aide stammered. "His room is made up, and his bag is not packed. Apparently, he has not been here all night."

"Get back here as fast as you can. I will be waiting for you outside at the front doors."

"Yes sir," the aide started to say, but the loud slamming of a phone on the other end made him recoil. He ran out to the black sedan which still had the motor running.

Moments later, he pulled up in front of the Apian Hotel, where the major reached for the door handle even before the sedan had come to a stop. He threw his two bags into the back seat and climbed in after them.

"Get me to the freight yard," he commanded.

The major's aide had heard that tone of voice before. No one needed to reach to close the opened door, as the centrifugal force of the driver stomping on the gas pedal did it for them.

*   *   *   *

The trip from the salvage yard to the freight yard had only taken a few minutes. Peter pulled the lorry though the open gates and looked around. There were no security personnel, no guards. Peter was alone. He drove the lorry into the yard and parked it next to the station master's shack. He turned the motor off and for the first time he could remember, he sighed a long breath of relief. He reached for his rifle and then cradled it in his arms and closed his eyes wishing the night to be over. It takes the average person seven minutes to fall asleep. Maybe it was the stress from the night's activities or just simple exhaustion, but Corporal Peter Kozlov was asleep in four.

*   *   *   *

The black sedan sped through the streets of Prague at breakneck speed. But the aide was only happy that the major's wrath was now directed at Corporal Peter Kozlov and not at himself. When they arrived at the freight yard, the major's car pulled into the open gates and stopped.

Hank had just taken up position across the street and had tucked himself into a narrow doorway as the black sedan roared by. Hank could see the Russian lorry parked a hundred yards ahead, to the left and behind a chain link fence.

The major's car slowly crept into the freight yard, then turned left coming to a stop behind the truck. Its headlights cast long triangles of yellow light. The aide popped out to open the major's door, but the major was already exiting the vehicle. He strode to the truck and banged loudly three times on the driver's door.

Peter Kozlov awoke, startled. His heavy breathing, despite only sleeping for a short time, had fogged the interior windows and windshield, giving the impression he had been there longer than he had. Taking his hand, he wiped a circle of clarity in the glass of the driver's side window. Standing outside was his father-in-law, Major Alexander Tkachenko. The sun was just coming up over the horizon.

"Get out of the truck!" the major commanded.

Peter opened the door and exited the vehicle with his rifle still in his arms. Alexander Tkachenko was known for his ability to yell. It was his trademark, and he did it well. Peter waited for the assault. It did not come.

"Explain yourself Peter," The major said, but without his usual hostility.

Commanding officers usually do not look for long-winded explanations and Peter was hoping not to attempt to give one. He was much more comfortable with the "YES Sir, NO Sir," responses usually demanded of him by the major.

It dawned on him the major had referred to him as "Peter," and not just "Corporal." He had come to almost believe the major had forgotten his name completely. Strangely, the major even seemed relieved somehow to have found him here.

"I don't understand the question, Sir," Peter said, regrouping.

"Have you been here all night?" the major asked.

"Yes, Sir," Peter told him. "There was a loose wire on the starter and by the time I fixed it and got here, no one was around." Peter found comfort in the woman's last words, "Find a half-truth in each lie, it helps."

"So, you stayed with the truck," the major said.

"Yessir. What else could I do, Sir? I had my orders."

"Has this truck been out of your sight at all tonight?"

"No Sir, absolutely not, Sir." Again, a truthful statement, other than the few moments he had slept. It was not a lie.

"And no strangers attempted to get close to it while you have been here?" the major pushed.

Peter forced himself to remain expressionless. The major had said 'strangers' and used the word, 'here.'

Well, they were now at the freight yard and the pretty woman, although he did not know her real name, was certainly not a stranger. Not after the night in his hotel room. The big man had even shared his sandwich with him, and the little fellow made him laugh even though he could not understand what he was saying. "Sir, no one has come close to this truck since I arrived here at the freight yard. Er, other than you, Sir." *That was close enough to the truth,* he thought.

The major relaxed, and Peter saw him lower his shoulders into a stance he rarely saw from him. He seemed to have had a burden lifted from those shoulders. He almost appeared...human, for just a moment.

Major Tkachenko sighed and then leaned against the cowling of the Russian diesel. As he felt the warmth of the engine compartment, the major stiffened. "When exactly did you arrive, Corporal?" the major asked with an eyebrow raised.

Before Peter could answer, the major barked at his aide, "Check the cargo, Lieutenant!"

The Lieutenant raced to the back of the truck, dropped the tailgate, and climbed inside.

"I don't remember exactly," Peter told him, hesitantly. He was happy enough to have delivered the truck and its contents to the freight yard undiscovered. He had never thought to check his watch. He prayed his half-truths would be enough to satisfy the major, but this time he was telling the whole truth.

"This truck is still warm, Corporal. What time did you get here?!" The stern and condescending look of the major was once again what Corporal Peter Kozlov had seen too many times.

From across the street Hank could see the major's body language stiffen and could hear the volume of his voice escalate.

"Well Corporeal, what time did you get here?!"

"Sir, I told you. I do not remember exactly," Peter stuttered, flustered. He started to cower once again but thought of the lady and her words again. "After this night is through, make your life your own," she had said.

The Lieutenant peered around the corner of the truck while still standing in the bed. "It's here Major, nothing appears to be touched at all."

"Of course, it's here," Peter said. "What did you expect? The truck is warm, Major, because I have been sitting here all night freezing my ass off guarding your tin can in a wooden box."

The major was a little stunned by Peter's angry tone of voice. He had never had the guts to challenge him before.

"I turned the truck on a while ago because I got cold. I let the heater run and shut the truck back off," Peter said growing tired of the Major's constant beratings. "It was payday last night, and while everyone else was back at the hotel I was sitting out here doing my job." Peter had once again noticed the major had relaxed when he heard the satellite was safe and sound.

But he was still the major. *That man could always find fault in you somehow*, he thought. Better to give him something to yell about and keep his mind off the cargo. "...I fell asleep!" he confessed with his tone rising. When he said it, he did not lower his eyes. Instead, he stared straight at his father-in-law, with anger welling up inside.

There was a short pause in the air. The mayor was a bit surprised at the outburst. Peter filled the space by shouting, "Is that what you wanted to hear, Major? Yes, I fell asleep. I screwed up...again. I have been out here all night, and was up all day yesterday, and I shut my eyes for a few minutes only to find you banging on my truck and yelling at me as usual!"

The lieutenant ducked back into the truck waiting for the explosion from the major. Hank did the same with the small doorway he stood in, thinking, *Oh shit, this is about to come apart at the seams.*

Major Tkachenko was not used to being talked to in such a manner, but his relief in finding the satellite was safe and sound, had softened him just a bit. "Peter, be careful. I am still your commanding officer."

The emotions of the last twenty-four hours had popped, and Peter had had his fill. He was tired. Tired of too many things. "That's the problem, Major, you have always thought of yourself as my commanding officer. You have been yelling at me since the day I met you, and it only became worse since I married Maria. I'm sick of it, sick and tired of it. I haven't been home in six weeks. We have a baby on the way and instead of being home with my wife, I'm here with you in this damn freight yard at this Godforsaken hour with you doing more of the same."

The major unexpectedly took a step back. Insubordination was one thing. An occasional gesture behind his back, maybe a whispered comment the lower ranks thought could not be heard; it was all part of the territory when you are an officer.

But this was different. There was a raw honesty in Peter's tone and in his words. Peter was standing up to him. Maybe the boy he had always thought Peter to be was becoming a man for a change.

Peter was surprised when the major said, "Go on."

Thinking a good defense is always the best offense, he risked speaking his mind in its entirety. Hell, at this point he really didn't care anymore.

"I fell asleep, so bust me down to private, take part of my pay and make it that much tougher for Maria back home. In fact, do me a favor, drum me out of the Army altogether. I can live with the shame if it means being home with Maria. I was never cut out for the military, and both you and I know it. I never wanted to be a soldier! You demanded it! What were you thinking? Perhaps if you yelled at me enough, I might become more disciplined, more like you? And what makes you think being more like you is what is best for your daughter?! She married me for who I am not who you are. I hate it," Peter told him. "I just want to paint. If it means painting houses to put food on the table, then so be it...I just want to go home." Tears had welled up in his eyes and he wiped them away. He was spent with emotion and feeling defeated.

Alexander Tkachenko...*Major* Alexander Tkachenko had raised his eyebrows in surprise. *No one had spoken to him like that in twenty years,* he thought. Then he did what no one could have expected. He paused...and then...he laughed.

He laughed, long and loud, committing his body to the laughter. Not in a condescending way. Not in a way which makes a man feel like a fool or less than.

He had not laughed like that in many years and enjoyed the feeling. Peter did not know what to say or what to do.

"Did you just yell at me Peter? Did you just put your father-in-law in his place?"

Peter started with his usual apology, "...I..."

"No, I think you did," the major said, laughing even more heartily. He grasped his son-in-law by the shoulders with both hands and held him at arm's length. "You did well tonight, Peter! You took it upon yourself to do your job, and you have no idea how important that is," he said, thinking of the earlier call from his commander. "I am proud of you."

The major turned away from Peter while still holding him in his grasp. "Lieutenant," The major barked, "Go back and gather up the corporal's belongings. This man has a train to catch in less than an hour; He's going *home*!"

The major's aide scrambled down from the truck and ran to the black sedan, fingering Peter Kozlov's room key which was still in his pocket.

Hank removed his newsboy cap and wiped a bead of sweat from his brow. He slapped the silly hat which was three times too big for his skull back into place, gathered the little bicycle with the pink basket, and started peddling as fast as he could towards the safe house.

Off to the East, the horizon had turned from subtle pink to the colors of autumn leaves, and the sky was fading from blackness to a beautiful hue of lapis blue.

Chapter 40

The Safehouse

The garage was a flurry of activity when Hank returned. Tony was hefting large boxes into the van as the rest of the team was scurrying to pack up what was left of the gear. Gravda and her team had arrived back at the safehouse five minutes after 6:00 a.m., and those extra few minutes after the hour had been the longest of Brad Ray's life. Nervous Bob had been beside himself.

"We will give them a few more minutes," Brad had told him on three separate occasions. "If they're not back in ten minutes then we'll go."

Bob was so apoplectic Brad almost offered him an "aspirin" to shut him up. Brad knew he was just kidding himself, and he had no intention of dolling out the little pills Hank had given him...but still, the man's tension was getting on his nerves.

When Gravda used her key to enter the side door, Brad could not have been happier to see her. Bob actually cried.

"How did it go?" Brad asked.

"Well, so far so good. It should be at the freight yard and

Hank should be right behind us."

Gravda then turned to the engineer who had milled the rod and duplicated the seal and said, "Nice work, everything went back together just the way it should have." As Big Tony, Joe, Steve, and the NASA engineer entered the door, there were handshakes all around. Bob was giving hugs.

"How do the photos look?" she asked.

"Beautiful," Brad told her. "We have 170 done, and all of them came out clear. I still have two more rolls to develop but we can get to them later." He turned to Joe and said, "You're a damn good photographer, Joe. I'm impressed."

Bob spoke in an excited voice, "Betty, you won't believe this, but a lot of stuff on that satellite is stolen technology from America!"

Gravda turned to Steve and smiled while saying, "Really?"

Bob went on to explain all about the solar panels and film canisters, but no one was really listening.

Gravda walked to the kitchen and pulled out her hidden stash of the finest Russian vodka and looked around for glasses. She was just walking out of the kitchen with glasses in hand when Hank pulled up and banged on the rollup door. Tony once again reached for his sidearm.

"I think it's just Hank," Gravda said.

"Oh, I know it's Hank. But if he punches me in the nuts again, this time I am really going to shoot him," he said smiling. Tony only opened the rollup door about two feet, making Hank crawl in under the door.

Hank looked up from the floor. "You're an asshole."

Tony laughed. "You think we're good?" he asked.

"Yeah," Hank said. "I think so."

"The package got delivered?" Gravda asked.

"Oh, it got delivered, and just in the nick of time," Hank told her. "I thought you said the Russian's weren't getting to the freight yard until seven? At five minutes after six, your Air Force major came flying up with his driver and the first thing they did was check the back of the truck. He didn't look happy either," he added.

"And?" Tony asked, urging him to continue.

"Well, the major seemed satisfied everything was in place. In fact, he even seemed to be relieved. But then there was a lot of yelling, though strangely enough, your young corporal was the one doing the most of it," Hank looked towards Gravda. "What has me bothered is why the major showed up so early, and why he had the driver quickly look in the back of the truck," Hank said. "It was almost like he expected it not to be there...I think...he was tipped off."

"Tipped off?!" nervous Bob yelped.

"He showed up early and in a hurry for some reason," Hank explained. "You might want to hold off on that bottle of vodka and any celebrating..."

Steve turned to Gravda and said, "Betty, we now know James Webb has a leak at NASA. We just don't know how big the leak is. It is possible."

"Oh, dear God, they're on to us," Bob said, hopelessly.

"Relax," Gravda said. "Webb doesn't know *when* we would attempt to get any eyes on the satellite, he only knows a team is working on it. No one at NASA or his team knows we are currently in Prague. You two engineers are on loan, but it was for an unspecified amount of time. Allen Dulles is the only man who knows we're here."

"You think it is just a coincidence then?" Tony asked.

"I don't believe in coincidences, but for now I think we're okay. If the major *was* tipped, he still doesn't have all the information. He couldn't have. I think the major was just being cautious, and even if Peter had said something, he has no idea where we are. So, what happened after that, Hank?"

"That's the weird part, because that's when the corporal really started yelling at the major."

"And when you say 'yelling,' what exactly do you mean?" she asked.

"I mean he was angry, he chewed off a piece of the major's ass," Hank said. "I know, I didn't think the kid had it in him either. He just blew up and let the major have it. I was worried the major was just going to snap and shoot the poor kid."

"And then what?" Tony asked.

"Okay, here's really the crazy part," Hank said. "The major looked stunned by all of it...and then laughed. And when I say laughed, I mean belly laughs, like they had just shared the best joke ever. Then it was hugs all around. The whole thing was crazy. It makes no sense."

The smile on Gravda's red lips had started before Hank had even finished the story. She beamed brightly and handed a glass to everyone in the circle and began to pour. Her entire team looked at her a bit confused, especially Bob who was still in his usual panic.

"It makes perfect sense," Gravda told them. "Where I come from there is an old saying. 'Sometimes, even the biggest bear needs to be trained.' I think young Peter just trained his bear," she laughed.

"So, we're good?" Tony said, hoisting his glass into the air.

"Oh, we're good. Peter will never say anything to anyone, I am sure of it. And the Russian major thinks he dodged a bullet. Steve, I do agree there is a leak at NASA, and I think I know just how to plug it! Let's get the rest of this stuff packed up and get the hell out of here."

Everyone pulled their glasses to their lips in unison, and when the burning perfection of potatoes and distillation hit their guts, even nervous Bob had no choice but to smile.

Chapter 41

Washington, Just After Midnight

The phone had rung only once before the tired and haggard man picked it up and said, "What do you have for me, Allen?"

"Nothing yet, Mr. President. I'm still waiting for some kind of confirmation."

"Damn it, knock off the Mr. President crap. That stuff is for nine-to-five, and this is definitely not nine-to-five. What the hell do you know?"

"Jack, I don't know anything yet, I'm in the dark on this one. I told you I would call you around midnight and I knew you would be waiting. As soon as I have some information, I will let you know."

"Well, that certainly puts my mind at ease," the president said sarcastically. "What the hell is the delay?"

"I don't even know at this point if there is a delay. It's how things like this work. I'd say don't worry until we have concrete reason to do so. Give it some time. The hardest part is always the waiting game. I was just keeping you informed."

"Well, you just informed me you have nothing to inform me and you're the guy I count on for answers, Allen. I'm not hearing any answers. I would rather hear the news from you than have to read it on the front page of Pravda in the morning. What is your plan 'B' if this goes in the toilet? And don't give me your speech about plausible deniability! Remember the international ramifications if your people get pinched!"

"There are provisions in plan if things were to go south. The prime directive was there to be no violence towards any Russians. I have two teams in play. One at the dismantling site with the satellite and the other a safehouse not far away to develop photos and do analysis as well as any parts fabrication needed to reassemble it and return it within the needed time frame. My field operatives are well trained and well versed on how to extract themselves from difficult situations. They know what they are doing...."

"You asked me for two civilian employees of NASA. What about...."

Kennedy did not know about Steve, Joe, and nervous Bob. Even Allen Dulles knew little about them other than their employment records. He had put full faith in Gravda to pick her own team. He interrupted the president by saying, "Civilians are a liability in a covert operation: You pay me to make the tough decisions, Jack. I've listed them as expendable in the name of national security."

There was no response from the president other than a long and audible exhaling of air.

"Jack?"

"Call me when you actually know something Allen, I'll be in

my office. Let's hope we know something positive and soon."

"I will Jack," Dulles said, before hanging up the secure phone line to the White House.

Chapter 42

The Safehouse in Prague

"What the hell happened to the phone?" Gravda called from the kitchen into the garage.

"Oh, yeah, sorry," said the engineer who had remained at the safehouse. "I melted it down to make the new seal."

"Where is the old seal?"

"I melted it down and destroyed it."

"And the length of rod we pulled out of the satellite?" she asked.

"Brad dug a hole out back and buried it I think."

"Good thinking," Gravda said. "TONY!" she called out.

Tony popped his head around the corner and asked, "What do you need?"

"How much longer?"

"Five minutes, no longer."

"Good, don't worry about the portable dark room or the cots upstairs. I have a cleaning team coming from the consulate and they will be here at 7:00 a.m. Make sure everything else is loaded and be prepared to pull out of here when I get back. I need to make a phone call."

Gravda reached into her purse and laid five-hundred kornos on the counter next to what was left of the phone. It was equal to almost a two-month salary for the average worker in Czechoslovakia. She had no idea how much Allen Dulles had paid to secure the safehouse, but money bought silence, and it would be more than enough to pay for a new phone.

"You want someone to go with you?" Tony asked.

"Might not be a bad idea. I need to find a phone booth. We'll take the Skoda," she said, walking back into the garage.

"You expect me to fit in that thing?" Tony asked.

"Just get in," she said, walking to the tiny sedan.

Tony slowly wedged himself into the front passenger seat and even as he set it back as far as it would go, he looked ridiculous. His knees were jammed into his chest and his newsboy cap was bent over from the headliner.

Hank looked over and laughed. "Reminds me of my circus days, only we got twenty people in a car that size."

She deftly pulled the car around the van as Steve raised the overhead door. She leaned out the window and said, "I need to find a phone. Be ready to pull out of here in ten minutes." She stepped on the gas and the little car puttered out into the early morning sunshine.

*   *   *   *

They drove three blocks up and turned left until they found a main road. Almost in passing, Tony said, "You did well tonight, Betty. I'm not trying to be condescending, and I'm not saying it just because you're a woman...I'm just, saying."

"Would you have said it if I hadn't been a woman?" she asked.

"Well—" Tony said pausing.

Gravda interrupted his pause. "Well then, consider yourself condescending, big guy," she smiled. "Times are changing Tony, and this whole project worked out tonight because it was unexpected. I usually choose to work alone, simply because then there is no one else to worry about. Well, tonight I worried a lot. I don't like the feeling. It's enough in our line of work to save your own ass, and adding people to the list just makes it that much more difficult." Gravda saw a phone booth just ahead and started to pull over. "...How many notches, Tony?" she asked.

Tony understood exactly what she was asking.

In the days of the Old West, gun slayers would take a knife and carve a notch in the butt of their gun whenever they had killed another man. Some would lie and carve fictitious men's lives into the wood hoping to impress others. *Lives were not trophies*, she thought.

Tony paused and said, "Four. But I try not to think about it."

As Gravda Nemiroff climbed out of the car, she walked to the passenger side window and leaned in to say, "Nine, Tony, nine. And that's the difference between you and me, I never think about it. But if any one of the men here tonight had been injured...or worse...and it was on my watch...it would be all I could think about for the rest of my life. This is it for me, Tony. I have one more phone call to make, then I am out, I'm done."

Tony did not know what to say. He sat there and watched the beautiful Betty Miller stride up to the phone booth and drop a coin in the slot.

* * * *

"Yes operator, I would like to make a collect call to London, please."

"The number, please?" the operator asked.

Gravda gave her the number of a switchboard which had been standing by and waiting for her call.

"Whom should I say is calling?"

"It's Betty," Gravda told her. "I am hoping to reach my Aunt Mildred. Thank you, operator."

When the call was connected, both parties continued the rouse until they were sure the busy operator had moved on to other duties. "Aunt Mildred, It's Betty. I just wanted to see how you were feeling, I know you have been sick lately," Gravda said.

"Oh dear, I am fine, but I hadn't heard from you in a while, and I was worried. Is everything okay?" the British switch board operator and agent asked.

"Couldn't be better," Gravda told her. "Everything is as it should be."

"That's wonderful," the agent said. "I am sure Uncle Allen would love to hear the good news, let me get him for you."

The call was forwarded, and Allen Dulles picked up on the first ring.

"It's me," Gravda said. "Everything is back in place."

"Good," Allen Dulles said. "Any problems?"

"Nothing major," she told him. "There does seem to be a

leak in a water pipe that runs through the attic though. But everything is secure, and at this point there is no water damage."

Allen Dulles knew immediately what she meant. James Webb had a spy on his team at NASA. "How bad is the leak?" he asked.

"Well, it looks like a lot of the plumbing was put together with scavenged parts, but I think I know just how to punish the plumber," she told him. "I should be leaving here in just a few minutes and would love to talk to you more about it. I should be home later tonight, where would you like to talk?"

"Why don't we meet at the big house on Main Street," Allen Dulles said. "Is 9:00 p.m. okay with you?"

"Of course, Uncle Allen. I will see you there."

Gravda hung up the phone and stood there for a moment. She had never been to the White House before.

Chapter 43

Washington, D.C. 12:37 A.M.

The phone rang, and once again, it only took a single ring for the person to pick up.

"What do you have?" the president asked.

"It's been returned," Allen told the President.

"Good, any problems?"

"I don't know all the details yet and won't until I can debrief my primary. But the satellite has been returned, and apparently, everything went according to plan. It seems the Russians borrowed some of our technology to make the thing work...and it means we have a leak in James Webb's operation."

"Shit," the president said. "Do we know how big a leak?"

"Well, Jack, NASA is a governmental agency, and there are bound to be leaks somewhere. But this one is big enough that someone was able to pass on classified information to the Russians which helped them build the satellite. However, you can actually consider this to be good news, Mr. President."

"Allen, damn it, how the hell can you consider a leak in one of my agencies good news?"

"Jack, if they could have built the damn thing on their own, they would have," Dulles explained. "This operation wasn't just about finding out what they know, it was about finding out what they *don't* want us to know. I think when this is all over, you might just have a few more trump cards in your pocket."

"I see your point. When will you be able to de-brief your agent?" Kennedy asked.

"I have a plane waiting in Prague now, it will fly my primary to London this morning, from there we have booked a ticket on a Pan Am flight to New York leaving Heathrow airport at 2:00 p.m. Flight time with a refueling stop at Gander Newfoundland is roughly eight hours. There is a five-hour time difference between London and here. With another flight from New York, my agent should be on the ground here in Washington by late afternoon or early evening. I have set up a meeting tonight at 9:00 p.m. to get all the details, and I think it is a meeting you might want to preside over. I want you to hear this firsthand."

"Where is this meeting?" the President asked.

"In the one place I know will be the most secure."

There was a very long pause. "The Oval Office?"

"I know it was a little presumptuous on my part, but I think what she has to tell us should be for our ears only."

The second pause on the President's end grew. "...Your primary on this operation was a woman, Allen?"

"Not just any woman, Jack. You're going to want to meet her and thank her. I think this woman might have just handed you the moon!"

Chapter 44

Exodus from Prague

Big Tony would not let the topic go. "Betty, you can't just walk away from the CIA. It doesn't work like that," he told her.

Gravda laughed. "You have been watching too many spy movies, Tony. If I want out, I walk, plain and simple. I have spent my whole life running from my past, and I think it's time I start thinking about my own future."

As she drove the little car back towards the safehouse Tony said, "Betty, you're not naive and you're certainly not stupid. People like you and me know a lot of things, things certain people would not be happy about others knowing about. You catch my drift?"

"Wow, that sounded like compassion there, Tony. And yes, I caught your drift. I know how the game is played." She patted his knee, which was still buried in his chest from the small seat and the smaller car. "Thank you," she said. "I understand what you're saying and appreciate your concern, I really do."

In another block, they would be back at the safehouse. "What about you Tony? How much longer are you going to do all of this?"

Tony just chuckled. "I'm a street kid from Detroit. I grew up stealing cars to make money. I thought I had wised up and worked hard when I managed to get a degree in political science from the University of Michigan. But here I am, still doing the same shit I was doing fifteen years ago. The only difference is now I am sanctioned by a government who pays me well to do it. Breaking and entering, larceny...and worse, if need be. It's just like working for a mob boss, only now the boss sits in an oval office and the pay is better. It's a job, Betty, and I need the money."

"Do you ever just want to be normal, get out, live your life?" Gravda asked.

"To do what?" Tony asked gruffly. "This is what I know, Betty. Can you picture me teaching some damn course on polisci in some community college for a tenth of what I make now? It is what it is," he explained. "This is the only normal I know."

Gravda understood exactly what he meant.

As they pulled up to the safehouse, Tony tried one last time to make her re-think her decision. "You can't just disappear."

"I don't plan on just disappearing. That would just mean looking over my shoulder forever. No, I plan on telling Allen Dulles personally."

"Oh, just gonna call him on his personal line, huh?" Tony asked, with just a hint of friendly sarcasm in his voice.

Gravda smiled that bright smile of hers and said, "No, I thought I might tell him tonight at dinner. It will also give me the chance to break it to 'your mob boss,' at the same time."

Tony was stunned. He raised an eyebrow knowing she was not kidding, yet still asked, "...The president? The president of the United States!"

"Yes, Tony, I have a meeting at the White House at 9:00 p.m. So, if you don't mind, let's get the hell out of here. I have a plane to catch."

Silence. As she left the car, he could only say, "Holy shit, Betty Miller, who the hell are you?"

The question was rhetorical, as Tony was left to pry himself out of the compact Skoda.

*   *   *   *

Joe was the first to meet her at the door. "Everything okay?" he asked.

"Yeah, Joe, how are you holding up?"

"Me, I'm fine. Tired, but fine. You must be exhausted though."

Gravda thought back to his whispered comment as she fanned sleep on the little cot upstairs. Was it all just twenty-seven hours ago? It felt like a lifetime.

"You're a good man, Joe. Let me ask you, after last night, do you still think you're boring?"

"After last night, I could use a little more boredom in my life, Betty," he told her honestly. "I am starting to think maybe photographing landscapes in a tropical destination for a few months wouldn't be bad idea."

She smiled once again as they met eyes. "Yeah, a little bore-dom does sound very nice right about now," she said.

Joe was immobile. The eyes he could not look into at the kitchen table yesterday morning were now eyes he could not pull away from. The tiny flecks of brown surrounded by hazel flashed for just a second. A man who took few risks, one who had doubted everything...took a chance. Keeping his gaze he said, "The only problem with boredom is, doing it alone, is well, really boring."

"I hate that type of boredom," she furrowed her brow and smiled in agreement.

Joe reached for her hand, and she met him in the middle. A delicate and well-manicured hand, fully capable of holding a gun and disabling the largest attacker, was still soft and delicate. Their grasp lasted for just a second.

In that moment, Gravda Nemiroff had made her second major decision of the day.

*   *   *   *

"Are we packed up?" Gravda asked her team.

The unnamed engineer from NASA who had stayed behind at the safehouse said, "Yes, everything except for Brad's photo lab, the chalkboard, the lathe and the cots upstairs. What do we do with them?"

"Leave 'em," Gravda told him. "I have a cleaning team who should be here in just a few minutes. Gather round guys, please."

The team she had handpicked and assembled dropped what they were doing and surrounded her. Each one thinking about last night's activities with a feeling of exhaustion mixed not only with a sense of relief that it was over but with a deep-seated emotion which comes from knowing they had done what no one could have expected. They had pulled off the impossible.

"The significance of what we did here last night may not be understood for many years, if ever," she told them. "This was a highly unorthodox operation, but we accomplished what we came for and I truly want to say thank you. No one will ever receive a trophy or medal for what happened here. You're just going to have to except my gratitude as your pat on the back. Once we leave here, this night never happened."

The solemn moment was broken when Hank being Hank said, "Roger that, over and out." Roger chuckled and Tony swatted Hank's cap hard enough to make it spin on his head backwards for having broken the mood.

She singled out Tony first. "You, yah big galoot, thanks for all your help. You're not as tough as you think you are, and I want you to remember what we talked about earlier." She walked over and hugged the mammoth man.

He stood stoically, not quite knowing what to say but finally mustered up, "If you ever need someone on a future team, you call me. I'd work with you any time." He meant it.

She turned to her two civilian NASA engineers. "Everything you saw here tonight was classified at the highest levels. You are never to speak of any of it to anyone except for James Webb, and even then, it should be behind closed doors. There is a leak and means your walls have ears."

The engineer who had remained at the safehouse to replace the seal was surprised. "There is a leak...at NASA?" he asked, stunned.

"The satellite was built with a lot of American parts and most of them were classified," Steve interjected. "It means the leak has to be one of the guys on your team."

"It also means you can't trust anyone, no matter how well you think you know them," Gravda explained. "The leak could be anyone, even your best friend at the office."

From the look on the two engineers' faces, you could tell

they were doing a mental inventory of the faces they had seen around the conference table just a few short days ago.

"The leak is my problem, not yours. We had a close call tonight, but I'm sure the Russians don't know we're here. So, the less you say the better."

The engineers nodded in agreement.

"This was all way out of bounds on your usual responsibilities and you both did a fantastic job," she said. "There won't be any bragging rights, but you might have just turned the tide in favor of us in the Space Race. Congratulations, gentlemen. Don't forget to pick up your passports and wallets on your way out."

She turned her attention to Steve and Bob. "Look at you two! From desk jockeys to field operatives now, huh? Both of you will find a fat little thank you in your next paychecks. I couldn't have done this without you. This was far beyond your usual call of duty. Thanks for trusting me and doing your part."

Steve smiled. "It's the most excitement I have had in a long time. I won't ever complain about a desk job ever again."

Bob said, "I miss my desk..."

Hank had wandered off to the kitchen and returned with a brown paper bag. It was the same type of bag Tony had packed his sandwich the night before. He had blown air into it and was preparing to explode it while standing behind Bob, but the look Gravda gave him made him re-think the idea. Disappointed in not having one last opportunity to make Bob jump out of his skin, he acquiesced and grumbled.

"You did well, Bob," she said. "You and Steve will have plenty of work doing the analysis of the photos from your desks back home. Webb will need the information and your opinions could very well change the direction of our future space program. Again, nice work."

"Brad, Joe, you make a good team. Nice work out there."

Turning her attention to Hank, she simply pointed his way and curled her index finger three times, indicating he should walk over. Gravda walked back a few steps to separate them from the rest of the circle and Hank followed. Bending down on one knee, she asked, "Are you satisfied this operation is complete?"

She had not bent down as a way of being condescending towards his size, but more to speak quietly so others would not hear. Before he could respond, she added, "You and Tony were the only ones recommended to me by Allen Dulles. That alone told me he wanted someone here to keep an eye on things. I don't blame him, Hank. I have been playing this game for a long time and I understand how the rules work. You were Dulles' eyes on this one, weren't you?"

Hank looked at her with a little bit more of earned respect, yet said nothing, allowing her to finish her thought.

"It's always about covering someone else's ass...right? and I was the un-known entity on this one. Up until this project, I have always worked alone. But this operation was my idea, and the objective was way out of Allen Dulles' comfort zone. I knew it when I proposed it," she said. "It's why it worked. No one in their right mind steals a Russian satellite on Soviet soil, right?"

"Yeah, your plan took a lot of balls and some brains to pull it off," Hank said. "It could have gone bad ten different ways, and I certainly wasn't a big fan of plan 'B'. How did you figure out I was the overseer on this one?"

"It was simple. Tony had his sidearm. My orders explicitly

said no gun play on this one. So, Tony wasn't carrying a gun to protect anyone from the enemy...He was here to make sure the enemy never found out who we worked for."

Hank just nodded.

"Tony is no sociopath though," Gravda added. "We all have our jobs to do, but it doesn't mean we enjoy it. The job needs to be done and you do whatever you must to see it through. I like Tony, he is a good man. He would never have turned that gun on any of us...unless he had his orders...It meant the order had to come from someone else."

The usual joker Hank had appeared to be became very serious. With Gravda still on one knee bending down to whisper, he said, "I don't get to make the rules. This whole operation had bad news written all over it even before it began. An untried team of NASA boys and two CIA desk jockeys from Washington with, no offense, a female lead who had never led an operation before...I was shitting my short pants before it even started."

He paused before adding, "You're the one who pulled this off. I don't know how you did it, but you did. Yah got some serious brass ones on yah, lady. I don't think anyone else could have made this one work. Now give me my hug and let's blow this joint while we still can."

Gravda pulled him into her arms and honored his request. *He had earned it*, she thought.

Hank smiled and said, "Well, there's a first. Never had the boss hug me after a mission."

Gravda laughed.

"Just so yah know, dame, I'm keeping the little bike," Hank said, smiling.

*   *   *   *

"All right guys, this is it! Get ready to pull out of here," Gravda said loudly. "Brad, I want all the photos and negatives; I'm taking them with me. Hank, you will go out the same way you came in. Steve, you and Bob will hitch a ride with Tony."

Tony looked at Gravda. "It's going to be a cramped ride, the van only seats six."

"I know," she responded. "Joe will ride with me."

Joe seemed surprised but said nothing. He tried hard not to change his facial expression.

Brad handed her four large manila envelopes and two smaller envelopes containing the negatives. "How many rolls are still yet to be developed?" she asked.

"There are only two," Brad stated, and reached into his vest to retrieve them and handed them to Gravda.

"Nice job," Gravda said, reaching for the canisters of undeveloped film.

Hank interrupted by asking Brad, "Hey, you got any aspirin?"

"Why, do you have a headache?"

"Not today I don't, but yah never know when one will pop up. I like to be prepared."

Brad was more than happy to hand back the cyanide pills. "Take them. I didn't want them to begin with."

Hank placed them back into his canister. "Good, I never wanted to give 'em to you in the first place." They shook hands and Hank started to climb onto his bicycle head for the door.

Gravda watched the transaction and fully understood its

meaning.

"Hank before you leave, give me your lighter. I have one more thing to do and then we're out of here."

Taking his lighter, she pulled out the second set of photos of her and Peter Kozlov. Lighting the corner of each one, she dropped them onto the concrete floor watching the burning corners curl up and wither in flames. Each one changed from full color to sepia tone and then to ashes. Her promise was complete.

Two minutes after they had left, a nondescript van pulled up and three men in dingy coveralls climbed out. Fifteen minutes later, the same van pulled away loaded with cots, photo developing equipment, a chalkboard, and a large metal lathe. There were now no traces of the nine interlopers having ever stepped foot in the grimy garage.

Chapter 45

Prague, 10:00 A.M.

The flight time from Prague to London was just under two hours. The empty Boing-707 had sat on the tarmac of a private airstrip just outside of Prague waiting for Gravda's arrival. The crew of four were dressed in Lufthansa uniforms and the plane's markings indicated it was part of the same airline.

Of course, neither were true. The 110-passenger jetliner had been commissioned by the CIA in late 1959 and was used mostly as an airborne command center. Its interior had been outfitted with a conference table and seating for up to twenty. Large plush recliners gave additional seating for rest and relaxation. The latest radar jamming equipment in the cockpit had prevented the Russians, or anyone else for that matter, from even knowing the plane was currently on the ground in Prague.

Gravda and Joe had driven to her hotel with enough time to bathe, freshen up, and even nap for a little while before the first leg of the journey home. On the drive, Joe, asked the simple question, "And why am I lucky enough to be traveling with you?"

Gravda answered with her usual flash of a smile. "I never

know what the future holds Joe, but for right now, I want to find out more about you. If you're willing to take things slow and with no agenda, we'll see where each moment takes us."

"Is it okay to feel like a kid in high school? I haven't felt this way in a long time, Betty," Joe admitted.

"Joe, I don't even know what that feels like. My life has never permitted it," she said. "So just be patient and maybe one day I might just give you my locker combination…"

Joe had napped on the couch. It was Gravda who had stepped out of the bedroom, wearing little at all, who then surveyed the sleeping man on her sofa from the doorway. She whispered, "I could see you in my future." She then closed the door behind her and returned to the bedroom for a few more minutes of much needed sleep.

When she wheeled the small car onto the tarmac, the pilot met her at the foot of the stairs.

"I was told you would be traveling alone," he said.

"Well, it looks like the plans have changed."

Joe gathered up her four suitcases and thought to himself he had never seen her wearing the same outfit twice. She was quite the enigma, and he looked forward to knowing more about her.

Out of habit, Gravda pulled a handkerchief from her purse and wiped down the steering wheel and the door handles of the Skoda, making sure no fingerprints were left behind. The rental agency would be notified as to where to pick up the car but not until long after they had left Prague.

*   *   *   *

The flight would take the two passengers over Germany,

across Belgium, the northern tip of France, and across the English Channel to the South-Eastern coast of England, then on to London. From there, they would catch a Pan Am flight to New York. The first twenty moments of the flight were spent in silence. Joe was simply taking in the surroundings of the opulent space around him and the comfort of the near stranger he was traveling with.

"So, do you always travel like this?" he asked, finally breaking the silence.

Gravda laughed. "Not always, but I do enjoy the finer things in life. It's not really about the money, Joe," she explained. "That's just compensation."

Her comment had been honest but seemed sad. Joe looked into her eyes again and thought for a moment. Those green eyes could sparkle so easily, maybe even on demand, but they lacked the luster he had seen when their hands had met in the garage.

"When you said compensation…you weren't talking about a paycheck, were you?" he asked.

The brown flecks glistened just a bit. "No. I like fine clothes and fancy cars, but not for the same reasons normal people would. They aren't status symbols for me, there's no 'status' in what I do. I mean, money is just one way to compensate for the things I have seen and done. It's not…ego, if that makes sense?"

"I guess," he answered. "You're saying surrounding yourself with nice things helps you to forget the not-so-nice things in life?"

"Yes," she nodded. "It's rather ironic though. I think it's why so many people are driven to their graves in Cadillac hearses. Like somehow, they feel it makes up for the darkness. But it never does."

"Betty, every day is a new day. I'm starting to realize you can't change the past, even if you wanted to. But it doesn't mean your future has to be the same. You're a chameleon. In London I saw you go from dowdy to fabulous just by fixing your hair and what you chose to wear. They don't hand out Oscars to spies, but you're the greatest actress in the world." Joe let the air around them grow silent for a moment before he added, "Sooner or later though, the makeup has to come off and the spotlights fade away. That's when you have to decide who you really are."

His comment hit home. She was a chameleon. So much so in fact she wondered if even she knew who she was any more. She started to slip into her own head, but Joe's next comment brought her back.

"Betty…and I doubt that's even your real name…but right now, your real name doesn't even matter to me. I don't know a damn thing about your past, and I've got to be honest, I don't know if I could handle knowing all of it. But I do know this, there is something about you. For the life of me I can't explain it. There's something there which seems pure and strong and kind, and I like that person no matter what their past has been. I won't ask you any questions."

Gravda smiled at his sincerity and his sweetness and then laughed a bit. "Joe, I don't know if I would have the right answers anyway."

Joe reached for her hand. "You're braver than I am. I couldn't have led the operation, and I wouldn't have wanted too either. But you did it. I have a feeling though there is something which might require even more bravery on your part though."

"And what is that?" she asked.

"Trusting someone who cares and allowing them to be a friend. It's a pretty good start," Joe told her.

She clutched his hand a little tighter, as a silent way of saying thanks. Ever observant by training and intuition, with few things ever escaping her vantage point, she thought of the man who had risked so much by reaching for her grasp at the garage. He had just borne his soul while asking for nothing in return.

There was a very long pause while both their hands entwined before she spoke. Their grasp became a handshake by her doing.

She said softly, "My name is...Gravda."

"Nice to meet you Gravda," he said slowly and with intent. "My real name is..." he paused while making a goofy face, not knowing what else to do. "...Joe."

Her laughter was real. For the first time in her adult life, she truly embraced a man by her own choice, and for the right reasons.

Chapter 46

Washington D.C.

Gravda had paid for Joe's first-class ticket from London to New York, and again for the short flight from New York to Washington. She understood a man's ego can be eggshell thin and had told him it would wind up on an expense report Allen Dulles would be paying for. She had not been kidding.

As they both sat in the backseat of the taxi taking them from Washington's airfield to The Willard Hotel, she told him, "I have one more thing I must do tonight, and I would like you to be there with me, if it's okay. Afterwards, we can get down to your plan of some serious boredom."

"Sure, Gravda, but what is it?"

"You don't happen to have a suit and tie, with you, do you?"

He laughed. "No, I didn't know I would be needing one. Where are we going?"

"I thought it might be my little surprise for later tonight," she said mischievously. "It's just one evening and a little excitement won't kill you."

He chuckled. "I don't know. I have seen your brand of excitement."

"No, I think you'll enjoy this. But you'll need to look presentable." She leaned forward and told the driver, "Change of plans. Please take us to Raleigh Haberdasher, it is on F Street North-West."

Raleigh Haberdasher was named for its first location in the Raleigh Hotel on Pennsylvania Avenue and was opened in 1911 by Clarence W. Grosner. The emporium catered to the ultra-wealthy and the most influential men of Washington. The original store was moved to an impressive and opulent location on F Street North-West in 1923 and remained there until its closing in 1992.

When the cab pulled up to the impressive storefront, Joe got out first and held the cab door open for her. Joe reached into the side window of the Studebaker taxi to pay the 80-cent fare, handing the driver a dollar and telling him to keep the change.

As he turned to escort Gravda to the front door, an impeccably dressed Italian man greeted them with his arms outstretched. "Bianca," he cried, "So good to see you! You 'ave been gone for so long-a!"

Joe said nothing, but thought to himself, *how many names does she have? What am I saying, she's a spy!* Still, it left him wondering just how many layers there were to the beautiful woman.

Gravda hugged the man and kissed him on both cheeks, then bantered with him for a few seconds in flawless Italian. She turned towards Joe, and said, "Mario, this is my friend, Joe. He needs a fine suit and tie. Along with some shoes. The whole works. Can you help me?"

The man smiled. "For you Bianca, anything. When will you need it by?"

Bianca grimaced. "Well, that's the problem Mario, we have a meeting tonight at nine and my friend came a little under-dressed. Can you help us?"

Mario furrowed his brow then broke out in a broad grin. "Come on, come on. I see what I can do!" He ushered them into the expensive shop. "What did you have in mind?"

Joe noticed how Mario had only spoken to Gravda, not him.

Gravda stepped back and took in Joe's broad shoulders and slim waist. She had never taken the time to notice these things before. As observant as she was, things like that are distractions while on a mission, unless the information might benefit her. Thoughts like those are better left to silly girls with less on their minds. Her connection had been made by his manner and the way in which he carried himself, but she liked what she saw. "Let's put him in an Italian continental suit. Grey, mind you. I'd say a three-button-straight front jacket, pants with no pleats, and wingtip oxford shoes...black."

Mario looked at Joe and eyed him up for a second before saying, "As usual, Bianca, I agree with you completely. Let's see what we can find for your friend."

Gravda grabbed one arm and Mario grabbed the other while Joe hung on as they escorted him deeper into the store. He wondered how many suits she might have picked out for other men before him. They ushered him to a three-way mirror and Mario reached into his vest pocket for a measuring tape. Before he could begin, she said, "Jacket size thirty-eight, regu-lar...I would say a thirty-two-inch inseam. Shirt size fifteen and half neck with a sleeve length of thirty-four." Joe was stunned, as her assumptions were correct. "Mario let's try him in an eight and a half shoe. Bring us a nine though, some of those European styles tend to run small."

"I'm impressed," Joe said.

"In my line of work, it pays to pay attention to the details."

Mario retuned with a gorgeous suit crafted from the finest Italian wool in the color of soft dove grey. Mario held the jacket up and Joe turned his back with his arms outstretched so the tailor could slide the jacket up over his shoulders.

Joe felt the silk lining graze across his body as the jacket came to rest and fell perfectly over his frame.

"I'm so sorry, but off the rack will have to do for tonight," Mario told Gravda. "I can hem the pants and take in the waist, but I won't 'ave the time to tailor the jacket."

Gravda faced Joe and ran both her slender hands down the length of the lapels and stepped back to take a better look. "It won't be necessary Mario, it's perfect."

Joe reached for both her hands and led them to his lapels once more. "Oh, do that just one more time," he said smiling.

She complied willingly, the malachite in her eyes sparkling.

"He will need a shirt and tie to go with it too, Mario. Would you, please?"

Mario dutifully ran off to find the perfect match.

Joe looked in the mirror and admired the cut of cloth and the fit of the jacket. Then by force of habit, he reached down to the cuff and pulled the price tag up so he could read it. He was stunned. "Gravda...this suit is $200!" Embarrassed and feeling a little shamed, he said, "I can't afford this."

She put her finger to his lips. "Don't worry," she told him.

"No, I have never paid more than $30 for a suit," he said. "You have already paid for two airline tickets. I'm sorry, I couldn't accept this."

"Well if it makes you feel any better, we will call it a loan. Listen, tonight's meeting is unfamiliar territory, even for me. But having you by my side would mean a lot to me," Gravda said. "Besides, you look handsome," she added. "I'm sure we can work out some sort of repayment which will be...mutually beneficial to both of us."

Uncomfortable as Joe might have been, the glint in her eyes gave him no choice but to acquiesce. She was a woman who was used to getting what she wanted.

With everything picked out and the task completed, she asked Mario, "Can you please have it all sent to The Willard Hotel, and by 8:00 p.m.?"

"Of course, Bianca, of course," the tailor told her. "Now go, you two 'ave better things to do then to stand around my shop all day!"

Gravda kissed him on both cheeks again and thought to herself, the man was exactly right.

*　　*　　*　　*

The Willard Hotel is a Washington landmark and one of the most opulent hotels in the country. It resides at the corner of F Street and Pennsylvania Avenue and has been the favorite resting place for ten American presidents, dating back to the days of Zachary Taylor, Millard Fillmore, and Abraham Lincoln. John Wilkes Booth had dined there on the day of Lincoln's assassination. The guest list included the most wealthy and influential men of America. Mark Twain wrote two of his books while staying at The Willard and it has been said more handshake deals were settled in the lobby of the hotel than in Congress. Later, Martin Luther King would prepare his "I have a dream" speech in his room the night before his march on Washington for Jobs and Freedom, August 28, 1963.

The lobby of the hotel was impressive. Ornate columns of pink marble supported the high, intricately carved ceiling while thick red rugs adorned the marble floor. Gravda strode confidently to the front desk and asked for her key to the suite she occupied on the sixth floor. Hand in tow, Joe found himself looking over his shoulder at the impressive architecture as she guided him to the elevator.

As the doors to the elevator closed behind them, Joe said, "Wow, so this is your idea of boring, huh?"

"It is when you have no one to share it with."

"Gravda," he said holding her at arm's length. "Your life is a lot...faster paced than mine. Be patient with me, some of this will take me a while to get used to."

"I'm not asking anything from you, Joe," she told him.

"And I won't ask anything of you that you aren't willing to give freely by you own decision."

"Well let's start with this," she said, leaning towards him and kissing him hard on the lips.

Joe wrapped his arms around her slender waist and kissed her back with ferocity, surprising even himself. They lingered together in each other's arms long after the elevator's doors had opened.

"Now there's something I could get used to," he said.

Her suite was grand but without pretense. Unlike any hotel room he had seen before it was obvious this was her primary residence and not just a room for rent.

Resting her key on a table by the door she told Joe, "Make yourself at home, I'm going to freshen up."

Joe looked around, taking it all in. There seemed to be nothing here which could tell him more about the beautiful woman he was sure he had already fallen for. His own home, as modest as it was, spoke volumes of his interests. Camera equipment was everywhere, fishing gear, and books. There were no books here at all...In fact, nothing personal he could see.

Then he noticed, resting on top of the baby grand piano, a photograph. Picking it up he saw bright smiling eyes, which looked familiar, and a gigantic walrus mustache. *So, she does have a past,* he thought. He put the photo back where it had been sitting, making sure to put it back exactly as it was, fearing he may have intruded.

"There is a bar over in the corner," she called out from the bedroom. "If you want mix yourself a drink."

A drink sounded like a pretty good idea, Joe thought. Walking over, he opened the double doors and found it to be well stocked. Finding the gin, he poured two fingers and reached for the tonic water. Just as he was about to sit on the sofa there was a knock at the door. The bellman had arrived with Gravda's four bags and his lone suitcase. Feeling the need to be extravagant, Joe handed him a five and said thank you.

"Your bags are here," Joe called out, still facing the door.

"Wonderful," she said, from right behind him.

He had not heard her bare feet on the lush carpeting as she had snuck up behind him. He turned, startled, only to see her freshly scrubbed face, which looked even more beautiful than what makeup could produce. Her black hair was pulled into a tight ponytail, and she was wearing only a lace and silk slip. He almost dropped his drink.

"We can worry about the bags later, Joe, let's find out what else you might feel up to getting used to..."

Chapter 47

Washington Later That Evening

The packages from Mario and Raleigh Haberdasher had arrived promptly at 8:00, and although neither of the young couple had slept, both felt refreshed and renewed. The bellman had knocked twice before entering with his passkey.

Gravda spoke behind the closed bedroom door, "Thank you, just leave them there, please." She rested her head back on Joe's shoulder once again and he stroked her hair.

"Are you going to tell me where we're going tonight?" he asked.

"Nope," she said. "A girl has to have her surprises."

Joe laughed heartily. "You...are nothing but surprises, girl."

"Come on, let's get dressed. I think you will find tonight to be a night you won't want to miss," she told him. She got out of bed and sauntered to the bathroom. The faint light of the Washington summer evening outlined the perfection of her naked body through the shear drapes as she disappeared behind the bathroom door.

Joe held his hand over his heart and asked himself for the third time in twenty-four hours if he had completely fallen in love. He flopped back over and buried his head in her pillow with the intent of just smelling the lingering's of her soft perfume. Under her pillow he felt a soft lump and reached for it.

First confused, then truly surprised, he retrieved a small blue teddy bear. Its fur was worn thin by many years of hugs and stained by too many years of tears. He held it up to get a better look. One button eye was missing and the stitching on its torn shoulder had been delicately mended with mismatching thread.

Earlier he had thought this dwelling said little about its mysterious occupant, but he had been wrong. The photograph had told him much, but this little worn bear told him everything. He imagined its usual place of prominence was that of resting on her pillow, ready to welcome her home on the chance occasion she would return shortly. We all have secrets. We all have things in our lives we wish we could forget. The secrets themselves are not the burden; it is never having anyone to share them with which stifles the soul.

She must have quickly stashed it behind her pillow for reasons he fully understood were not yet his to know. Still, he wondered. Was it the irony of the toughest woman, he had ever met having an even softer side than he imagined. Or perhaps she wasn't ready to reveal herself. Either way, it did not matter.

Joe held the bear at arm's length and whispered, "Hey buddy, I'm not here to replace you. Maybe between you and me, we can make sure the incredible woman in there never has to cry again." He smiled at the ridiculousness of talking to a stuffed animal, but by staring into its one intact button eye, he realized this teddy bear had heard much before. "Can you handle one more secret?" he asked the bear. "I think I am madly in love with the woman behind that door. But don't tell her just yet. I'll make you a deal, if you will keep my secret for a while, I will be patient until she is ready to tell me all of yours." Placing the bear back under her pillow, he rose, then walked out to the living room to gather his new clothes, smiling all the way.

*   *   *   *

Joe felt a little out of sorts, but at the same time he felt good about wearing some nice clothes and having the most beautiful woman he had ever met hanging on his arm. At twenty minutes until nine o'clock, the air in Washington was still warm and inviting. Their destination was only two blocks away, so she decided they could walk and enjoy the evening. Her little black Givenchy dress was all the rage, but on her, it truly appeared like Givenchy had designed it with her form in mind. A simple innocent strand of pearls around her neck was the finishing touch.

He felt like the luckiest man in the world.

They walked casually. Chatting, getting to know one another better. Then she stopped him by putting her delicate hand on his shoulder. "We're here," she said, smiling.

Joe had been so fixated on the conversation he had not noticed any of his surroundings. When he looked up, he saw the massive wrought iron gates, and the unmistakable silhouette of the White House, bathed in lights.

He dropped her grasp. "You're shitting me!"

Gravda laughed. "Nope."

Joe could only stammer, "I...but."

She put a finger to his lips and said, "It's okay, I'll do the talking, come on."

She pulled his hand towards the gate and met the guard standing there at attention. "I have an appointment at nine."

"Your name?" the guard said, bored by his routine.

"X", Gravda said, then added, "And friend."

"I have you listed as just one individual."

"Things change," Gravda informed him. "Make a phone call if you must."

"Stand here," the guard told her sternly.

Stepping inside a small shack he picked up the phone and in hushed tones Joe heard him say to someone on the other end of the line, "Yes sir, but she is not alone, she has someone with her." After a few seconds of unheard conversation, the guard said, "But sir I have no record of her guest!" Another second later, he stiffened to attention and said, "Yes sir, right away, sir."

Hanging up the phone, he looked harshly at Joe, then said to Gravda, "Mr. Dulles is waiting for you." He opened a gate for them to walk through. "Someone will meet you at the front doors. Stay off the grass."

Gravda and Joe started up the semicircular driveway of 1600 Pennsylvania Avenue, NW. The grass the guard had spoken of was the North Lawn, and to their left they could see the simple yet elegant fountain, now lit for nighttime viewing. Its round design was framed by a circle of red carnations, and Gravda had heard before the president hated the damn thing. "With the Russians having nuclear weapons why don't you just put a Goddamn bullseye on the front lawn," he was quoted as having said.

Both the East Wing and the West Wing were purposely blocked by view by dozens of large trees Franklin D. Roosevelt had commissioned back in 1934. Now stately White Oak and American Elm trees grew in groves, blocking prying eyes from seeing inside the mansion. A wide avenue of grass was all which allowed tourists to see the structure with a clear view from Pennsylvania Avenue. Roosevelt had complained, "The eyes of the world were already on the White House. I don't need them looking in my windows too."

As they walked, Joe felt uncomfortable. Although they had permission to be there, he felt he was still somehow trespassing and would be singled out and asked to leave immediately by a silent and stern voice.

Gravda felt his grip tighten and understood. "Would you believe me if I told you I was nervous too?" she said.

Joe stopped and turned her his way. "You don't seem to be the type of woman who gets nervous about anything."

"This may surprise you, Joe, but I am human," she told him. "On the flight, you said I was an actress, and you couldn't have been more correct. But tonight, the stage is a little bigger than I'm used to."

"What you pulled off in Prague was impressive," Joe said. "You accomplished everything you set out to do. Think of tonight as the encore," he smiled.

"It's a little more than that, Joe," she said, putting her hand on his chest. "It's also my curtain call. After tonight...I'm out...I'm quitting."

"You're serious," Joe said quietly.

"Yes, I am serious."

"Why?" Joe asked. "And more importantly, why now?"

"When you play as many roles as I have Joe, sooner or later, you just become detached from everything you know about yourself. I don't even know who I am anymore," she said, sadly.

"Well, let's both find out who you are together then," Joe said, looking deeply into those green eyes.

She grabbed his hand tighter. "I like that idea."

The north portico of the White House appeared to be supported by four large columns when viewed from the passersby on Pennsylvania Avenue, but it is not. Twelve columns hold up the massive roofline, taking up almost half as much space as the depth of the entire mansion itself.

The first set of four columns stand in front of the slimmest of macadam pathways, allowing skilled chauffeurs to slither their limousines between the outer columns and the two additional inner columns which bare the weight of the front portico. Protocol demands drivers enter only through the same Northwest gates Gravda and Joe had entered. Doing so also requires passengers to disembark only from the passenger side of the car facing the front doors. The small width of the pass does not enable both sides of a car to be opened without striking the massive blocks of marble supporting the primary exterior columns.

They continued their pace through this ribbon of asphalt and onto the six marble steps leading to the marble porch. If ever there was a structure epitomizing the concept of "the grand entrance," it was this.

A young marine in full dress uniform said, "Right this way." He turned his back and walked away at a fast pace, making them struggle to catch up. "Usually, you would be required to wear badges," the guard said over his shoulder, "But I was told to escort you to Mr. Dulles as quickly as possible." The young marine turned and walked backwards as he spoke, knowing the route well. "Don't wander off, just follow me, please."

"I was hoping to maybe find some silverware from the dining room as a souvenir," Joe joked.

Gravda elbowed him, but she also giggled.

The guard did not. At a fast clip, the guard took them through the main entranceway, then made a hard right, splitting his turn in a perfect ninety degrees. Gravda and Joe found themselves looking at a long hallway which split the White House in two from front to back.

The entire building seemed to be vacated. Apart from the gate guard and their Marine escort, neither Gravda nor Joe had seen another human being. As they walked the length of the Center Hall with its vaulted ceiling, the plush carpet muffled the sound of Gravda's high heels and Joe's new wing-tipped shoes. They came upon the double doors leading to the Palm Room which stood between the White House ground floor and the West Wing and acts as a staging area for visitors, providing access to the Rose Garden.

The doors stood open as if anticipating their arrival. "This way," their guard told them. They once again stepped outside and walked the full distance of the covered pavilion known as the West Colonnade. With the White House strangely vacant of personnel, the sound of Gravda's heels now echoed loudly off the tan-colored granite tiles and white columns, before disappearing into the warm spring air as they headed towards the West Wing and the President's office.

When they reached the doorway to the West Wing, the guard stopped and said, "He is waiting for you," and opened the door.

In the small reception area of the West Wing stood Allen Dulles, director of the CIA Standing five foot and nine inches, the silver-haired man with round-rimmed style glasses puffed heartily on his burl wood pipe. The smell of cherry Tabaco filled the small space and lingered in the air. His grey mustache and quick eyes seemed more fitting for a doting grandfather than the head of the largest intelligence agency on the planet. His three-piece suit was impeccable, and the crisp and heavily starched collar of his white shirt made Joe thankful Gravda had directed him to dress appropriately.

"Oh, my dear," he said directing his comment to Gravda while reaching for her hand, "Welcome home."

His greeting seemed more like a kind uncle greeting his niece than a man of such power. "What do you have for me?" he asked, with eyebrows raised.

Gravda reached into her oversized handbag and retrieved the envelopes of developed photographs, negatives, and canisters of undeveloped film. "I think these are going to make you very happy, Allen." she said in a sultry voice.

He took them without investigating the contents. "And who is your friend? I wasn't expecting this."

"This is Joe," she said. "He took those photographs, and I thought his insight would be helpful in our debriefing."

Dulles seemed instantly satisfied by her reply and reached his hand out to Joe.

They shook hands. "Mr. Dulles," Joe said nervously.

While taking a long drag on his pipe and gripping Joe's hand in a vice, he said in a billow of cherry scented smoke, "Relax, Joe. Call me Allen."

He turned back to Gravda and asked, "What did you find?"

"Well, let's start with basics," she said. "They're not as far ahead as we thought they were. They have been stealing U.S. technology all along to get to where they are. The Russians are masters at improvisation, after all," she explained.

Joe, feeling confident enough to interject, said, "The radioactive protective film they used in the Luna 3 came from American high-altitude balloons we launched over Alaska a few years ago. Those canisters aren't exactly high-tech."

"Go on."

"The big news is the Russians got the photos from the back side of the moon by using light sensitive glass panels stolen from Corning. They used a simple electric relay switch to activate the cameras. Their concept was…actually brilliant…if it is okay to say."

"It is," Dulles told him. "I want real answers and real observations, not just the information you might think I want to hear. What else did you find?"

Joe looked at Gravda and she just nodded.

"The satellite was oriented with the cameras pointing towards the dark side of the moon," Joe went on to explain. "That side of the moon receives just as much sunlight each day as the side we see, but since the moon revolves so slowly, we never see the far side from here on Earth. In reality, it is not the dark side at all, but more properly called the far side of the moon."

Dulles nodded. "Joe, 'X' here asked for you personally on this mission, so forgive me for not being able to remember every detail in a dossier. But I don't recall you having a background in aerospace."

"I don't sir, but I did a hell of a lot of listening in the last twenty-four hours to the people who do."

Dulles puffed hard on his pipe. "Okay...continue."

"They used our own solar collectors to capture the reflected sunlight from the surface of the moon to trigger the relay switches to an electric motor which opened the aperture on the top of the capsule and started taking photographs. The same panels were used to trip an electric timer to snap the photographs and to keep the satellite in orbit around the back side of the moon. The timer was set to pulse at three-minute intervals to the booster rockets keeping the craft in orbit around the moon. They used the same boosters to rotate the craft while it was out or radio range so they could avoid overheating issues. You wanted us to look for some type of on-board computer system, but there was none. They used the simplest of parts to make the thing work, and even then, they had to borrow parts from us."

"Interesting," said Dulles turning his attention to Gravda. He asked, "Did you run into any snags?"

"It took longer to disassemble the satellite than I had hoped," she explained. "And we had to make two modifications to get the damn thing back together, but it's back in place and it will take the Russians a long while to figure out it was ever touched."

"What modifications?"

"Every nut, bolt and screw were labeled and returned to its exact location, but there was a three-foot aluminum rod supporting the weight of the nose cone to the interior of the satellite." She paused before adding, "We were able to get the nose cone off, but the rod was stripped at its mounting bracket on top of the photo development equipment. I made the decision to cut it and have one of your NASA engineers fabricate a new rod to replace it."

"Okay, I understand, but why is that a problem?" Dulles asked, looking concerned for the first time.

Gravda looked hard at her boss. "I told you exactly what I thought we might need for this operation, but someone on your end sent aluminum rod to Prague in English imperial measurements instead of metric. The Russian's only use metric. I had to cut it, or we would still be trying to reassemble the damn thing. We didn't have the time to mill down an entire three-foot rod to metric specifications so we just did the ends so it would fit. We also had to bore out the bracket on the top of the photo developer to make the new dimensions work."

Dulles exhaled a long breath of smoke and sighed. He took the time to rub the bridge of his nose between his eyebrows. "Noticeable difference?" he asked.

"Not to the naked eye," she told him. "It's one and a half-hundredth of an inch off, but if a Russian engineer ever puts calibers to it, then they will know we came calling."

Allen Dulles rubbed his chin. "In your opinion, what is the likelihood they will discover the tampering soon?"

"Slim to none," she said confidently. "The Luna 3 is a show-piece now. Khrushchev is using it as a propaganda tool. Besides, technology has changed a lot in the last few years, so I doubt they would be concerned in taking the time to dismantle it and check out every component for tampering."

Joe interjected, "There was a Russian seal attached to the photo equipment cover and we needed to cut it to access the interior. Your guys at the safehouse did an excellent job in replicating it to the exact dimensions as the original. Everything except for the rod and the bore size on the bracket is exactly as it was."

"Well thank you for your vote of confidence, Joe, but they *will* find the discrepancy on the rod eventually," Dulles said.

"Yes," Gravda said. "But when they do, they will also know we are aware of them stealing U.S. technology. It means they lose any bargaining chip on trying to embarrass our government."

Dulles thought for a moment, before saying, "Good point, and nice work. Anything else you want to tell me before I prep the president?"

"Just one more thing," Gravda said gravely. "The Russians may have been tipped off while we were there in Prague."

"Your patsy?" Allen Dulles asked.

"No, no way. Peter Kozlov had too deep a personal interest in keeping his mouth shut," Gravda told him. "But Major Tkachenko showed up at the freight yard just moments after we delivered the satellite, and he showed up in a hurry, as if he was worried about it. And the first thing he did was inspect the crate. Now, he did seem satisfied everything was in order, but I want to know why his interests were peaked to begin with."

"You mentioned there was a leak at Webb's NASA. Do you think there is a connection?" Dulles asked.

"Allen. They built the satellite mostly from parts off the shelf."

"Off *our* shelves," Joe added.

"The tech they stole from us was already a year old when they used it. And that was three years ago," Gravda stressed. "It means somebody has been selling or giving the Russians information for a while. Webb has only overseen NASA since February. The leak was formed much earlier than his tenure. It could be the same person, but I don't know. It could be more than one person, or even several at this point."

Dulles removed his glassed and muttered, "Well…Okay then. If your Russian major *was* tipped off, then I must consider the possibility the leak could have come from *my* department as well. This was a need-to-know mission, and there were only a handful of people who knew you were there. I will consider it on my end."

"No, I don't think it came from your end. My gut tells me we need to look at a senior engineer, someone close to retirement age," explained Gravda. "It has to be someone who has been in the system for a while…Otherwise it is a Soviet plant, and then we really do have a problem."

"Any suggestions, then?"

"Yes, I have a few. If it's one man, I think I know just how to catch the bastard."

"Good. Let's go tell the president the good news," Dulles said.

"The president?" Joe stammered.

Allen Dulles removed the pipe from his mouth, inspected its contents, and reached into his vest pocket to retrieve a lighter. Looking over the top of his glasses he looked at Joe and said, "Yes, Joe, this *is* the White House."

*　　*　　*　　*

Allen Dulles led them from the lobby of the West Wing through the doors of the Roosevelt room directly adjacent to the Oval Office. Usual protocol at the White House requires all guests to check in with Evelyn Lincoln's desk before speaking to the President. But this was not a usual meeting, and the hour was growing late.

Allen Dulles knocked just once on the outer door and the voice on the other side, a voice Joe had only ever heard on television or on the radio, told him to enter.

John F. Kennedy was perched upon the corner of his desk. He chose this spot as he hoped it would reflect a more casual nature. He had found doing so relaxed those who entered the Oval Office for the first time and tended to speed up the process of acquiring information. "Allen, come on in and introduce your friends," he said smiling warmly.

"Mr. President, this is our primary on the mission to Prague. And this is Joe, he was the primary photographer on sight."

"Allen, I have told you before. There is no need for the Mr. President stuff after hours, we have known each other to long for that." As the president spoke, he un-perched himself and walked over to greet them.

His words had not been a rebuke of the CIA director—in fact it was a rehearsed script used several times to put new-comers at ease. Ever the politician, Kennedy grasped Joe's hand firmly and said, "Hello, Joe."

"Mr. President," was all Joe could say.

Stepping to his side, Jack Kennedy looked at Gravda, sizing her up. At six feet tall, he stood a good half foot above Gravda, even with her two-inch heels. "So, you're Allen's secret weapon, huh kid?"

His comment was not meant to be condescending but more complimentary. But it still sounded pretty condescending to both Gravda and Joe.

She flashed a humble smile. "Well, I'm not so sure of that."

"It sounds like you got the job done, so it certainly says something," the president remarked. Still gazing at her, he tilted his head ever so slightly and asked, "Have we met before?"

"Yes, Mr. President, but just once."

Joe was surprised to hear this, but did his best to not react.

"Refresh my memory."

"Two years ago, at a private cocktail party at The Willard. I was...a guest...of your brother."

Robert Kennedy, the current attorney general and younger brother to the president, was well known in Washington for his philandering. The press usually left his indiscretions go out of respect for the president, but even then, the president seemed to have acquired the "Kennedy gene" for indiscretions. Both Jack and Bobby had been raised by a man who had many public affairs. Joseph Kennedy's public affair with Hollywood starlet Marlene Dietrich undermined the senior Kennedy's bid for the presidential election in 1940. It seemed in the Kennedy clan; the apple did not fall far from the tree.

Gravda's phrasing said everything the President needed to jog his memory. "Yes, you wore your hair shorter back then," he commented.

"Yes, Bobby liked it short...it's why I grew it long." She held his gaze. "Plus, in my line of work, it pays to change your appearance as often as possible."

"Still, you're hard to forget," the President said candidly.

Joe again said nothing, but his surprise was hard to conceal. Yes, she had a past, and it was none of his business, but was the President of the United States openly flirting with her?

Allen Dulles stepped in to say, "Bobby is the one who brought her to my attention, Jack. She has been working for me for almost two years now."

"Well then, it was a good choice. I can see how she could be very persuasive."

What an asshole, Joe thought to himself as the president put his hand on Gravda's shoulder and led all of them to the two couches facing each other in front of his desk.

"Tell me about Prague and please, don't leave out any details," he said, "I want to know everything."

Gravda spoke for the next hour, first explaining her responsibilities in London, and then the plan to secure the satellite and expedite its return. Allen Dulles and Joe interjected when appropriate. The president was attentive and inquisitive, asking questions throughout to gain more information. While she left out some of the sordid details of her night in Peter Kozlov's hotel room, she still matter-of-factly stated her methods of hooking her fish.

Joe almost expected the president to ask if those photos were in the envelopes Allen Dulles still had in his hands. He'd be disappointed to learn Gravda had burned the last copies back in the garage in Prague.

When the briefing was about to be finished, Kennedy turned to Dulles and slapped his knee on the couch they shared across from the pair. "Damn it, Allen, we have those bastards!" Looking back across the coffee table he said, "Good work, really good work!"

"We still have one issue to attend to Jack," Dulles said, seriously. "There is a hole in James Webb's team, and they may have been tipped we were there in Prague."

The President's elation escaped him like air from a balloon. "After the Cuban affair I don't need this shit! How deep is this hole?"

"We don't know yet," he answered.

"How the hell could the Russians know our exact whereabouts when this was classified at the highest levels?"

Before Dulles could respond, Gravda interrupted and said, "I don't think they did."

Both Allen Dulles and the president turned their attention towards her as she continued. "I think Major Tkachenko's reaction was precautionary. I think he was out to cover his own ass. Prague was the most unlikely place for us to have tried to secure the satellite. It is why the operation worked," she said. "The Russians are good but not that good. Their intelligence agency is bogged down with bureaucracy and even worse...fear. They move slowly because everyone is afraid to make a mistake. Tkachenko was at the freight yard an hour earlier than expected because he was worried he might have something to explain to his superiors. If he was confident someone was up to something, he would have shown up in force."

She gave them a moment to consider her hypothesis and then continued. "I think he got last minute intel," Gravda explained. "I think our leak at NASA is one man, and I think it is the same man who sold them the information about solar collectors and the radiative protective film. I think this man also informed them we were out to get a look at the Luna 3. The only NASA people who knew we had any intentions of doing so were the men in Webb's recent meeting."

Allen Dulles took in her statements and thought for a moment. "It makes sense."

"I am betting the Russians will step up their security for the rest of their world tour, but I don't think they even have a clue the horse is already out of the barn."

"You need to find the damn leak, Allen," the President said.

"I have an idea," Gravda said.

All eyes turned once again to the pretty spy who had already done the impossible.

"What did you have in mind?" the president asked.

"Have James Webb call another meeting, same cast of characters," Gravda said. "You can leave your astronauts out of it; I am sure they have already been vetted with thorough background checks. Have him preference his comments in future tense. 'We're hoping to get a closer look at the satellite soon, what should we be looking for?' The next stop on their world tour is Mexico City in two weeks. It would be the logical place for any operation to take place. Let the Russians think we are trying to gain intel, and by doing so, they won't have any idea we already have it."

"I like it," Kennedy responded.

"If Webb has a mole in his team, then the meeting should drive him to his Soviet contact. High priority information with a timeline in place. Tail all of Webb's team and see who scurries to tell someone else."

Allen Dulles had sat silent. "I agree, it's a good idea."

"So, make it happen! I want the meeting in the next twenty-four hours."

"I would keep the NASA boys who were with us in Prague out of the meeting though," Gravda said to Dulles. "Give them a while to decompress, they went through a lot over there. I know they're needed but give them a couple of weeks off with pay to get them out of the picture and to reward them for what they have already done. Remind them of their duty to the country and their vow of silence, and believe me, they won't even tell their wives what happened. Those boys are strait-laced, and I don't think lying is one of their skill sets. Plus, I wouldn't want a facial expression or a wrong word to tip the mole. If anyone asks why they are not there, just inform Webb to say something like, 'a few of our guys are working with the CIA right now to advise them on the matter.' Those comments alone should drive our leak to his contact."

Kennedy leaned forward, drawing closer to Gravda. "Let the Russians think we're about to attempt to get our hands on the Luna 3, and they stop thinking we ever tried in the past. I'm glad you're on our side, young lady." He reached forward and put his hand on her knee. "I can see big things in your future. This one was the big leagues, and you stepped up to the plate!"

Gravda removed his hand as she said, "Thank you, Mr. President. But it brings me to my next point...and maybe my last." Turning her direction towards Allen Dulles, she rose, and said, "Allen, I will help you to wrap up any details on this one. But when this is over, I'm out. I'm done!"

In his surprise, Allen stood almost by reflex and uttered, "Gravda, you can't be serious, you're kidding right?"

The moment the words came out of his mouth, he knew he had broken his own cardinal rule. No names...ever. Catching himself in his own slipup, he staggered.

Gravda quickly let him off the hook. "Allen, it's okay. Joe already knows."

The president, completely unaware of what had just transpired, looked first at Dulles, then at Gravda, and then back again, like a spectator at a tennis match.

But Allen Dulles understood. He understood completely. And just like the kind old uncle he appeared to be, he smiled.

Chapter 48

Washington, D.C. - The Meeting Continues

Allen reached across the coffee table and shook Gravda's hand. "Keep in touch. Nice work." He extended his right hand towards Joe, forcing him to rise. "Thank you for your service." He held the grasp and squeezed it tightly. "I guess this means I will be expunging your name from my payroll list as well. The best to both of you."

With the president still sitting and looking a little bewildered, Gravda turned to him and said, "Goodnight, Mr. President." Then she turned her attention back to Dulles. "I think we can find our way out, Allen."

As Gravda and Joe retraced their steps from the grand entrance of the White House, along the driveway and towards the gate, Joe finally said, "Did the President of the United States just blatantly come onto you?"

"Why yes, I do believe he did," she said, somewhat unaffected. "Men like him are used to power. It makes them think whatever they want, they're entitled to. I have had to dance around that crap my whole life, Joe."

Joe was silent until they had moved onto the sidewalk of Pennsylvania Avenue. "It bothered you, didn't it Joe?" she said.

"What, that he found you attractive? No, I understand that part. I'm not jealous or even insecure if that's what you're asking. I'm not the first and I certainly won't be the last man who thinks of you in that way."

"What is it then?"

"His arrogance," Joe spat. "Maybe I am naive, but I expected better of the president for some reason. His display of self-centeredness was disgusting. I have no rights to you Gravda, but seriously, I found myself wanting to punch him in the mouth, just out of principle."

Gravda laughed. "It probably wouldn't have been your best career move, but I thank you, Prince Charming."

Joe returned the laugh and said, "Well...speaking of career moves. Did I just resign without ever having said anything?"

Gravda grimaced. "Oh yeah, I think you did. But hey look on the bright side. It means we will have more time to spend together."

"Oh, well then, I made the right decision. Even though I didn't really make the decision. Yesterday I was employed and now tonight you said, "Oh we'll just go for a walk." How was I supposed to guess it would be to The White House...*The White House*! Gravda I have to tell you. Your idea of excitement is still more than I am used to."

"Wasn't meeting the president exciting?"

"Well, at first. Then, it was almost like finding out there is no Santa Clause."

"Welcome to Camelot," she said.

They continued to walk, and she gave him some time to process everything he had been through.

He finally said, "Allen Dulles seemed nice man though."

"He is, Joe, I trust him. Well...as much as anyone can trust someone in this business. But you should remember this is Washington, and not the Old West. The good guys don't wear white hats and the lines between good and bad are drawn with a very thin pencil. Time is the only one who gets to judge who is good or evil, and even then, it is usually the team which wins who gets to decide. I am sure the Russians would look at our little mission from a different vantage point."

"They stole technology from us," Joe said.

"And then we stole it back," she said. "It's all just a game to the big players Joe, and the pieces on the board are always changing. It's why I want out now, before I become just another pawn. Allen Dulles is the closest thing I still have to a father fig-ure, but he makes decisions every day which cost people their lives, and it's people like me who carry out those orders."

"Have you ever had to..." he started to say and then stopped. "Don't answer that, I said I wouldn't ask you any ques-tions."

"You can ask me any questions you want Joe, but the an-swers may be things you really don't want to know. If I were as innocent as you, I would only have one name instead of many. If the Russians had caught me in Prague, they would have sen-tenced me to death as a foreign spy. It's what I am. Those are the rules of the game. It's why I don't want to play their game anymore. And believe me, I have done far worse things than grand theft satellite."

"Well, I still like you," he said, grinning.

"You're sweet Joe. I think it is what I most like about you."

"You like me more than Kennedy?" He asked teasing.

Putting her arm around his waist and her head on his shoulder as they continued to walk, she said, "Well other than his wealth, power, and extremely good looks, there is one thing you have he doesn't."

"Really, what's that?" he asked, smelling the perfume in her hair.

"Me."

*   *   *   *

Moments after they had left the President said, "Did I just miss something here, Allen? Did she just quit?"

"I would say so, Jack."

"What are you running here, a steno pool or an intelligence agency? Control your people for God's sake!"

"Jack, she's not the type of woman anyone controls. She is bright, resourceful, and extremely good at what she does."

"All the more reason she stays onboard," the president said. "You know how important the end prize is in all this. We can't afford to have someone with her knowledge out there doing whatever the hell she wants. I think your taking your eye off the ball!"

"Well, she has done everything I ever asked of her, and some of the things I've asked for haven't been very pretty. She has earned the right to make her own decisions."

"That's bullshit. If she is that good, then we need her on the team. An asset is only an asset when you have it under control.

Especially when it's a woman."

Allen Dulles laughed but found nothing humorous about the president's statement. "This is not your typical woman we're talking about, Jack. I wouldn't expect you to understand."

"Oh, I understand," Kennedy said. "...You're fond of her, aren't you?"

He stood up. "Yes, Jack, I am. I also have tremendous respect for the lady. She has earned it. And I know that is something you don't understand." His last comment was heated. "The CIA is *my* organization. I know I report to you, and I mean no disrespect, but I will handle my people the way I see fit. That woman is not one of your starstruck little bimbos you parade around here after hours. You and I have been friends for a long time, and I am telling you, let this one go. Just let it be."

"Allen, if this woman is no longer an asset, than it means she is now a liability. With what she knows, and all there is at stake here, you might have to make some tough decisions. I won't be embarrassed again like I was on the Cuba fiasco!"

"Dammit Jack, you and I have known each other for a long time," Dulles said without mincing words. "I kept you in the loop on this operation purely out of respect to our friendship. It was a covert operation and I have told you things off the record to preserve your culpability! She accomplished everything and more of what I asked of her and dammit, she might have single-handedly moved our space program up by two years or more. Please, don't challenge me on this one."

"I am not challenging you on anything Allen, but I am still the president. And you report to me, don't forget it. Someone must think of the bigger picture and what is best for the country."

Allen Dulles paused before making his last statement. "Mr. President, this country has been built by people like her who have risked their very lives to serve what they think to be a better good. Do not diminish their contributions to that cause simply because it may conflict with your ability to cover your own ass. I am fully aware of her little tryst with your brother Bobby. It was almost three years ago, and it was Bobby who brought her to my attention."

"Well, that in itself could be a problem," Kennedy said.

"Are we still talking about the country, Jack, or are we just simply talking about you?" Dulles was becoming disgusted by the conversation and the implications.

"Scandals rock an administration, Allen...the woman knows too much."

"That woman has kept her secrets much better than any of you Kennedys ever have. It's why you need people like me in the position I'm in Jack! I am going to say it one more time. Let. It. Be."

"I don't like your tone of voice. Allen, remember who you're speaking to."

"Oh, believe me I remember, but sometimes it is only your true friends who will remind you being president doesn't also make you God." He paused long enough to let his last comment sink in. "Mr. President, my full report will be on your desk tomorrow morning."

Allen Dulles turned and walked out of the Oval Office, knowing a friendship of many years was now over.

President John Fitzgerald Kennedy, went back to sitting on the edge of his desk, still wondering what the hell just happened.

Chapter 49

Goddard Space Center, Greenbelt, Maryland

"Gentlemen, thank you for coming on such short notice," James Webb told the assembled group of engineers. "Same ground rules as before boys, this is top secret and what we discuss here stays here. Do I make myself clear?"

All the men nodded but Robert Lawson squirmed a little in his seat. *Maybe this time Alex will meet me at the zoo,* he thought.

"I received a phone call from Allen Dulles at the CIA late last night, and gentlemen, it looks like we are going to take a shot at getting a better look at The Luna 3 after all."

"When?" one of the engineers asked.

"Two weeks from now, when the Soviet tour is in Mexico City," Webb stated.

An excited buzz was heard throughout the room as the engineers turned towards each other.

"Quiet down," Webb barked. "You've had some time to

think about it, and Dulles wants to know what questions you want answered. This is your opportunity to find out what the Russians might know that we don't. So, let's split into teams of three and write down your questions. Let's tell his spy guys what they should be looking for."

Robert Lawson asked, "How are they going to get a closer look at it?"

"I don't know, Robert, and I don't want to know. Some stuff is way above my security clearance, and I'll leave it up to them. I've told you all I know. Our job is to simply tell them what to look for."

"Oh, I was just curious."

"Let's get to work," Webb directed as he walked to his desk, sat, and folded his hands together.

As his men scurried excitedly to put their thoughts to paper, James Webb sat and observed his team through new eyes. Each man was eagerly discussing the topic at hand or writing.

Except for one. He was looking off into space. James Webb had the first name for Allen Dulles to consider.

Chapter 50

Washington D.C. - 8 Hours Later

Robert Lawson once again sat in the same booth at McMillian's Tavern. He was disappointed. He had hoped Alex would accept his generous offer of paying his thirty-cent entrance fee and would meet him at the zoo the following day, as he had recommended. The Smithsonian's National Zoo sits on 163 acres in the heart of Washington D.C.'s Rock Creek Park and was founded in 1889. Lawson had never taken the opportunity to visit it, although he had thought of doing so many times. *Some things are just more fun when you're with a friend. I did really want to see the big cats though.*

But Alexsey Baryshev had told him if the information was so important, it was better for them to meet tonight. *It always seems like Alex is too busy to just spend some quality time with his best buddy instead of just talking about work.*

Ten minutes later, while Lawson was just about to finish his second cherry soda, Alexsey Baryshev slid into the booth across the table from the skinny, gaunt-faced engineer. Alex took the time to take off his hat and rest it on the table, looking at Lawson with an incredulous look. "What do you have for me Robert?" he asked.

"How was your day?"

"Good. Robert, what do you have?"

"Yah know, for two friends who have known each other as long as we have, we don't really socialize very much."

"Oh, I know, Robert, but you know how it is when you have a boss. It's always work, work, work," the Russian agent said, noticing the man's usual frustration. Alex was used to Lawson's quick change in temperament and had grown accustomed to his little snits. "So, go on, tell me about your day."

"Do you have an envelope for me, Alex?" Lawson asked, still feeling put off by the urgency.

"Well, it all depends on what you have to tell me," Alex said, knowing just how to play into Lawson's need for approval. "I bet it's good though. You don't usually call me so soon after our last meeting."

"Oh, it is Alex," Lawson said excitedly, forgetting the earlier slight. "It is!"

"So, tell me," Alex said, feigning equal excitement.

"Oh, okay, so James Webb, he is the director at NASA, and also a good friend," Lawson began. "He pulled his most brilliant engineers into another meeting again today, and you won't believe what he told us."

"What?" Alex asked, with enough false enthusiasm to pour lighter fluid on Lawson's enthusiasm.

"Well…I told you the last time we met the astronauts and some of the engineers wanted to get a closer look at the Luna

3 satellite. Do you remember?"

"I do."

"Well, Webb told us the CIA is going to put their top agents to work at getting their hands on it."

"When?"

"In two weeks," Lawson said excitedly. "In Mexico City."

"You're sure?" Alex asked.

"Oh yeah, Mr. Webb said only his most trusted employees were being told. He said it was top secret. If you and I had not been friends for so long, I would never have told you."

"Well thank you Robert. Did he say anything else?"

"The objective of our meeting was to give the CIA pointers on what to look for once they had the satellite in their hands," he said. "I'm still worried they can track those Corning glass solar collectors back to me though. Alex, I don't want to get into any trouble."

"Robert, you're a brilliant man," Alex said, hoping he sounded convincing. "Hundreds of people worked on developing those solar cells, and you're one of Webb's most trusted employees. They would never suspect you in any of this, you're too smart for that."

"Thank you, Alex. You're right...I am."

Lawson then spent the next fifteen minutes once again explaining the nuances of space flight and satellite reentry trajectories, but Alex had long since stopped listening. He had what he came there for.

"You've done very well, Robert," Alex complimented. "You will find a little extra in your envelope this time," he said reaching into his suit pocket. "I'm sorry, but I must be going." He rose to leave.

"Wait, Alex, maybe we can go back to my place, and I can show you my model railroad collection."

"Robert, I would love to, but I have another meeting I need to attend to. Maybe next time?"

"Yeah, maybe next time," Robert Lawson said, once again in a snit, as he tucked the envelope deep into the waist band of his trousers.

*　　*　　*　　*

As Alexsey Baryshev exited the bar, he looked both ways before walking off to find a payphone. The two men parked in a non-descript sedan across the street hunkered down and looked at each other. One of the men had sat in the booth behind Robert, nursing a beer for all but the last few moments of their conversation. "That's him," he said.

"Do we follow him?" the other man asked.

"No, let him pass the information on, but get a couple photos of him for later."

Five minutes later, Robert Lawson walked through the door at McMillian's Tavern and headed straight for his grey 1958 Pontiac. "He's the one we follow," the man said. "Get on the radio and tell them he is on his way."

The trip from McMillian's at 1264 Wisconsin Avenue to just outside Arlington Virginia would take twenty minutes. It gave Allen Dulles' men plenty of time to prepare for the engineer's arrival home. Robert Lawson, NASA aeronautics specialist and traitor to the United States, pulled away from the curb with the sounds of Patsy Cline's latest release blaring from his car radio. *"Crazy...I'm crazy for feeling so lonely...I'm crazy for feeling so blue…"*

Alexsey Baryshev rounded the corner and dropped a coin into the payphone slot. The Red Army colonel at the Russian embassy picked up his private line on the first ring. "What do you have for me?"

"They're going after the satellite!"

"When?"

"Two weeks from now, in Mexico City."

"You're sure?"

"Positive."

"Good work Alexsey, good work."

*   *   *   *

Robert Lawson never looked in his rear-view mirror or he might have seen the car following him from a distance. His mind was solely on his friend Alex and how he works so much and if he just socialized more, he would probably be happier. He parked his car in the driveway, which was two mere strips of concrete with grass growing between them and headed towards the house. It was just after 9:00 p.m. and the sun had just started to duck behind the roof lines and chimneys of the small houses which lined the quiet street.

He walked through the unlocked door without worry—in 1961 few people felt the need to bar their doors and lock their windows. Dropping his keys on the entryway table, he reached for the light switch.

At the same time, someone reached for him.

Lawson, ever awkward, did not even flinch, with the words, "Who are you?" escaping from his lips.

"You've been a very busy boy, Robert," said the man, now holding his left arm high up on his back, causing a pain Lawson had never felt before. The man led Lawson into the cramped living room, still decorated and untouched from the days the residence was owned by Lawson's mother before her death in '56. Sitting in a chair was a similar man in another dark suit, white shirt, and skinny black tie. Calmly, almost as if talking to a child the man said, "Robert, you and I need to have a talk."

The jab of the needle embedded deep into his thigh made Robert Lawson jump. The man who held his arm behind his back dropped the syringe to the faded carpet and held on. Ninety seconds later, he relaxed his stranglehold and lowered the NASA engineer into a sitting position on to the sofa. "Robert...can you hear me?" the man sitting in the chair asked.

Just after midnight, the two men in black suits had everything they had been directed to discover and more. A phone call to Allen Dulles had dispatched an ambulance and squad car to the little house on Baker Street from the parking garage underneath the CIA headquarters. The few neighbors who even noticed through slightly parted drapes at such a late hour never saw the two men in black suits climb into the police car as the tall NASA engineer was wheeled to the waiting ambulance on a gurney, a starched white sheet pulled high up over his head.

The obituary had already been written and would appear in the Washington Post two days later.

Robert Lawson, age 47, Senior NASA aeronautical engineer, passed away early Wednesday morning from what appears to have been a coronary embolism. He had no next of kin. James Webb, director of NASA, expressed his sadness at his passing and gratitude for Mr. Lawson's contributions to America's space program.

Robert Lawson was never to be heard from again.

Chapter 51

The Russian Embassy, Washington D.C.

Dmitry Ivanov, Alex Baryshev's handler was pleased to file his report from the basement of the Russian embassy there in Washington. The Red Army colonel attached to the K.G.B. was soon to retire but it did not hurt to have one last feather in his cap before doing so. He sealed the envelope and placed it into a diplomatic pouch which would be flown to Moscow later in the evening, as it was every time it was marked as urgent. The subject matter would not be the primary topic of conversation later tonight when honoring his commitment to dinner with his lifelong friend, but he was looking forward to bringing it up.

Tonight, was the recently promoted General Anton Petrov's last night before returning to Moscow, and both were looking forward to lengthy stories of long forgotten memories much more so than work. As the vodka flowed and the night became early morning, both men were smiling and had run out of stories to tell and steam enough to tell them. It was then the colonel said, "This spy game is always about knowing something someone else does not know. It's not very often a lowly colonel like me can boast about knowing something a big-shot-recently-promoted general doesn't."

With what would be his last drained shot glass of vodka for the night, General Anton Petrov said, "And what exactly might that be, my friend?"

"I got a phone call earlier tonight...."

*   *   *   *

"So, Mexico City, you say? It makes perfect sense. I will inform my subordinates and increase security."

The following day, Major Alexander Tkachenko was informed of the Central Intelligence Agency's intent to gather further intel on the backup to the Luna 3 satellite. His efforts to thwart the capitalists in their endeavors would garner him a promotion later the next year. Twenty-four-hour guards were posted for the upcoming exhibition in Mexico City, and additional wax seals were added to the exterior of the satellite. Those seals were marked by an indentation from the signet ring the major had worn on his ring finger for almost twenty years.

No one thought to look at the interior of the Luna 3 or investigate any possibility the Americans had already achieved the impossible. That information would only come out many decades later. Long after the promoted Lieutenant Colonel, the man who had been placed in charge of the satellite's safe keeping, and father-in-law of Peter Kozlov, had died from a heart attack in 1965.

Peter Kozlov, the patsy, was honorably discharged from service to the Russian military, with the recommendation he return home to bear witness to the birth of the major's second grandchild. He would go on to father three more children, all of them girls. His dreams of painting were somewhat realized with a career spanning more than thirty-five years working for the Gorkovsky Avtomobilny Zavrod (GAZ) motor company, where he painted buses and large commercial vehicles. He eventually worked his way up into management and retired in 1996 at the age of 58.

He and his loving wife, Maria, still live close to the factory he spent most of his life working for in the picturesque river city of Nizhy Novgorod, located roughly 400 kilometers east of Moscow. He spends most of his free time doting on his wife and twelve grandchildren, as well as sketching pictures of the local landscape.

*   *   *   *

Allen Dulles had quickly become disillusioned by the man he had once called a friend and now occupied the Oval Office. Throughout the rest of the summer of '61, the President continued to exert pressure on him to tie up any loose ends from the Prague mission.

Dulles knew exactly what he meant but had refused to do so. The Bay of Pig's fiasco would not go away, and the press was still looking for a scapegoat and Dulles knew it was coming. The man who had served as CIA director since February 26, 1953, was to be put out to pasture.

On November 28, 1961, President Kennedy pinned to his left lapel the National Security Medal in a well photographed press conference at the CIA Headquarters in Langley, Virginia. The next day, the White House released a resignation letter signed by Allen Dulles.

The following morning, Allen Dulles picked up the phone in

his private study at his home in Langley and dialed a number from memory. The phone on the other end, six hours away, rang only twice.

The pretty brunette on the other end had walked happily to the phone.

"It's me," he said.

"Allen, it's good to hear your voice."

"I resigned yesterday," he told her.

"Okay…" she said, letting the gravity of his comment sink in.

"I can't protect you anymore," he said. "The man's ego is out of control. Watch that pretty little back of yours, alright?"

"What about you Allen, are you alright?" she asked.

"I'm fine," he told her. "I'm not worried about me. If he keeps up with his own personal agenda, eventually he is going to become his own national security threat. Just be careful, young lady, I am worried about what he thinks he is capable of."

"Thanks for the call," she said.

"It's probably my last to you. I'm out of the loop now."

"I understand."

With sadness in his voice, she heard him say, "Take care of yourself, and take care of Joe. You two are good together, and he is a good man."

She placed the phone back in the cradle, knowing Allen Dulles had already hung up.

"JOE!" she called out.

Final Chapter

Late December 1961

The Balearic Islands are an archipelago off the Eastern coast of Spain in the Mediterranean. It is recognized for its sandy white beaches and teal colored water so clear small boats appear to hover in the air instead of being docked. Mallorca is the largest island, and it is best known for its scenic coastline and the majestic Tramuntra mountains bordering its north.

Gravda had awoken just before dawn and had thrown a robe over her naked body to watch the sunset coming up over the horizon from the East. In December, the temperature would later rise to the lower sixties Fahrenheit, but right now the chill in the air was invigorating.

As she stood by the railing of the deck overlooking the ocean, she allowed the thin cotton strap of Joe's terry cloth robe to fall open as she felt the chill of the early morning air dance across her body. The familiar tingle made her smile as she looked over her shoulder at the man she loved, still fast asleep, and wrapped in the warmth of high-thread-count cotton sheets and comforter. She knew he would jest protest of her chilled skin, but both would enjoy her favorite way of 'warming up,' once she returned to bed.

* * * *

As the sun continued its journey and the temperature rose, she awoke to the sounds of Joe in the kitchen. The aroma of fresh-brewed coffee and bacon and eggs on the stove made her gather her scattered hair and rise. She stretched like a feline and reached for the panties she had seductively dropped on the floor by the bed the night before. Looking back to the bed she winked at the teddy bear Joe had placed next to her on her pillow. She then padded into kitchen with bare feet putting her arms around Joe's waist and snuggled her head into his back.

"You stole my robe," she teased.

"Your robe? This is mine!" he said lovingly. "Did you sleep well?" He slid the robe off his lean body and slipped it onto her shoulders.

"I have slept better in these last few months than I can ever remember," she told him.

He kissed her forehead "Good. Now, go sit down. I have coffee for you."

She sat fixated, watching as Joe orchestrated the timing of toast popping up, eggs cooked to perfection, and bacon being pulled from the pan. He flitted back and forth with fluid movements of one who is happy and confident at home. She continued her gaze. Bare-chested and with blue jeans now an inch too big for his waist, he glided from station to station as he assembled their meal.

"You're going to make someone a very good wife someday," she teased.

Looking over his shoulder, he smiled. "I was thinking the very same thing about you, my dear."

He brought two plates to the table, and she thanked him with a kiss, holding both cheeks in her delicate hands.

"I like the new beard," she said. "It makes you look rugged."

He winked.

For a man who had spent so many years in a dark room, the Corsican sun had changed him for the better. Their long walks on the beach together and the almost nightly aerobics sessions after dark had transformed his body into lean muscle, and she thought his new-found copper color made his eyes look much bluer than before.

*   *   *   *

The time was 10:00 a.m., and already the very large man in the black leather trench coat and ill-fitting news boy cap was complaining about the heat. The sweat dripping from his brow was not just due to the fifty-degree temperature though, but for the reason he had been ordered to be there.

They were parked on the winding gravel driveway leading uphill to the modest villa perched onto the side of the mountain overlooking the ocean. As the large man looked up to his right through the windshield, he could just make out the edge of terracotta-colored roof tiles over the tops of the trees.

The man who sat beside him in the passenger seat looked at him and said with a snarl, "Dumbass, you're sweating like a pig. Why did you wear a stupid overcoat to begin with?"

"Just shut up," the larger man said.

The two did not know each other. They had met for the first time late last night, and it hadn't taken long for the driver to detest the arrogant little prick sitting next to him. His cold cockiness and slicked-back black hair, along with the mirrored aviator sunglasses, made the bigger man want to punch his fist right through his skull. But he was there to follow orders...even if he didn't like them.

"Come on, let's get this over with," he said.

"You know the plan," the smaller man explained. "You're the only one who can positively identify her...Don't screw this up!"

As the Spanish agent climbed out of the car, he left the door ajar to hasten their departure. He leaned back into the open window and growled, "You coming?"

"Yeah, I'm coming," he grumbled.

"Good, now move your fat ass," the man ordered as he started the long walk up the driveway.

Asshole, the bigger man thought to himself, feeling anger starting to rise. As he started to extricate his large frame from the small sedan, he smiled ever so slightly as he allowed his right elbow to glance against the horn button.

The single staccato toot was short-lived but startling. The smaller man turned angrily and strode back to the driver's side of the car.

"What the hell is wrong with you?!" he barked in whispered tones. "You're an idiot! Why don't you just phone ahead?!"

"Hey, I'm sorry," the man said, pulling himself the rest of the way out of the car, now standing at his full height of six foot seven inches. "You picked the stupid little car, not me."

"I was told you were a professional. You better hope no one heard that."

Towering over the smaller man and reminding him of it by

taking a step forward, he said, "Or what?"

The agent took a defensive step backwards. "Or you then get to explain back to the new boss in Washington what went wrong. This is all going in my report."

"No one heard it," he said. "We're right beside the ocean and we're still four hundred yards from the house. Let's get on with it. There won't be any more mistakes."

Walking away the smaller man grumbled, "There better not be."

Big Tony had never disobeyed a direct order from a superior before. His loyalty to the CIA was nearly legendary. It was not his place to think of the bigger picture. He had always figured when you're asked to do something, the people in charge must know what they were doing. His job was not to ask why.

He was now re-thinking his thinking. He did not like being treated like a buffoon.

Tony looked at the man three steps ahead of him and, with the only sound being their muffled steps as they made their way up the driveway, he reached into his overcoat.

Aiming his gun at the back of his head, he pulled the trigger without hesitation. He watched the crimson explosion of grey matter and skull fragments as the man fell limply face-forward to the stones. The subtle *"Pssst"* of his silenced weapon did not even disturb the birds in the nearby trees.

Walking slowly, he bent down and grabbed the carcass by its left ankle and dragged it to the shoulder of the driveway, where, in one swift motion, he picked it up and hurled it into the wooden ravine lining the driveway to the left. Retracing his steps, he bent down and picked up a shattered pair of mirrored glasses and tossed them in the same direction as far as he could. He scattered fresh stones over the gooey red trail with his size thirteen shoe and looked up towards the quiet house.

He smiled.

Slowly, he took his left hand and wrapped it tightly around the still warm silencer and began to slowly unthread it. He was in no hurry. Placing it into the pocket of his black leather trench coat, he raised his weapon high into the air and pointed it towards the ocean.

This time the birds did not just flinch, they thundered out of the trees in a cacophony of flapping wings and cries, as the echo of the boom of his .45 caliber rippled off the hillside and traveled upwards towards the house.

"Oh, I bet they heard that," he said chucking to himself. "Now run Betty Miller, please...Run, as far away as you can!"

Tony took off his cap and reverently bent down and gently laid it down in the middle of the stone pathway.

He turned his back and returned to the sedan. Climbing agilely and without difficulty, he put the car into reverse and slowly backed down the driveway to the main road.

"Dammit...that's the second time I have given away my favorite hat," he said aloud. *But maybe this time, someday...I might get this one back...*

Epilogue

Author's Notes

The decade President Kennedy spoke of in his Address to Congress on May 25, 1960, would later become one of the most tumultuous times in American History. What had begun as an era of hope and optimism would later spiral into an eddy of political strife and social disillusionment for many.

In no other time in American history did the span of just ten years change so much for so many. The generation before had won a world war, but war is nothing new. This was different. Ever since prehistoric man sat outside a cave and stared up into the night sky, they dreamed of what they all knew was unobtainable, unrealistic, impossible. The Soviet-American Space Race forced the entire world to redefine the definition of what human beings can accomplish and even what the word impossible ever meant.

Technological innovations came at a pace which had never been seen before. Along with it came the mounting frustrations of blatant inequalities between the status quo and those who had never been invited to join their ranks. Like a coiled spring pressed and pressured for many years, the lever holding back the torment of civil unrest was released within the 60s, with no chance of ever returning it to its former self.

Parents who had grown up in a time when children should be seen and not heard were now the guardians of a generation who spoke out loudly about everything. The counterculture revolution made most people over the age of thirty shake their heads in a state of bewilderment. Fathers who had been indoctrinated to the concepts of short hair and white starched shirts were now no longer looking at themselves as the prototype for their offspring but the antithesis of their creation. Long hair and bellbottom jeans were the anti-Christ to men who had faithfully served during World War II, and now they witnessed their sons burning draft cards and protesting the conflict in Vietnam. Mothers who had hoped to raise well-behaved daughters were now challenged to accept their little girls demanding equality in pay and respect, all the while burning their bras in public demonstrations and speaking out.

America represented a stark dichotomy between time and space. As technology outpaced itself, those with civil consciousness demanded social change at the very same rate. As an author and historian of America's past, I can tell you social change in this country has always traveled at a much slower pace.

The Space Race of the 1960s was not born out of a quest for new advancements in technology, or the worthwhile endeavor of a better quality of life through innovations in discovery. Those were simply the offspring of research and design. The later advent of laptop computers, cellphones, global positioning systems, as well as smoke detectors, and even memory foam mattresses were never the goal. Those items we take for granted today were just the byproducts of the hard work and dedication of 500,000 employees and 20,000 companies hired by our government to beat the Russians before they could beat us.

The primary quest of President Kennedy's and NASA's race for the moon was primordial. The motivation was based solely on fear alone. One we, as American's, have harbored since the very days of the inception of our nation. The fear of other people outside of our borders will one day force us to change what we have always thought to be *our* divine right to live as we judge to be best.

The Early Redstone rocket program pioneered by German scientist Wernher von Braun, the Atlas program which became Gemini, and eventually the Apollo program, were not just technological marvels for the ages but our way of combating the militaristic fear of the Russians getting to the moon before us. We weren't so worried about losing what was thought to be our rightful place on the word's stage and newspaper headlines as much as we panicked thinking of the possibility of Soviet missile bases on the lunar surface pointed towards us. President Kennedy was deft enough in politics to label our Space Race as a national agenda and not a military cause, but like so many other political objectives, please do not be fooled by the smokescreen of political rhetoric.

At the time of this writing, and in the 240 plus year history of this country, there have only been thirteen complete calendar years where we were not at war with another nation or fighting ourselves within our own borders. There are those who will argue this fact, but their argument is one of pure semantics and the definition of the word, "war." It is my strong opinion, when any government demands individuals, whether in uniform or clandestinely, to take the lives of others, and then justify those actions with the mandate of maintaining status quo, then those in charge have created a state of war. Most of these so-called "conflicts," which have been encouraged and sup-ported by those at the upper echelons of American govern-ment, have never been fully sanctioned by the United States Congress with a formal declaration as an end to peace time. 58,279 American soldiers, many of which had been drafted and not volunteers, lost their lives in Vietnam between the years of 1965 and 1973, in an 'armed combat' situation which had started eleven years before we became involved, and then lasted almost two years after we pulled out.

This may surprise many, but The United States Congress has *never* voted as a collective Legislative branch and declared war on another nation since the end of World War II. Korea. Vietnam. Panama. Somalia. Yemen. Syria. The first Gulf War, the second Gulf War, Afghanistan, present day Ukraine, all are officially listed on paper as, congressional "authorizations of military force." Semantics and the difference between words like 'war' and 'armed conflict' might make governmental lead-ers sleep better but it does not offer much solace to those who have lost loved ones.

The 1960s represented to many an obvious dichotomy be-tween good and evil, right versus wrong. At the same time hip-pies and flower children preached the message of free love in the San Francisco Bay area, water cannons and attack dogs were being unleashed on the young black populace of Amer-ica's south. Membership in the Ku Klux Klan rose rapidly in the early 60s and its swell in membership came mostly from young, white, family men who attended Christian churches on Sundays and were well-thought-of as dutiful citizens by their neighbors. One side fought the dogma with civil disobedience and peace-ful demonstration, while the other resorted to the more com-mon way of getting a point across—violence and intimidation.

Both sides were equally passionate, and both felt equally compelled to do so. One side struggled for radical, fundamental, social change, and the other fought to repel change at any cost.

Sadly, this has become the story of America, which continues to this day. We have always been quick to embrace technological advancement as Americans. But social evolution and enlightenment have always come at a much, much slower pace. President Kennedy's mandate of putting a man on the moon and safely returning him back to this globe was accomplished on July 20, 1969. The words of Neil Armstrong, as he stepped off the ladder of the Eagle landing module, were heard and seen by the largest television audience in history. People of all faiths, race, creeds, and color, were galvanized together for one moment as never before. From space, no borders exist. Borders are only lines drawn on maps by men in power and none are visible from outer space. For those few sparse moments in world history, we all thought of ourselves for the very first time as a global community. "One small step for man...one giant leap...for mankind."

The message was beautiful, even poignant. Had we learned from it, the world would be a better place indeed. We easily embrace the technological advancements garnered by the Apollo missions. But the true message and the beauty of his statement has once again been long forgotten. How many bigots today have smart watches strapped to their wrists and cell phones in their pockets?

I contend the culmination of the Space Race and the 1960s was not only our end of an age of innocence, but perhaps our last desperate chance at finding it. The president never bore witness to his greatest contribution to American technology, having been shot in the back of the head from a window of the schoolbook depository in Dallas on November 22, 1963.

One week later, newly sworn in President Lyndon B. Johnson appointed Allen Dulles to the Warren Commission to investigate the president's assassination. Johnson had done so in hopes the fired CIA director might be able to keep the commission from digging any deeper into the highly illegal activities Kennedy had mandated to his onetime friend. Before Allen Dulles' resignation, President Kennedy had demanded of the CIA chief find a way to assassinate Fidel Castro, the dictator of Cuba. Dulles refused, and Kennedy went to J. Edgar Hoover of the FBI instead. Several attempts were then made, but all of them were once again mitigated disasters. One of Castro's ex-lovers was asked to put poison in his drink. Another involved a plan to plant an explosive device in one of Castro's cigars. Allen Dulles had been correct. President Kennedy, in his arrogance, had become his own national security risk.

*   *   *   *

As an author, I take it on as my passion and personal responsibility to hold the magnifying glass to world events in hopes of making others see details either missed or ignored by headlines or history books. It is not my intent to re-write historical facts. When writing historical fiction, I often find myself torn between what little verifiable information is available and how to fill in those blanks. *Stealing the Sky* is such an example.

In the spring or summer of 1961, the United States and the CIA *did* indeed steal, disassemble, photograph, and return to the Soviet Union the backup to the Luna 3 satellite. Recently declassified and now public documents will bear witness to that fact. The exact location of the theft, whether it be in Prague or Mexico City has never been disclosed. I took it upon myself to create the timeline with what information was available to me. The exact number or names of civilian NASA engineers involved in the caper has never been disclosed and remains classified at the highest levels. *Stealing the Sky* is the culmination of over two years of research before putting pen to paper.

For a writer, the Freedom of Information Act passed in 1967 can be a treasure trove of possible stories worthy of telling, but with governmental bureaucracy and redaction seldom is the whole story released to the general public in anywhere near its entirety.

The historical characters within these pages such as Allen Dulles of the CIA, James Webb of the National Aeronautics and Space Administration, and President Kennedy, are real. I have done my best to portray each one as accurately as possible with the information at hand. I freely admit to having created scenarios and conversations which are purely of my imagination but are founded in the extensive research I have done.

The names and or lives of those individuals actively involved in the mission to steal the Luna 3 have never been released by the United States Government and never will be. Therefore, the fictional characters within these pages are just that, and of my own making. Most of history is only the half of the story those with secrets are willing to share….

Thank you for reading *Stealing the Sky*.

The Author,

Dan Hughes

Follow me at: facebook.com/danhughes.tv

Join me at my website: www.danhughestv.com

Made in the USA
Las Vegas, NV
24 October 2023

79668295R00195